Praise for
In the Company of Women

"This provocative, practical book deserves a wide readership."
—*Publishers Weekly*

"Thorough, thoughtful . . . sophisticated."
—*Boston Sunday Globe*

"Thought-provoking, politically incorrect."
—*Time*

"Powerful, eye-opening, smart reading."
—*Susan Estrich, author of* Sex & Power

"*In the Company of Women* addresses how and why female workplace relations break down as well as how women can inspire each other to new levels of excellence."
—*John Gray, Ph.D., author of* Men Are From Mars, Women Are From Venus

"One of the most important lessons I learned in Congress is how powerful the unified voice of women can be. This book provides insight and tools that can help women become an even stronger force . . . by creating alliances out of conflict."
—*Patricia Schroeder, former member of Congress, and President and CEO, Association of American Publishers*

"Being one of the few women in a male-dominated field made me realize how important it is to form alliances with other women. This book will teach you how to build the relationships that will help put you over the top."
—*Lillian Vernon, Founder and CEO, Lillian Vernon Corporation*

"How do you preserve a harmonious . . . relationship with your former friends and keep them from stabbing you in the back when you least expect it? *In the Company of Women* provides an excellent roadmap. . . . Run, don't walk, to your nearest library or bookseller and read this book!"
—*Pittsburgh Post-Gazette*

"As I worked my way through the corporate environment and into my own business, I never understood why 'one of us' was more eager to chop off my legs than was 'one of them.' But now I get it! This book showcases something most of us have always known but rarely articulated: that the 'steel skirt' can be as deadly to women at work as the glass ceiling."
—*Linda Novey-White, CEO, Linda Novey Enterprises, recipient of the Avon Women of Enterprise Award*

"Finally! After years of 'politically correct' discussions of women's relationships, *In the Company of Women* provides an explanation for why women make our best friends—and our worst enemies."

—*Pat Palleschi, VP for Management Planning, The Walt Disney Company*

"Alliances are one of the keys to women's success. *In the Company of Women* explains the sociological and biological research behind why women's alliances are so important and gives valuable insights into keeping them strong."

—*Carol Gallagher, Ph.D, author of* Going to the Top

"Based on twenty years of research, this is a rare gem of a book that is such a compelling read I literally couldn't put it down. The stories, the causes, and the solutions all rang true: I found myself nodding my head and even saying 'Yes' out loud every few pages. If you want better work *and* nonwork relationships with women, *In the Company of Women* is for you."

—*Ginger Applegarth, author of* The Money Diet *and* Wake Up and Smell the Money

"A hands-on guide to fostering healthier, more productive relationships with the women in our lives. What a terrific and inspirational read!"

—*Judy George, CEO and Founder, Domain, and author of* The Intuitive Businesswoman

"If this insightful and instructive manual had been around when I was starting out in management, it would have saved me much heartache and second-guessing. I had to learn the hard way that career success results in isolation from female peers. I plan to make *In the Company of Women* required reading for all my management staff—male and female. I can't imagine a better way to improve the effectiveness of my company than through enhancing my team members' ability to understand one another, to resolve conflict, and to offer support."

—*Margo Provost, Chairman and CEO, Log Haven Restaurant Group*

"Every working woman will find herself here. Heim and Murphy will make you smile and think 'Been there, done that' or 'Wish I had known that' over and over. For any woman who wants to take control of her career, for any managers who want to support the careers of the women on their teams, this book provides the perspective, the psychology, and the how-tos."

—*Beverly Kaye, President, Career Systems International*

IN THE COMPANY

Pat Heim, Ph.D., and
Susan A. Murphy, Ph.D., MBA

with Susan K. Golant

JEREMY P. TARCHER/PUTNAM
a member of Penguin Group (USA) Inc.
New York

OF
WOMEN

Indirect Aggression Among Women:

Why We Hurt Each Other

and How to Stop

Most Tarcher/Putnam books are available at special quantity discounts for bulk purchase for sales promotions, premiums, fund-raising, and educational needs. Special books or book excerpts also can be created to fit specific needs. For details, write Penguin Group (USA) Inc. Special Markets, 375 Hudson Street, New York, NY 10014.

Jeremy P. Tarcher/Putnam
a member of
Penguin Group (USA) Inc.
375 Hudson Street
New York, NY 10014
www.penguin.com

First paperback edition 2003
Copyright © 2001 by Pat Heim, Ph.D., Susan A. Murphy, Ph.D., MBA
with Susan K. Golant, M.A.

The Library of Congress has catalogued the hardcover edition as follows:

Heim, Pat.
    In the company of women : indirect aggression among women : why we hurt each other and how to stop / Pat Heim, Susan Murphy, with Susan K. Golant.
        p.   cm.
    Includes bibliographical references.
    ISBN 1-58542-115-4
        1. Women employees.   2. Women—Communication.
3. Women—Psychology.   4. Female friendship.   5. Teams in the workplace.
I. Murphy, Susan, date.   II. Golant, Susan K.   III. Title.
HD6053 .H387   2001   2001033102
650.1'3—dc21
    ISBN 1-58542-223-1 (paperback edition)

Printed in the United States of America

10   9   8   7   6   5   4   3   2   1

Book design by Mauna Eichner

To our best girlfriends,
in gratitude for the lessons all of you have taught us
about how wonderful women's relationships can be.

ACKNOWLEDGMENTS

Writing this book has been among the most rewarding professional experiences of our lives. We have been on a pilgrimage—almost a spiritual journey—as we've delved into and discovered new and wonderful elements of womanhood. The three of us worked on this book together for nearly a year with nary a squabble among us. What a joy from start to finish! We are all grateful to one another—cohorts in this particularly savvy Girl Gang and mutual admiration society—for a deep understanding of human nature, many laughs, untold kindnesses, and sheer persistence. This has been a learning experience for each of us, one that we will always cherish.

Susan Murphy suggested we write about relationships among women in the first place. She would not let the project die, and she never wavered from her vision. Pat Heim provided the philosophical framework upon which we eventually hung so many useful concepts. Susan Golant took the ideas and made them sing. Her knowledge of the primate world was invaluable in shaping our understanding of female behavior.

We are also indebted to Michelle Berry, who added "researcher" to her job description and amazingly ferreted out every article we asked for. At a critical moment early in the writing, Kathryn Tobin, senior director of research and advisory services at Catalyst, sent us the Tend and Befriend findings that helped us focus on a critical body of recent research.

Wendy Hubbert at Tarcher grasped the importance of this book immediately, and frequently asked discerning questions that challenged our thinking and added insights to our theories. Her careful editing brought clarity to our ideas and, on occasion, breakthrough understanding. Wendy's enthusiastic belief in this project gives us hope that a small group of committed individuals can, indeed, change the world. As ever, our agent, Bob Tabian, deserves credit for assiduously looking after our interests.

We are also grateful to our wonderful families and dear friends. Pat Heim thanks Serge Lashutka, her husband and greatest cheerleader and supporter. Special mention goes to Susan Murphy's sisters, who early in life taught her the value of female love and friendship. She is thankful to Jim, her husband, for his love and sense of humor. Susan Golant is forever grateful to her family. They provide the wellsprings of love and support from which all of her work derives.

As nobody can do more mischief
to a woman than a woman,
so perhaps one might reverse the maxim and say
nobody can do more good.

ELIZABETH HOLLAND
nineteenth-century writer and salonist

CONTENTS

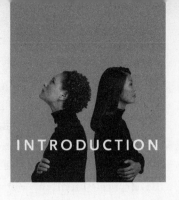

INTRODUCTION

WHEN WE ASK MEN who their best friend is, most will identify their wives. When women are asked the same ques-
tion, they usually name other women. It's not that women don't love their
husbands or that men care for their wives more than their wives care for
them. This imbalance arises from the profound emotional ties to and need
women have for one another. Even when a woman finds the male love of her
life, the bonds she shares with her female friends usually remain unshaken.

Contrast those close and intimate female attachments with the response to a question we often ask in our gender workshops: "When a woman
gets promoted, who is the first to attack her?" The answer is always a re-
sounding "Women." It matters little if the group to which we're speaking is
male, female, or mixed or if it's composed of engineers, nurses, accoun-
tants, computer programmers, chemists, salespeople, administrative assistants, or top executives. Without fail, in our twenty years of conducting
conferences and workshops about gender differences in business, almost
every participant we've encountered has acknowledged that women damage other women's career aspirations. It is ironic that on the one hand,
when a woman is in emotional pain, she will seek out a female friend for
consolation, while on the other, it is often another woman who put her in
that predicament in the first place.

We first became aware of this destructive dynamic among women in the early 1980s. At that time, we were both executives in a Fortune 500 organization where—as in most companies back then—the women employees had little power and held hardly any positions of significance. Still, there were at least a few women in leadership positions in the corporation, and it might be assumed that they would have helped each other and the women beneath them in the corporate hierarchy. But did they lend a hand? Did they offer advice or mentor their up-and-coming female colleagues? Did they praise other women on successful projects? Did they band together for strength in a male-dominated atmosphere or did they help each other move up through the organizational ranks? Some did, but, unfortunately, most did not. In fact, we noticed that many women in this large corporation often did the opposite. They actively sabotaged one another.

For example, within three days of several new employees having joined the organization, they learned through the informal grapevine that Christine, the most senior woman in the company, was living with the CEO (and therefore, it was whispered, "should not be taken seriously"). And what's more, they were told, she started as a secretary (so "she couldn't really be very competent or educated"). It was almost always women who tipped off new employees to these revelations. Rather than being proud of Christine or feeling "Isn't it great that we have a woman in the top-management ranks?" her female colleagues chose to discount her position.

They never mentioned to the new hires that Christine had earned an MBA from Harvard and that her work as a secretary had occurred when she temped at the company the summer after graduation in order to unwind from the rigors of school. Minor details.

Christine's mistreatment at the hands of other female co-workers at this company and many more similarly distressing incidents awakened in us the realization that we were witnessing a problem that women face every day in the workplace. It seemed to us that *women consistently failed to support other women and even actively undermined their authority and credibility*. This new awareness disturbed us; such behavior was detrimental to female advancement. Besides, the sniping and backbiting also made all our lives miserable. We needed to understand why women behaved as they did in order to help them find a way out of this destructive behavior. Thus began an odyssey for both of us, an odyssey that eventually led to the writing of this book.

THE SEARCH FOR AN ANSWER

As a management development specialist at the national headquarters of this large company, Pat's quest for understanding was facilitated when, in 1982, a female vice president approached her for help. "Can you conduct a communications workshop with my employees?" Karen asked her. "I'm having problems in my unit. My boss says my managers are poor communicators. He says they're so darned sensitive about negative feedback from each other, and they're always going straight to him, bad-mouthing their co-workers. What am I supposed to do?"

"But you're talking only about the women!" Pat said. Intuitively, she had sensed these employees were all female.

"How did you know?" Karen replied with astonishment.

"I've been reading all the research I can find on gender differences in the workplace, and the problems you've mentioned are often unique to women," Pat explained. She agreed to conduct the workshop for Karen's female managers, and it was a wild success. Soon word got out, and the female executives in the company asked for their own workshop. When Pat left the corporation to become a private consultant on gender differences, she continued this important work, interviewing women from around the country and conducting workshops for those who feel they are targets of other women.

For her part, Susan, a health care executive and a leadership development consultant, found that after each leadership workshop she led, both male and female managers would quietly come up to her to admit something along the lines of: "All this leadership material is interesting, but my main problems are with the women who work with/for me." The men felt helpless about conflicts among their female employees, labeling these problems "catfights." They kept their heads down, hoping the women would resolve these battles themselves—although often they didn't. And, like Christine, many female managers felt bloodied by women in lower positions. Both men and women were pleading for help.

As the years passed we realized that between the two of us, we speak to about fifty thousand people each year at more than one hundred corporations and public agencies such as Microsoft, Procter & Gamble, General Motors, the Federal Reserve Bank, and the U.S. Army, as well as professional societies including the American Association of University Women and the American Medical Association. What we had first noticed during our own stints working at large corporations was typical of something we now saw in the workshops we gave all over the country in every field of employment. Women's work relationships with other women tend to be more conflictual than their relationships with men or men's relationships with one another. Women sabotaged and undermined one another; they snubbed one another and gossiped.

After having maintained our relationship as colleagues for many years, and after discussing the issue of female-to-female hostility at length, we finally decided to join forces and devote more time to this problem to better define it, discern why it exists, and even come up with some solutions. We pooled the data we had compiled and, in 1997, we developed a Web site (*www.heimgroup.com*), where we posted a questionnaire that assesses the preferences of and difficulties in working for or with people of the same or the other gender. We asked people to respond to questions including:

- Whom would you rather work for, a man or a woman?

- What has been your most difficult situation with other women?

- What (or who) caused the problem?

- What did you do about it?

- How did it turn out in the end?

We were astounded at how many individuals took the time to share their experiences and their gruesome tales of betrayal and sabotage. Respondents included men and women in a broad range of industries. Many of the participants recounted emotional stories, often providing their phone numbers so we could call for more of the gory details. We followed up with one-on-one interviews and focus groups. These people were in pain and saw no way out. Their responses to our questions proved to us we were right about the significance and pervasiveness of this issue.

HERE'S WHAT WE FOUND

As a result of our years of research, we can say that relationships among women often polarize at two extremes: either they're truly wonderful or they're quite terrible. There is little in between—the friendly acquaintances. Men, on the other hand, tend to occupy this middle ground with one another, usually having neither intensely intimate friendships nor hateful enmities. The good news is that the ratio of positive female relationships far outweighs the bad: only a handful of other women will really burn you. However, those one or two fallings-out that do occur can be awfully hurtful, perhaps because we women all have such high expectations of our female friends.

The incontrovertible truth we found is that *when women work together, they often experience conflict with one another—a phenomenon that is referred to most often by men as a "catfight."*

WHAT ARE "CATFIGHTS"?

Men generally use the term "catfight" derogatorily to describe women's behavior that looks irrational and highly inappropriate to them. But whenever we raise the issue or utter the word in a roomful of women, every single one nods her head in recognition. We don't generally use the word ourselves because we see these clashes as very real and not at all irrational or inappropriate.

But even though the term conjures up images of women having physical hissy fits in the office—which, let's face it, doesn't happen all that often—we use it in this book because so many women know that by "catfight" we mean *a negative interaction with a female colleague.* Though it is a traditionally chauvinistic term, it is still a useful shorthand that all of us understand. We'd like to consider this book a politically correct—free zone, and to that end, please know that we are not trivializing women's hurtful and often bitter exchanges when we label them catfights, but are merely calling them by a quickly recognizable term.

So what is a catfight? Let's take a moment and consider what fighting cats—the furry feline variety—look like in the real world. Usually, cats fight over territory. They try to scare each other off without a physical tussle; only rarely will angry cats swipe at their opponents. Rather, cats will arch their backs, hiss at each other, and bare fangs and claws. Their fur may stand on end, and you can hear a deep threatening growl emerging from their throats. Holding their ground, they attempt to stare each other down. Eventually, the loser slinks off, only to appear another day to fight again. While dogs go straight for the jugular when they fight and often leave each other wounded and bloody, most cats do not attack each other violently.

Why have women's battles been referred to as "catfights"? Perhaps because we, too, do not resort to physical violence when we feel affronted or encroached upon. Instead, we use many forms of what social psychologists call *indirect aggression* that for biological and sociological reasons, which we will explain in chapters 3 and 4, has been part of our arsenal throughout the millennia. Indirect aggression is covert aggression: we are mounting an attack in such a way that we hope to remain hidden, and we do this to protect ourselves; we disguise our hostile intentions in order to avoid retaliation and social condemnation.[1]

How does this indirect aggression manifest itself among women? We don't necessarily arch our backs or bare our fangs, but if we are engaged in a conflict with another woman we may use many other oblique strategies to get at this person whom we perceive as having hurt us in a particular way. These strategies can include:

- *Gossip:* Gossip has many functions, some of them positive, as you'll see in chapter 5. However, malicious or destructive gossip can be used to tear down another woman. A supervisor in San Diego wrote to us that "women are nonconfrontational and will talk about me as their superior behind my back. I cannot get my women subordinates to tell me the truth about what they want or what they'd like me to change. I only hear about it through the grapevine."

- *Spreading rumors and divulging secrets:* These are excellent ways to hurt another woman without her knowing the source of the problem. A young doctor from Detroit wrote to us, "I went through residency with a woman more than twelve years older than I. We had become friends. However, after she joined my medical group, she began spreading rumors about me, sometimes revealing information that was true but should not have become public knowledge. My credibility was totally ruined, and when I found out who was spreading these vicious rumors, so was our friendship."

- *Publicly making insinuating or insulting comments:* One woman in Kansas City was hired by an attorney to come into an office and assist a woman who had worked there for ten years. They had a fine professional relationship for two years until trouble suddenly erupted. "It all started when she was updating personnel files and discovered I was making the same amount to start out that she made after working there all those years," she wrote to us. "For a year and a half, she tortured me by cutting me down to her friends on the phone (like I couldn't hear—sitting four feet from her)."

- *Undermining and sabotage:* The word *sabotage* comes from *sabot*, the French term for a wooden shoe or clog. At the dawn of the Industrial Age, if someone wanted to halt production at a factory, he merely had to fling one of his *sabots* into the gears of the machinery, and the deed was done. Today, of course, there are many ways in which we can undermine one another. For example, the only woman project manager for a large construction company in Cincinnati complained, "The female receptionist will not give me phone messages from anyone except my nine-year-old. She has told me that I act too 'manly.' My manager will not intervene because he thinks we 'girls should just work it out!' This is a very serious problem. I don't even know when my clients are calling me!" How can this manager do her work if her subordinate won't carry out her function?

- *Purposefully snubbing and withdrawing friendship:* Many of us remember childhood threats of "I won't be your friend anymore," if we wouldn't go along with a playmate's demands. Well, some habits die hard. As one snubbed former office friend wrote, "She gets back at me by not speaking to me except in short grunts when asked direct questions, ignoring me when I talk, glaring at me, and storming around the office like we'd just had a fight when no words were exchanged."

All these strategies can make for a singularly uncomfortable work environment, especially if, as often happens, other women are enticed into joining the fray.

Have You Been the Object
of a Destructive Conflict?

Ask yourself the following questions:

1. Have I ever felt undermined by another female at work?

2. Have I ever felt unjustly snubbed by a female co-worker?

3. Have I ever heard secondhand that a female co-worker is upset about something I said or did?

4. Have I ever performed most of the work on a project and had a female co-worker take the credit?

5. Have I ever shared a secret in confidence with a female co-worker and found that she had leaked it to others?

6. Have I ever had untruths spread about me and been the victim of malicious gossip?

7. Have I ever been told, "It's nothing!" when I asked a co-worker with an icy demeanor if something was bothering her?

8. Has any woman tried to diminish my power by making herself look better at my expense?

9. Has a co-worker gone to my supervisor with a complaint about me without discussing it with me first?

10. Has a female co-worker ever "forgotten" to tell me about a meeting, phone call, or message that was very important to me?

If you answered "Yes" to at least one of the above questions, then it's likely you have at some point in your life been on the receiving end of another woman's particular wrath. Whether or not you were consciously aware of the special challenges that can arise when working with women, you knew enough to pick up this book. Perhaps you were the subject of nasty backbiting and gossip, or maybe you noticed that a female subordinate consistently refused to follow your orders and never completed assignments on time.

Perhaps you realized that you just can't stand your female supervisor who constantly puts you down and makes you feel insignificant. Possibly you've been suffering in silence, believing that no one else has had to put up with this kind of pain or fearing that others will label you "difficult" if you complain.

YOU'RE NOT ALONE

A recent study of one thousand women conducted by the American Management Association found that 95 percent of the research sample felt other women had undermined them at some time in their careers.[2] And another study showed that woman-to-woman sabotage has increased by 50 percent during the past ten years.[3] Although women may not talk about their conflict with one another, this is a problem that likely affects most of us.

We've seen the sabotage scenario play out over and over again, though positions, professions, and levels change. As Hillary Rodham Clinton was readying herself to run for the New York Senate seat, a spate of newspaper articles trumpeted the erosion of female support for her. A *New York Times* article, for instance, explained, "[Mrs. Clinton's advisors] say that they are also struggling to overcome psychological factors not normally at play in political campaigns—specifically, the attitudes of women toward Mrs. Clinton's marriage, ambition, and the power she derived from the most powerful man in the world."

Consider, too, Barbra Streisand. The winner of all the entertainment industry's major awards, she has sold eighty million records, earned untold millions of dollars, and is a cottage industry unto herself. Perched at the top of the heap, surely she should feel immune from female hostility. So why is it that in a recent article heralding the bestowal of yet another honor—the Golden Globe's Cecil B. DeMille Award for contributions to the field of entertainment—she complained about the treatment she receives from other women?

"What I've done, going into a man's world, was tough," she admitted. "You get attacked, but mostly by women. That's the irony. I've found that women are the most competitive and vitriolic [people]. The worst reviews I've gotten were from women. . . . When they're out to get you, they're out to get you."

You're Not Difficult

Moreover, if you've picked up this book, you need to know that you're not difficult or odd. As we will explain, there are significant biological and sociological reasons why female workplace relationships are uniquely challenging. There may be people, however, who quail at this concept and ask, "How can you say that women are different at work? After all, isn't the business world a level playing field when biological differences like physical strength don't come into play?" In our long quest for equality, many women understandably don't want to go down a path that implies that there's a difference between men and women at work. In this postfeminist society we'd like to think that we're all the same—but we're not. Due to our biological heritage and social learning, males and females actually grow up in distinct cultures. Like it or not, we have come to the conclusion that men and women are different from each other.

However, rather than just being different from men because of who we are and how we've been raised, we can appear to be "problematic." There are many ways in which men and women are alike, of course, but it is the subtle differences between the genders that cause us to be judged and to be judgmental of others.

The problem of female-to-female conflict has never been addressed before, and without such external validation, it can feel as if you're struggling with a personal failing rather than a cultural dynamic. But the truth is, when we raise the subject in all-female groups, the women laugh (and groan) in recognition and are eager to embrace the issue. In mixed company, however, the squirm factor is almost palpable. Females in the room seem shocked that we would even mention such a forbidden topic around men. They certainly don't open up and share. It's as if their edgy silence is telling us, "Catfights make us look bad. We don't want to acknowledge that we're capable of this kind of behavior. Don't let them know we do this. It will only give the men more ammunition to perceive us as fractious and difficult."

Even though this issue is so pervasive, rarely do we see much written about it. It's as though this is women's dirty little secret. When someone does dare bring the topic to light, though, it seems to hit a nerve immediately. When *Frequent Flyer* magazine published an article "Ms. Treatment on the Road" about the poorer service women travelers often receive from female flight attendants, they received more letters about it than *any other article they had ever published.* When a woman wrote the "Ask Annie" columnist in *Fortune* magazine about the abuse women heap on one another, Annie replied that she wasn't sure this truly happened. Annie received 266 letters, and more than 200 of the respondents told her she was all wet. The pain and anger women feel toward other women tend to be stuffed inside but pierce the surface and then gush forth.

One of our goals in writing *In the Company of Women* is to validate your reality. By the end of this book, we want you to be completely confident that if you experience problems with your fellow women in the workplace, it doesn't mean that you're a difficult person. We have spoken to thousands of women who have been undermined and may have even lost opportunities for professional advancement because of sniping, sabotage, and catfights. It is part of the cost of keeping this secret and holding on to a pretense that women are always "nice" and supportive toward one another.

THE PRICE WE PAY

Let's face it. Female-versus-female workplace imbroglios can undermine our career progress and even our organization's profitability. They can create an unpleasant, stressful, unproductive work environment, draining our mental energy from our job responsibilities and refocusing our attention on solving taxing interpersonal conflicts. They can interfere with our overall level of satisfaction in our work and—when we wrestle with these problems mentally and emotionally—adversely affect the day-to-day quality of our lives and even our health. They can have a negative impact on female advancement in general, when women create and then align themselves with negative stereotypes of petty squabbling. Indeed, recently an executive explained to Pat why his company, a huge consumer products company, had a man running its Women's Initiative Program. "The executive vice president hired a man for the position because women do all this bickering," he said flatly. "The EVP didn't want to deal with it."

We've heard from other male executives who are afraid to hire and promote senior women because they "always turn out to be a bitch." A physician in Newport, Rhode Island, wrote to us that her biggest problem was with a secretary who could not accept the fact that she was the surgeon, had an agenda, and was not there to take orders from her. "I repeatedly tried to 'negotiate' and used every conflict management tool I knew," she explained. "Her actions were damaging enough that they contributed to my having to seek legal assistance and resigning my position."

Clearly, female bickering is incredibly costly to us. In order to avoid such hassles, some women choose to hide their talents, which may thwart their advancement. Another woman, Leslie, wrote to us, "My biggest problem in working with women has been my ambition to achieve and my higher than average intelligence. I found that other women would usually feel threatened by me. I did my best not to overemphasize my abilities, and I actually dramatized any difficulties that I had." Of course, Leslie's boss would also assess her performance and behavior and might form a diminished view of her abilities based on Leslie's fear of offending female co-workers. In the same vein, a junior executive sensitized to the need that she had to keep a "flat structure" in the office told us, "I do not like to be identified as 'the boss.'" Imagine a male executive saying that! And imagine, too, how this woman's higher-ups might interpret such an attitude—that she's not really senior executive material.

Damaging conflicts with women can cause us intense emotional pain and stress, especially when women enlist others to help fight their battles— a favorite technique. One executive working on an overseas assignment had a doozie of a quarrel with a co-worker/roommate. "My roommate was justifiably fired because she caused a conflict. I, on the other hand, had been given a promotion. After her sudden firing (of which I had no prior knowledge), our group of seven female co-workers decided I was somehow responsible and proceeded to sabotage my/our apartment and spread vicious rumors. It was a terrible experience. I had to continue working with the group, knowing what they had done. I never spoke to them again, and they never spoke to me."

Fights like these can interfere with our life satisfaction, our sense of well-being, and ultimately our mental and physical health. They may embitter us and can even cause us to avoid working with and/or for other women—a blow to women's political momentum. Several of our respondents declared that they would think twice and three times before working for a female boss again, if ever. As one woman from Austin, Texas, told us, "Before her promotion, Fran was friendly and seemed to care about others. Afterwards, she was just an extension of her male boss, and others were there to be used and abused." Another woman from Seattle admitted, "Unfortunately, there is *nothing* I enjoy about working with women. I find them to be petty, tyrannical, emotional (usually about issues that call for logic), spiteful, and vengeful (have I missed any stereotype clichés?). They are mistresses of micromanagement. I am, too, but I micromanage my *own* time! I have spent a great deal of my life working with women (and occasionally for—a mistake I will *not* repeat again in this lifetime) and, except for an occasional bright spot, I have never failed to be disappointed by my female co-workers."

Aside from the expenditure of vast stores of emotional energy, these conflicts also cost us and our companies real dollars. As productivity increases in our nation, we have more to do in less time. It's therefore critical to communicate effectively the first time around and maintain supportive work-based alliances. Damaged relationships between you and your female co-workers can disrupt communication (effective listening decreases when you're stressed) and information sharing, which may lead to lowered productivity, mediocre outcomes, and high turnover. On the other hand, a recent Gallup survey showed that having a "best friend" at work correlates with high job satisfaction, high productivity, and high retention rates.[4] How well could the woman who was working overseas fare if she and her seven co-workers had stopped talking to one another?

Now consider the words of this Chicago municipal employee: "My most difficult situation came in working for a woman who took offense at my presence from the very beginning. I am not sure what, if anything, I did to offend her, but I was never able to get off on the right foot with her, or even get to the point where things were neutral between us. I heard from a friend years later that her boyfriend had asked her who I was on the first day, and she felt threatened, but I don't really know what the story was. She ran hot and cold, from wanting us to be best buddies one day and then insulting me in the worst ways the next. I never knew what to expect." We imagine that constantly walking on eggshells because of a co-worker's erratic attitude had made it very difficult for our correspondent to concentrate on her job.

The director of a medical diagnostic laboratory in Minneapolis told us of a technician she employed who liked to be in control. "She has to feel needed and doesn't seem to respond to suggestions about how I want things done. I have engaged a program director to be her direct supervisor. We delineate specific performance measures for evaluation to eliminate any discrepancies in expectations, which seems to work. And I avoid spending time in the laboratory while she's there." What a lot of time and energy this conflict must have consumed.

The cost is too high for these problems to be ignored and to go unresolved. It is imperative that all of us understand and arrest woman-to-woman sabotage before the damage hits catastrophic levels—especially since 53 percent of the workforce is now female and more women than ever are being promoted within organizations. Corporations consulting with and/or receiving services from female-run companies also need to understand what causes these conflicts, considering that the number of women-owned businesses has doubled in the past twelve years. In 1999, women owned 9.1 million U.S. companies, employing 27,000,000 workers— 33 percent of U.S. businesses with a total revenue of $1.6 trillion.

When the landmark book *Games Your Mother Never Taught You* was written in the mid-1970s, the career choices for women were far more limited to teacher, nurse, and secretary. But in the new millennium, as more of us enter the executive ranks in organizations, the challenge of women's workplace relationships will only become more crucial. We control more financial and political power than ever before in history. According to Carol Gallagher, author of *Going to the Top*, today women earn more than 35 percent of MBAs (versus 3.6 percent in 1970) and more than 42 percent of law degrees (up from 5.4 percent in 1970). Women now make up 48.9 percent of all managerial and professional jobs—fully double the percentage we held two decades ago.[5] Our numbers are dramatically changing the face of working America, but we need to take care to stop damaged relationships from reducing productivity and financial viability.

When you as an individual understand how to build business relationships with female co-workers, you can alleviate the potential for sabotage and its concomitant heartache. But companies as well as individuals need to understand what causes female-to-female hostility since a lack of knowledge regarding these dynamics can needlessly create problems. For instance, by increasingly pitting women against other women to reach certain sales goals, many organizations inadvertently trigger catfights that will harm team relationships and can result in poorer performance in the long run. By contrast, a deep understanding of why women relate to one another the way they do will enhance outcomes. With insight into the interpersonal dynamics that underlie catfights, companies can effectively restructure their reward systems to bring out the best in their female employees.

HOW THIS BOOK CAN HELP YOU

Having found yourself embroiled in a bitter wrangle, you may have asked yourself: What do I do if I'm the one being attacked? How can I effectively manage women who are creating problems for one another? What's the best way to maneuver if I'm part of a team whose members are sabotaging one another? How can I better handle my own feelings of resentment about my female boss or colleagues? About a friend who has just gotten a prized promotion?

In the Company of Women will help you address and resolve these nettlesome problems. This book will help guide you through the confusing thicket of woman-to-woman conflict in the workplace. In part I, we'll explore what catfights really are and why women engage in them. In chapter 1, we'll look at the three major components women need for fulfillment at work: relationships, power, and self-esteem. In chapter 2, we'll describe the groundbreaking formula we've discovered called the *Power Dead-Even Rule* that helps explain how female relationships work and why they sour. In chapters 3 and 4, we look at the biological and sociological underpinnings that clarify why indirect aggression has been functional for women through the ages, although today it is not the most effective technique. In chapter 5, we will illuminate the "Bitch Factor"—drawing together the many reasons that women act the way they do.

Part II—filled with real-life examples of problems and concrete solutions—will focus on strategy. Now that you know what's causing the problem, here's what you can do to solve it. This section of the book is devoted to helping you avoid destructive conflicts and/or turn them into productive collegial activity. Here we give advice on the problems that inevitably arise when promotions occur, how to resolve female-to-female quarrels, and how to lead other women, all with an eye toward maintaining empowering female alliances.

There have been books about male-to-male conflict and male-to-female conflict in the workplace—indeed, Pat has even written a successful one with our co-author, Susan Golant, *Hardball for Women*. However, this is the first book truly to develop a theory of why we behave the way we do toward one another, the first book to help you sort through your particular issues with other women. We present a model that you can apply to your life immediately. Understanding what sparks a conflict may help defuse the confusion, pain, and anger that you feel when you come under another woman's attack. You'll be able to analyze what's going wrong in the relationship and strategize about how better to resolve the issues. Using our model, you will even be empowered to foil these destructive conflicts before they begin.

In *In the Company of Women* you will learn about:

- Your attitudes about working with other women and how you can improve them

- The biological and evolutionary mandates that clarify why we have been socialized to behave toward other women the way we do

- Why there is so much commotion among women when one of us is promoted

- How to build relationships with female superiors, colleagues, and those who report directly to you

- Leadership skills unique to women

- The language (verbal and nonverbal) we use that can inflame female interactions, and how to enhance work relationships by becoming conscious of what you're communicating

- Building a dream team especially among female co-workers who are unfriendly toward you and/or one another

- How you and your female colleagues can inspire one another to greatness rather than tear one another down

All in all, *In the Company of Women* will teach you that you can face the challenges of dealing with other women, and that when you do, we all win in the end.

PART I

CONFLICT

Why

Women

Behave

the

Way

They

Do

ONE

The Golden Triangle: Relationships, Power, and Self-Esteem

RELATIONSHIPS

POWER ⟷ SELF-ESTEEM

THE DIAGRAM ABOVE is what we call the "Golden Triangle," and it shows how relationships, power, and self-esteem are the three key elements essential to women's overall happiness. There is a complex relationship among these elements—how much or little we have of one can affect how much we have of another. In this chapter, we'll look at what each of these components means to us, and how the balance of the elements within us and compared to other women affects the likelihood of our becoming involved in a destructive conflict.

Relationships are our connections to other people: friends, family members, colleagues. They are crucial to our sense of well-being; they actually help us define who we are. The *power* variable refers to the external force you wield in the world. This can take several forms, such as your position or title at work, your relationship to the boss, your attractiveness, your net worth, your boyfriend's/husband's status, your clothes, your sense of humor, your personality, and so forth. These are real or perceived tangible factors that you and others can actually observe. *Self-esteem* represents internal power—your feeling of inner strength and self-worth. Generally, strength or weakness in this element is far more hidden from the world.

Let's look at each of these elements in greater depth.

RELATIONSHIPS

It has become almost axiomatic that women live in a web of relationships. We have developed a great facility for relatedness, and we need these connections in order to maintain our sense of personal well-being. Jean Baker Miller, a clinical professor of psychiatry at Boston University of Medicine, explains that for women, "all growth occurs within emotional connections, not separate from them . . . To feel 'more related to another person' means to feel one's self enhanced, not threatened. It does not feel like a loss of a part of one's self; instead it becomes a step toward more pleasure and effectiveness."[1]

Relationships are such a critical element in the world of women that they are also central to our dealings in the business world. At the office we also tend to think relationally and work along relational, not hierarchical, lines (we'll get into this more in chapters 3, 4, and 5). Women often define career success by their ability to create affiliation with others and develop relationships in the work setting: "In my time at the Acme Company, my boss became my best friend, and ten years later, she's still my best friend." Organizational psychologist Carol Gallagher has found that the ability to maintain positive relationships was among the four critical success factors in the careers of the two hundred high-ranking senior executive women she studied. "The ability to develop relationships is imperative in crossing the threshold to the next level," she writes in *Going to the Top.* One of her interviewees explained, "On a scale of one to ten, I would give relationships a ten . . . I don't think you can get ahead without them."[2]

The maintenance of relationships in the workplace is also far more important to women than to men. In Susan's doctoral research into twenty-one career values (such as risk taking, economic security, and altruism) across three generations of men and women (Gen-Xers, baby boomers, and mature workers), she found that no matter what the age, *the importance of social interactions in the workplace is the most significant difference between the genders.*[3] Social relationships were also significantly more important to women than to men, ranking fourth out of the twenty-one values. Susan's research and dozens of other studies have proven that women value both social interactions and friendships significantly more than men do. They consider interpersonal relations important in their career development. They derive meaning in their lives predominantly through these interpersonal relationships and by observing and learning from others as well as their own life experiences.

Because of our focus on relationships, women are more likely to judge and care about people based on their innate qualities rather than their position in the corporate hierarchy. Consequently, female executives are more likely to adopt a collaborative leadership style, to share information and involve others in the decision-making process. We need our colleagues to make our work fulfilling and enjoyable, but also so we ourselves can be maximally productive. We therefore are more likely to pay attention to and address emotional issues at work. We often make concerted efforts to get along with our female colleagues. We share feelings and use heartfelt empathy to help assuage upset feelings or mitigate a difficult situation.

Women who have met with success in terms of concrete achievements but not what's called "affiliative success" often feel empty, lonely, and isolated. Susan consults in the financial industry with the senior women at a Fortune 100 company and was surprised to discover that what many of the female executives there want is not tactical advice such as "If Fred does this, and I respond in this way, what do you think will happen?" but empathy. During their consultations, the women pour their hearts out about the pain they feel, often from the other women in the company. For instance, two women had quit in Cynthia's department, and she believed their action was due to the way in which she had treated them. She spent almost an hour agonizing over how bad she felt, until finally Susan said, "Why don't you ask them why they left?"

The following week, Cynthia told Susan that she had phoned the women, and they both told her they had quit for other reasons. Whether or not her former employees were telling the truth, this executive certainly felt a lot better, believing her relationships had been preserved.

Because relationships are so important to women, it is all the more painful when they deteriorate. We will explore how this happens more fully in chapter 2.

POWER

Power is the ability to get things done. It is extremely important: without power you would find it impossible to reach your personal and professional goals. In 1959, psychologists John French and Bertram Raven at UCLA identified six kinds of power that both genders utilize inside and outside the workplace:

- *Reward power:* the ability to give something to someone. You can reward another with a promotion, gifts, or praise. You have something that she wants.

- *Coercive power:* the ability to punish someone, to demote her or otherwise harm her career progress. Derogatory comments can also fall under this category.

- *Legitimate power:* power conferred on you by the organization. You are given the title of vice president or appointed manager of the department or leader of the team.

- *Expert power:* power derived from your unique abilities or skills. You're the only person in the office who knows how to fix the computers, or perhaps you have expertise in managing the boss.

- *Referent power:* power based on your personal affection for or identification with another person or group. People do as you ask simply because they like and trust you. You have referent power over a friend who wants to please you.

- *Associative power:* power derived from whom you know and how you associate with them rather than what you know (expert power). You gain power by dropping names.[4]

Power exists in relation to someone or something else but never in a vacuum. It can be a double-edged sword, especially for women in the workplace, because it's much more straightforward for men to wield power on the job than for women. When men take command of a situation, they're perceived as resolute and authoritative. They are focused on winning and will often take charge. These can be positive, even comforting, attributes in a crisis. We might respect a powerful man, especially if he can provide structure and direction to a group during a time of confusion.

But women are in a more precarious position when they try to appear powerful. Unfortunately, power and friendship don't easily mix among women; acting as if you have power can skew female relationships. Friendship implies giving to another person and sharing, whereas power can result in your taking from the other person or directing her activity. To women, these do not feel like friendly actions. In fact, these behaviors could be perceived with downright hostility. Consequently, if you exert your power on the other women at the office in the same way that men do, you can easily provoke a catfight.

The Perils of Mixing Friendship and Power

Men more often experience "friendliness" with their co-workers, rather than friendships. They tend to be guarded when it comes to divulging intimate information about themselves to co-workers for the sake of their own survival in the hierarchical business world. Moreover, they are more apt to focus on their professional goals as well as on their own political survival in a corporation while women are often more focused on keeping their relationships with others intact.

Because relationships are so important to women, referent power (the power of friendship, mutual affection, and trust) can be more important to us than to men. And it's also the type of power that may be the most problematic. *Women have much higher expectations of power sharing with those they are closest to than men do.* Consider the following scenario: Your friend and former co-worker is promoted. She suddenly has more conferred legitimate power than you do. Chafing from the imbalance, you may feel tempted to withhold affection (your referent power), and a destructive conflict can ensue.

Or the opposite can occur: You genuinely like one of your employees and give her lots of leeway in her use of time. Such an employee can have a good deal of referent power over you. In fact, you may fear disturbing the friendship if you speak up, but you do eventually note that her work is slipping. Using your legitimate power, you talk with her about her unacceptable performance. You begin to use coercive power when you bring up her yearly evaluation. (She knows there are negative consequences to your disapproval.) As a way of evening out the power play, she withdraws her referent power from you. She goes to lunch with others without inviting you, throws work on your desk instead of handing it to you, and responds curtly when you ask about her family.

Some women managers will even back off from following through on discipline because they fear the damage it will do to their relationship with a female employee. The bottom line: you can't let referent power drive your management behavior, even though it may be attractive.

CHIP THEORY: WOMEN'S UNIQUE PATH TO POWER

It's wise to approach power in a distinctively female way in order to make it work for you. For example, consider the use of what Patricia Palleschi, a vice president at the Walt Disney Company, calls Chip Theory. This is based on a sense of equity: each of us is endowed with a certain number of chips of power—positive attributes or actions—that we constantly exchange with others. We possess, give, and get these power chips in three ways:

- *Interactions:* Saying "Hi, how are you?" whenever you meet a co-worker. Taking a genuine interest in her family, vacation, or new project at work.

- *As a birthright:* Some people are simply born with lots of chips—think of the Rockefellers. Fortunate chip-rich folks may be blessed with good looks, talent, great intelligence, athletic prowess—inherent qualities.

- *Active acquisition:* People proactively seek out chips. They will obtain an MBA or Ph.D., or they'll strive for the title of vice president. Some may marry handsome or rich significant others to increase their store of chips, or they'll frequent plastic surgeons who can artificially enhance their chip bank accounts by tucking their tummies or lifting their sagging eyelids and chins.

Although you may not have been aware of it until now, everyone with whom you interact keeps a chip bankbook on you. All day long you are gaining and losing chips with your direct reports, peers, and higher-ups. They know where you stand with them at any given moment, and you know where they stand with you.

Indeed, one of the most important rules in Chip Theory is that *we always make it equal in the end*—that is, if someone tries to take away our chips, we will find a way to even the score. For instance, if upon arriving at work, your warm and friendly greeting to co-worker Brenda is met with a flat "Oh, hi," you will probably greet this person much less effusively in the future. In fact, you may eventually stop saying hello to Brenda altogether. Conversely, if that colleague is kind and generous with her chips, most likely you will feel inclined to return them in kind.

Pat learned that lesson as a university professor. Her secretary, Sarah, worked in a windowless cubicle all day, and Pat knew that she valued relationship chips—the simple "Hi, how are you?" "What are you doing?" "What's new?" interactions.

One day, Pat was working with her boss, Kim, in Kim's office. Sarah came in, dropped off some typing for Pat, and left. Perturbed, Kim turned to Pat and asked, "When did you give her that typing?"

"This morning."

"Does she always bring it when she's done?"

"Yes, of course," Pat responded, surprised at this line of questioning.

"Well I gave Sarah typing to do three days ago, and she still hasn't finished it. She never brings my work to me when it's done. I always have to ask her for it." Kim hadn't been paying Sarah her interaction chips, and Sarah had found a way to make it even in the end.

The exchanges that occur at holiday time are another way to understand Chip Theory. When we receive a greeting card, we usually feel compelled to send one back. Gifts must be of equal value—when they're not, both the giver and receiver become uncomfortable. (Some people even keep extra presents around, just in case someone surprises them with an unexpected one.) Men usually don't value the exchanges of greeting card chips as much as women do; they will rarely send male friends birthday cards. Men will exchange tickets to Lakers or Yankees games, however, which hold much greater meaning and value to them.

When we talk about Chip Theory, people sometimes say, "But isn't this manipulative?" Our answer is, "Yes, indeed, it is." But consider this: We all started manipulating other people at the same moment—Day One, when we realized there was a connection between screaming and getting fed—and we have continued to manipulate every day of our lives since then. We have just become unconscious of it and more graceful at it.

We all need to manage our relationships with people, and wielding chips is simply an automatic tool to accomplish that end.

MAKING IT EVEN

Female managers often believe that because they're in charge, employees have to do what they say. But we've found that somehow, in some way, some-day, female employees will always make it even in the end. Jill was hired to manage a group of people who had to travel to relatively undesirable cities. When employees took these business junkets, they were allowed a "safe-arrival call"; that is, once they reached their destination, they could phone home to say "I made it" on the company's dime.

Soon after Jill took the job, she discovered there was supposed to be a dollar limit on these safe-arrival calls. She diligently went through old files and found that several of her employees had spent more money on their safe-arrival calls than was allowed. Rather than simply let this go but make an issue of enforcing company policy in the future, she went from desk to desk and collected $3.10 from Lila, $7.45 from Terri, and $11.52 from Debbie, and so on ad nauseum.

Until this moment, this had not been a particularly high-energy group, but the electric charge that ran through it and the team building that suddenly occurred were astounding. Mysteriously, employees soon began turning up at the wrong place at the wrong time with the wrong equipment. Over and over again. Jill was putting out one fire after another, which cost her far more in time and energy than the $100 or so she had collected from her profligate and loquacious employees. She kept thinking there was some glitch in the scheduling procedure and didn't realize that the glitch resided in the chip deficit she had created with her pettiness. That's what she really needed to fix.

Women have really good memories. We tend to hold grudges for a long time. The game is never over for us, so chip deficits can last a lifetime if they're not rectified.

DISPLAYS OF POWER

Ostentatious displays (see the box below)—the furs, the showy diamonds, the luxurious house, the flashy car—although they might not get you far if you're stranded in the Kalahari Desert, are all symbols of power in our society at which other women may take umbrage and seek to even the score. These various displays must be cautiously managed because female co-workers may become resentful of them.

Status symbols can entail more than simple material wealth. Suppose you have been promoted to manage your former co-workers. In such a case, it would be wise to manage your symbolic display of power. At least for the first few weeks, you might, for example, choose to do your own copying and pick up your own faxes rather than ordering a subordinate around. And when you are ready to ask for assistance, you might phrase your request as "Could you do me a favor and . . ." New hires might not have the same difficulties with you and would be coming on board with a different set of expectations for the relationship. But, as we'll elaborate in chapter 7, some management of the symbolic power display may be called for when your former peers become your subordinates.

DIAGNOSE YOURSELF: SYMBOLS OF POWER

Check any of the following symbols of power that may apply to you. These may inadvertently create obstacles when you are dealing with other women. Your awareness of their negative impact is important in order to avoid catfights:

___ Executive title   ___ Confidence

___ Graduate degree   ___ Striking figure

(continues)

___ Large office	___ Youth
___ Attention of boss	___ Financial freedom
___ Employees who report to you	___ Extravagant vacations
___ Promotability	___ Attractive partner
___ Special talent/ability	___ Successful partner
___ Expensive clothes/jewelry	___ Luxury car
___ Large/elegant home(s)	___ Classy neighborhood

If you have a problem with another woman, you must be extremely cautious about displaying these symbols of power. Such trappings only create more animosity. The woman is likely to interpret these symbols as your signaling that you are better than she is, further threatening the power balance. Even if your relationship with the other woman is positive, these symbols can create a problem. It's, of course, wonderful if you have these objects and attributes, but flaunting them can cause you trouble.

Body language (an open posture, head held high, expansive use of personal space), a confident air, and a condescending tone can also be construed as displays of power. At one of Pat's workshops held in Chicago, when a question about leadership styles came up, one man asked about Mike Ditka. Pat had to confess that she didn't know who he was—to her, an insignificant lapse—but at lunch later, a group participant sought to rub her nose in it. "I can't believe you don't know who Mike Ditka is," Diana said in a disparaging tone.

Pat explained that she isn't from the Midwest, and that she usually doesn't read the sports section of the newspaper, to which Diana coolly replied, "I would know who the coach is if you were talking about Los Angeles or San Diego."

"But I don't really care about football," Pat protested.

"I don't either, but I stay well informed on all topics" was this woman's haughty response.

Immediately, Pat had the impulse to go into full power-display mode and raise a subject such as the intricacies of the human genome project with this snooty individual, hoping that Diana wasn't knowledgeable on that topic, just so Pat could even out the conversation and the score. Instead, Pat held her tongue and tried to understand how Diana's world looked to her. She decided that if Diana did this to her, she probably did it at work too. Pat was running the workshop and had a great deal of legitimate and expert power that might have felt threatening to Diana.

Ironically, had Pat responded to Diana's power play, it would have backfired. Pat didn't feel diminished because she was ignorant about Mike Ditka—this was not something she cared much about. But Diana's seemingly arrogant display of power could have quickly triggered a destructive conflict with someone less aware or cautious, and it also might have made her seem unattractively supercilious to her assembled co-workers.

Your Power Profile

Power exists in relation to someone or something else but never in a vacuum. You can use this questionnaire to assess a troublesome relationship with a female co-worker.

Keeping this specific person in mind, think about how much power you're demonstrating with her, and whether it's positive power or negative.

	Not at All True 1	2	3	4	Very True 5
1. I have or can get resources that would be helpful to her.	___	___	___	___	___
2. I have or can get resources that she would like but I have held on to these.	___	___	___	___	___
3. I have shared resources with her that she wanted.	___	___	___	___	___
4. I am in a position to create negative consequences for her.	___	___	___	___	___

(continues)

	NOT AT ALL TRUE				VERY TRUE
	1	2	3	4	5
5. I have caused her to experience negative consequences, which she feels are unjust.	—	—	—	—	—
6. I have prevented her from receiving unwarranted negative consequences.	—	—	—	—	—
7. I have legitimate (position) power over her.	—	—	—	—	—
8. I have legitimate (position) power she thinks she should have.	—	—	—	—	—
9. I have legitimate power, and she is comfortable with how I use that power.	—	—	—	—	—
10. I have expertise that she believes could be of value to her.	—	—	—	—	—
11. At times I withhold my expertise that she believes could be of value to her.	—	—	—	—	—
12. I have shared my expertise that she believes could be of value to her.	—	—	—	—	—
13. I could develop a relationship of trust with her that she would value.	—	—	—	—	—
14. She does not trust me or value our relationship.	—	—	—	—	—
15. She trusts me and values our relationship.	—	—	—	—	—
16. I have contacts that would be useful to her.	—	—	—	—	—
17. I do not use my contacts to assist her.	—	—	—	—	—
18. I have used my contacts to assist her.	—	—	—	—	—

Now score yourself. For each question, transfer the number assigned to your answer to the appropriate column below. For example, if you said "very true" to statement number 1, place a 5 in the blank next to "Question 1" below.

QUESTION	QUESTION	QUESTION
1. _____	3. _____	2. _____
4. _____	6. _____	5. _____
7. _____	9. _____	8. _____
10. _____	12. _____	11. _____
13. _____	15. _____	14. _____
16. _____	18. _____	17. _____
Total _____ Power Potential	Total _____ Positive Power	Total _____ Negative Power

Here's how to evaluate your results. Let's look individually at your scores for your total power potential, the total positive power that you wield with your co-worker, and your total negative power.

POWER POTENTIAL

If you scored between 20 and 30, you have a great opportunity to have a positive (or negative) impact on this relationship with the woman you've kept in mind throughout this exercise. Take a look at the six kinds of power listed on p. 24 and consider which is most effective for you to use with this woman. If you scored below 20 but had one or more single scores at 4 or 5, you will need to target selectively how you use your power to improve the relationship. If you scored below 20 and your single scores were all between 1 and 3, it will unfortunately be much harder for you to have a positive impact on the relationship unless this woman decides to shift gears and become positive herself.

(continues)

POSITIVE POWER

If your score in the Positive Power column was between 20 and 30, you most probably have a good relationship with this woman. You have likely devoted a good deal of effort toward having a positive impact on her, for example by mentioning her to higher-ups or recommending her for a plum assignment. If, on the other hand, your relationship isn't great, ask yourself the question "Does she know what I'm doing for her? Is she aware that when I bring up her success on a project, I'm deliberately trying to make her abilities known?" We're not suggesting that you need to send a flag up the flagpole every time you are helpful to this woman, but she may not be connecting the dots of your actions. If you scored below 20 in this column and you have a substantial score in the Power Potential column, then it's time to generate some chips. What can you do for this woman that she would value?

NEGATIVE POWER

If you scored between 20 and 30 here, then a world of opportunity is open to you. If you are having problems with this woman, they may stem from your use of power. You may be pulling rank or seem insensitive to her concerns about her child. To correct the situation, think about how you can wield power more positively. How can you give assignments differently? You might ask more often about her family. If you scored between 12 and 19, you have not been using your power as well as needed for a positive impact on your relations with her. If you scored below 11, you are within reasonable limits in negative use of power, but you may still have opportunities to reduce this score. Focus on what you can do to increase your Positive Power with this woman.

The Friendship Quotient is another factor in this column. If the woman whom you were assessing in this Power Profile is or has been a friend, and you have a high Negative Power score with her, your problem may become more significant. If you scored over 20 points in Negative Power, add to that total:

5 points for best friend

3 points for good friend

1 point for an acquaintance or co-worker

Then reevaluate your new total score.

THE SELF-ESTEEM FACTOR

Self-esteem refers to how well you think of and value yourself, how much you're worth in your own eyes, and the power you allow yourself to have. Matthew McKay, psychologist and clinical director of Haight-Ashbury Psychological Services in San Francisco, explains in his book *Self-Esteem*, "One of the main factors differentiating humans from other animals is the awareness of self; the ability to form an identity and then attach a value to it. In other words, you have the capacity to define who you are and then decide if you like the identity or not."[5]

When you evaluate the level of your self-esteem, you look at intrinsic qualities such as whether you believe you're a useful person, how much you trust yourself, and how self-satisfied you feel. Are you pleased or unhappy about what you've accomplished in your life so far? How well do you relate to others? How comfortably do you accept responsibility for your actions? Whether your self-esteem level is high or low depends on how you feel about the following:

- *Your sense of value:* Do you feel that you have good qualities? Do you accept yourself and your emotions?

- *Your accomplishments:* Do you believe that you reach the goals you've set for yourself, you receive recognition for your efforts, and you continually work to develop your capacities?

- *Your relationships:* Are you able to get close to others, share, and establish a sense of trust?

- *Your abilities:* Do you have faith in your productiveness at your work and your capacity to act with self-control, make decisions, and shape your own destiny?

- *Your sense of responsibility:* Do you hold yourself accountable for your own failures? Do you take an active role in resolving any conflicts you are involved in?

- *How others perceive you:* Do your friends, colleagues, and family members treat you with respect? Do they appreciate your talents, abilities, and uniqueness?

As with your Power Profile, you can't define who you are in a vacuum. Rather, you do so through a world of cues that give you feedback about how the world sees you. It would be hard to hold a positive self-image if all those around you sent messages to the contrary—even if they were wrong. Sometimes others may even be *spitefully* wrong. They know they're being cruel in putting forth a negative assessment of you, but they somehow feel justified in their vindictiveness. Sometimes people will do their darnedest to make you feel bad no matter what, and once you take their opinion of you personally, your sense of self-esteem can be mired in an accelerating downward spiral.

All humans strive to feel good about themselves, and when our self-esteem is toppled, everyone feels a natural urge to right it. But self-esteem plays into our equation among women in quite a different way than it does for men. Women are more likely to "be hard on themselves" and "beat themselves up," therefore lowering their self-esteem. They are more likely to engage in negative self-talk ("I'm so stupid. How could I have said that?") and advertise their flubs ("You won't believe how I screwed up today!"). These self-defeating behaviors may be a temporary outlet for our feelings of frustration, but they almost invariably result in lowered self-esteem.

Interpersonal conflict can also diminish self-esteem. Says Carol Gilligan, author of *In a Different Voice*, "Women not only define themselves in a context of human relationship but also judge themselves in terms of their ability to care."[6] Since women highly value their caring relations with their colleagues, when they experience interpersonal discord, they often disparage themselves as inadequate, which cuts into their positive sense of self. This is especially true because women's conversations touch so many levels of one another's lives beyond the world of work: friends, family, menstrual cycles, restaurants, travel . . . When relationships break down, women are affected much more than merely at work.

One of the respondents to our Web site questionnaire described how complicated life became when she found herself enmeshed in a destructive conflict with her supervisor. "A woman boss gave my business partner and me our first break and became our mentor," she wrote. "But when we felt it was best for us to move on and 'spread our wings,' our mentor took it personally. She literally felt we'd betrayed her and couldn't understand how we could 'do this to her.' We ended up going to see her therapist with her to resolve this issue, but our relationship has never been the same." It was very likely that this supervisor's self-esteem was damaged when these two people decided to make a break. Perhaps she felt they'd personally abandoned her.

THE WOMAN'S DILEMMA

Women not only diminish their self-esteem through negative self-talk; they also fail to compensate for it by building themselves up when they experience success. We usually attribute our accomplishments to factors outside ourselves, such as effort ("I tried really hard"), task ease ("Anyone could have done it; it was easy"), or luck ("It just fell in my lap; I was in the right place at the right time"). Our success isn't our doing, we say, but our failings are. We don't have the ability, we think, saying things like "I'll never have enough willpower to lose weight," "If only I were smarter, I could do it," or "I have the memory of a flea." This is even true cross-culturally: a recent study of more than thirteen thousand children in twelve countries including Australia, Jamaica, Germany, Thailand, and Israel found that girls consistently blamed themselves when things went wrong.[7]

This unproductive way of defining our accomplishments and ourselves can easily become a self-fulfilling prophecy since self-esteem derives, in part, from the reflection of how we perceive the world responding to us. Let's say a woman says, "Gee, I just lucked out on this one; I didn't even know what I was doing. The stars were lined up, and it turned out that the data were available." If over time she's consistent enough in attributing her successes to factors outside herself in this way, people will eventually believe that she wasn't responsible for her wins and will reflect that attitude back to her. This feedback loop will ingrain in her psyche the belief "It wasn't me, it was other factors" all the more insistently.

Interestingly, men have the opposite tendencies. A man is likely to attribute his successes to his own abilities ("The reason I was successful is because you asked me to do this, and I'm good at it"), while he attributes his failures to factors outside himself ("I didn't get the job done because you didn't give me enough time"). The people around him are much more likely to believe that it must be his innate abilities that cause him to be so hot. And when he fails, it wasn't his doing. Give the guy a break! Just as with women, this feedback loop reinforces men's beliefs about themselves and their self-esteem.

Moreover, from the time they were little boys, males in our culture have organized their lives in terms of hierarchies (think sports teams, club officers, and so on). Everyone is either above or below someone else in the pecking order. Consequently, men are constantly trying to keep from finding themselves at the bottom of the pile. One of the ways they manage this is by behaving as if they are powerful even if they don't feel as though they are. If you act as if you're "hot" and the world begins to respond to you that way, it becomes another self-fulfilling prophecy that supports men's positive self-esteem.

Women, on the other hand, don't grow up in hierarchies. Their young lives are organized around "being nice" and sharing power equally. (As we'll discuss in chapter 4, there are no boss-doll players.) No one is in charge of this kind of play; girls form a cooperative group and build upon one another's ideas: "Okay, now I'm going to be the mommy!" "And I'm going to make the mud pies." There are no winners and losers in girls' imaginative games, unlike in boys' games with their team captains and star players. Of course, our socialization is changing, and more and more young girls these days engage in competitive sports, but in general women tend to flatten out the hierarchy among themselves; this makes their relationships more equal, but may look to the world as if they're putting themselves down in subtle ways: "You did a great job on the report," says Liz. When Mary responds, "Oh no, most of the information was already there. I just reorganized it," she appears to be negating her own worth. But in actuality, these two women are supporting each other's self-esteem.

TROUBLES TALK ENHANCES SELF-ESTEEM

In a similar vein, sharing difficulties, shortcomings, and areas of deficiencies in their lives is one of the major ways women bond with one another: "I'm a dummy in math." "I'm useless when it comes to applying new software." "My kids are driving me crazy." "My husband is always away on business, and I'm lonely." "I've gained so much weight." Communications expert Deborah Tannen calls this *troubles talk*,[8] and it's a useful way for women to maintain their relationships.

These sorts of interactions are a way to diminish the external power among women: if you are the one to start the troubles talk, you willingly open yourself up and thus give power to the person to whom you're speaking. Troubles talk can help if the woman you're talking to empathizes and joins you in your pain, but it can derail you if the empathy or help isn't forthcoming. If she makes fun of you or devalues your experience by one-upping you ("You think that's bad . . . you should hear what happened to me!"), you may be left feeling vulnerable, empty, and angry because such one-upmanship feels self-serving and is antithetical to women's culture. Your self-esteem can also decrease if a woman with whom you're sharing your troubles doesn't reciprocate and share a few of her own. If she does so, by demonstrating that you understand her pain and want to help her be comforted, you are extending yourself and can nourish and nurture her self-esteem.

YOUR SELF-ESTEEM PROFILE

The following questionnaire will help you assess your self-esteem. Bear in mind that this is a snapshot of how you're feeling at this moment, not an overall assessment of who you are. Self-esteem can vary according to life events and the situations in which you find yourself.

Place a check mark in the blank that most corresponds to how accurate or inaccurate you feel each statement is at the moment.

	NOT AT ALL TRUE				VERY TRUE
	1	2	3	4	5
1. I believe I have a number of good qualities.	___	___	___	___	___
2. When I set a goal, I reach it.	___	___	___	___	___
3. I find that I rarely can trust others.	___	___	___	___	___
4. I am very productive.	___	___	___	___	___
5. I have trouble saying "I'm sorry."	___	___	___	___	___

(continues)

	Not at All True				Very True
	1	2	3	4	5

6. New people whom I meet respond positively to me. __ __ __ __ __

7. I trust myself in a wide range of situations. __ __ __ __ __

8. I do not feel very successful. __ __ __ __ __

9. I am open to others even if they are different from me. __ __ __ __ __

10. I am able to do things as well as most people. __ __ __ __ __

11. I accept responsibility for myself. __ __ __ __ __

12. Others try to take advantage of me. __ __ __ __ __

13. I wish I had more respect for myself. __ __ __ __ __

14. My accomplishments are rarely recognized. __ __ __ __ __

15. I like to deal with people, and they like me. __ __ __ __ __

16. I can shape my own destiny. __ __ __ __ __

17. My failures are generally my fault. __ __ __ __ __

18. My co-workers treat me with respect. __ __ __ __ __

19. I feel others are worth more than I am. __ __ __ __ __

20. I continue to develop my capabilities. __ __ __ __ __

21. I get close to others and share. __ __ __ __ __

22. I act with self-control. __ __ __ __ __

23. I believe that the only kind of luck I have is bad luck. __ __ __ __ __

	Not at All True 1	2	3	4	Very True 5
24. People at work do not have confidence in my abilities.	___	___	___	___	___
25. I accept myself and my feelings.	___	___	___	___	___
26. I know I can accomplish anything I choose to.	___	___	___	___	___
27. I'm suspicious when I get a compliment.	___	___	___	___	___
28. I have difficulty making important decisions.	___	___	___	___	___
29. When I make a mistake, I have trouble admitting it.	___	___	___	___	___
30. My colleagues see me as a valuable member of our team.	___	___	___	___	___
31. I believe I am a useful person.	___	___	___	___	___
32. I wish I were able to reach more of my goals.	___	___	___	___	___
33. I become defensive when others give me feedback on things I've done.	___	___	___	___	___
34. I feel useless at times.	___	___	___	___	___
35. I take an active role in resolving my own conflicts.	___	___	___	___	___
36. Others speak negatively about me behind my back.	___	___	___	___	___
37. My self-talk is often negative.	___	___	___	___	___
38. I have much to be proud of.	___	___	___	___	___

(continues)

	NOT AT ALL TRUE				VERY TRUE
	1	2	3	4	5

39. I am a good listener and friend. ___ ___ ___ ___ ___

40. When I experience a setback, I find it hard ___ ___ ___ ___ ___
to get back on track.

41. I am competent to cope with and accept ___ ___ ___ ___ ___
life's challenges.

42. Others appreciate my talents, abilities, ___ ___ ___ ___ ___
and uniqueness.

SELF-ESTEEM SCORING

Self-esteem breaks down into six categories: values, accomplishments, relations with others, abilities, responsibility and/or accountability, and others' perceptions of you. To evaluate the level of your self-esteem in each of these categories, transfer your score for each statement to the blank below that corresponds to the number of the statement.

Value: This category is a measurement of how much you respect and trust yourself, how you see your unique qualities and your usefulness, and how positively or negatively you talk to yourself. Record the numeric values you gave to the following questions in Columns A and B below. Then total each column. To get your final score, subtract your Column B total from your Column A total.

COLUMN A	COLUMN B
1. _____	13. _____
7. _____	19. _____
25. _____	37. _____
31. _____	

Column A Total _____ Column B Total _____

Value Total (Column A minus Column B) _____

Accomplishments: This category measures how you feel about the goals you have achieved in your life, your level of success, and how strongly you believe that you can attain more. Add and then subtract your scores as above.

COLUMN A	COLUMN B
2. _____	8. _____
20. _____	14. _____
26. _____	32. _____
38. _____	

Column A Total _____   Column B Total _____

Accomplishments Total (Column A minus Column B) _____

Relations with Others: This category measures how you feel about yourself in dealing with others and whether you can trust and open up to them, participate in authentic communication, and develop deep friendships.

COLUMN A	COLUMN B
9. _____	3. _____
15. _____	27. _____
21. _____	33. _____
39. _____	

Column A Total _____   Column B Total _____

Relations Total (Column A minus Column B) _____

(continues)

Abilities: This category measures how you feel about your ability to be productive, to shape your own destiny, and to bounce back after a setback.

COLUMN A	COLUMN B
4. _____	28. _____
10. _____	34. _____
16. _____	40. _____
22. _____	

Column A Total _____   Column B Total _____

Abilities Total (Column A minus Column B) _____

Responsibility/Accountability: This category measures how well you feel you accept life's challenges, how much control you believe you have over your circumstances, and your ability to take ownership of and apologize for your mistakes.

COLUMN A	COLUMN B
11. _____	5. _____
17. _____	23. _____
35. _____	29. _____
41. _____	

Column A Total _____   Column B Total _____

Responsibility Total (Column A minus Column B) _____

Others' Perceptions of You: This category measures how you believe others see you, your innate worth, and your talents and abilities.

COLUMN A	COLUMN B
6. _____	12. _____
18. _____	24. _____
30. _____	36. _____
42. _____	

Column A Total _____   Column B Total _____

Others' Perceptions of You Total (Column A minus Column B) _____

INTERPRETING YOUR SCORES IN EACH OF THE SIX CATEGORIES

For each of the above six categories, notice where you have scored the highest and lowest. The possible range is −11 to +17.

Does it surprise you that you scored high in relationships and lower in accountability? Any score below +4 indicates a category that would be important for you to focus on when developing your self-esteem. For example, if your Value score is low, you might consider becoming more positive in the way you talk to yourself. If your Accomplishments score is low, consider making a list of and then celebrating all the important goals and successes you have already achieved in your life. Then note your current goals and develop a plan for attaining them.

OVERALL SELF-ESTEEM SCORING

Add the totals from:

_____ Value

_____ Accomplishments

_____ Relationships

(continues)

_____ Abilities

_____ Sense of Responsibility/Accountability

_____ Colleagues' Perceptions of You

_____ Grand Total for Self-Esteem

INTERPRETING YOUR OVERALL SELF-ESTEEM SCORE

The possible overall scores of the self-esteem questionnaire range from 102 to −66. If your score is:

+60 and above: Your self-esteem level is high and you have a healthy, respectful view of your personal worth. You have already done a lot of work on yourself to be at this level. Congratulations!

+40 to +59: This score is impressive, showing that your self-esteem level is solid in most areas. You have clearly spent time and effort on developing your talents, uniqueness, and relations with others around you. In order to raise your self-esteem score even higher, focus on categories where your score showed a bit of room for improvement.

+20 to +39: Your self-esteem level is fairly high compared with that of many women, although there are still some areas where you do not give yourself as much credit as you deserve. Focus on improvement in the categories where you are below +4, and your self-esteem level will increase to even healthier levels.

+1 to +19: Your self-esteem could definitely use a lift. You have a tendency to underestimate yourself and how well others perceive you. You may find it difficult to increase your sense of power with the low level of self-esteem you currently have, and you may wish to work on building your self-esteem (we'll suggest ways to do that throughout this book) in order to better your relationships with other women.

Less than zero: You have scored low in many categories, and this indicates you may not feel very good about yourself or your unique talents and personality. Your low self-esteem may have a negative impact on your view of the world, and it can diminish your ability to have authentic, healthy relationships with yourself and with others.

Assessment of Another Woman's Self-Esteem

Here's a "quick and dirty" quiz that you can use to assess the self-esteem of a co-worker who may be giving you trouble. You will find this information useful as you read chapter 2. Bearing in mind a particular woman colleague, answer Yes or No to the following questions.

Does Your Co-Worker Seem to:	Yes	No
Have respect for herself?	____	____
Talk positively about herself?	____	____
Reach goals she sets?	____	____
Accept blame instead of blaming luck or others?	____	____
Let in compliments from others?	____	____
Be a good listener and friend to others?	____	____
Have a sense of humor about herself?	____	____
Like herself?	____	____
Remain receptive when given feedback?	____	____
Be resilient after a setback?	____	____
Have confidence in her abilities?	____	____
Be able to say "I'm sorry"?	____	____
Admit mistakes?	____	____
Feel appreciated by others?	____	____

The more "Yes" responses you marked, the more positively you perceive the self-esteem of this colleague. If you marked "No" more often than "Yes," it is likely that you are dealing with a woman who has low self-esteem. Compare this general result to your own scoring on Your Self-Esteem Profile. If your score was low but you perceive this co-worker as having high self-esteem, or vice versa, beware of fireworks.

THE DANCE OF POWER AND SELF-ESTEEM

Up to this point, we have dealt with the issues of power and self-esteem as if they were two distinct traits. However, there is an interrelationship between the two. Having a high sense of self-esteem may not immediately enhance your sense of power, but research has shown that eventually there is a positive correlation between high self-esteem and high achievement (which can lead to the accrual of power). Conversely, a diminished sense of self-esteem could have an impact on your perception of your own external power. If you begin to believe that you're unworthy, you may unconsciously send out signals—downcast eyes, hunched shoulders—that you are, and accordingly people may treat you as powerless.

One of Pat's previously self-confident clients, Erica, was summarily and abruptly fired from a big job. Even though she felt the ax had fallen unfairly, at some point, while she was interviewing for new positions, Erica found her sense of self diminishing. In her own eyes she had now become a "fired person"—damaged goods. Her body language telegraphed her state of mind: her voice was hesitant, her walk seemed less assured, and she seemed to take up less space in a room. Because all these nonverbal cues could conspire to make her seem "smaller" in the world, in order to do well in her interviews, Pat advised Erica to pretend that she had confidence, to take on an outer mantle of power and act "as if"—even though she wasn't feeling quite that strong at the moment.

Does the dance of self-esteem and power work in the other direction? That is, if you increase your external power with a job promotion, an award, or some other tangible enhancement, will that suffice to increase your self-esteem? Logically one would think so, but this is a delicate matter that can depend on the level of one's self-esteem in the first place.

Some women are able to allow themselves to feel nourished by the perks of increased external power. Consequently, their self-esteem grows stronger. This was true of Carrie, a relatively new employee in a high-tech corporation. Although one of the youngest people on the company's sales force, she was energetic, outgoing, goal-oriented, and optimistic, and she sold rings around her co-workers. She was given the company's annual award for being among the top three salespeople in the United States. The honor reaffirmed Carrie's abilities, and she proudly and prominently displayed her plaque in her office. Most certainly, this external reward boosted Carrie's already high level of self-esteem and probably helped her succeed even further.

For other women, unfortunately, all the perceived power in the world won't build their self-esteem because they view themselves as so unworthy. Consider the short, tragic life of Princess Diana, a woman who held great external power but suffered from such low self-esteem that she appeared to feel perpetually unfulfilled. The seemingly extraordinarily powerful performer Madonna, known for her outwardly confident and attention-grabbing attire and behavior, revealed some years back in a television interview how vulnerable and insecure she felt at times because of the lasting effects of her mother's death when she was five years old.

Few of us attain such visibly powerful positions as Diana, Princess of Wales, or Madonna, but despite an outward appearance of strength, both these women seemed to suffer inwardly from the ravages of low self-esteem. Similarly, in the workplace, the veneer and accompanying accoutrements of power can be deceiving, and are often deliberately accentuated by a woman who has poor feelings about herself. Kathryn, for instance, an executive vice president at a financial firm, was physically lovely and very accomplished. She acknowledged to Pat, however, that when she receives compliments or awards, "they just go right through me. It's as if they flow out of the holes inside me. Nothing stays." Such a woman may never feel truly fulfilled unless she works at improving her sense of self.

THE IMPOSTOR SYNDROME

It's likely that someone like Katheryn suffers from what psychologists Pauline Rose Clance and Suzanne Imes call the *impostor syndrome.* This term describes what can happen when your external power exceeds your self-esteem; you feel like an impostor for having the power you don't feel you truly deserve. Occurring most frequently among high achievers (and especially females), the impostor syndrome includes a wide range of self-defeating attitudes such as:

- A persistent belief in your lack of competence, skill, or intelligence that flies in the face of objective data to the contrary

- A feeling that you are a fraud and the deep fear that you will be found out as such

- A sense that you don't deserve your success and the perks that come your way as a result of it

- A fear of your inability to repeat past successes and a conviction that your previous accomplishments were just flukes

- The belief that your successes have not come from your efforts or abilities but rather from fate, luck, timing, charm, or having manipulated others[9]

Ask yourself if you hold any of these common attitudes. Paradoxically, on some level, it may mean that you are doing well—achieving your goals at work, which is actually a good thing, even though it may not feel that way to you right now. You might want to review your accomplishments on Your Self-Esteem Profile on page 39 and focus on raising your internal sense of self-worth by welcoming your achievements and allowing them to feed you. In chapter 2, we will provide some strategies and resources to help you augment your self-esteem.

This can be crucial; when you're caught in the grip of the impostor syndrome, your negative feelings about yourself can paralyze your ability to succeed. And, unfortunately, they can also subtly and inadvertently fuel catfights. As you will see in the next chapter, it is instability in this very delicate balance between self-esteem and external power vis-à-vis your co-workers that can subvert all the good that may come from female relationships and get us into deep and distressing trouble with one another.

TWO

THE POWER DEAD-EVEN RULE

THOMAS E. BEALL, an executive at WorldCom, encountered a
difficult situation when he tried to promote one of his top
female employees. It was the fall of 1998. WorldCom's acquisition of MCI
had been going on for some time, and Beall was immersed in the accompanying issues of merging two corporate cultures. At the time, he was leading
a large team of telephone analysts for the internal Help Desk, covering all
three shifts as well as managing a team of four women in the Resource Management Support (RMS) group who were chartered to provide technologi-
cal support for the entire organization. "These women," he explained to us,
"were all demonstrated overachievers, and they all had more than their
share of native intelligence." Beall decided to promote one of the women in
the RMS group to team leader so he'd have fewer direct reports to deal with.

He discussed his idea with his senior manager and gained his instant
approval. When asked about the best candidate for the job, Beall replied,
"One particular employee, Maria, would be ideal. She has the background,
the experience, and the education to make a fine team leader." It never occurred to him to put the position up for grabs. "After all," he explained to
us, "there was a clear choice right in front of me. I was positive that Maria's
co-workers would agree and welcome her good fortune.

"How wrong I was!" Beall says. After talking with Maria about the promotion, he announced her new role via e-mail. But he was completely un-
prepared for the response. "The uproar was vehement, fast, and borderline

vicious," Beall told us. "With a group of guys, there might have been a little jealousy, but by and large, they would have congratulated the new team leader and gone on with their lives and work. Not the women! Nope! As a group, they immediately descended upon our senior manager in loud and tearful protest.

" 'Why wasn't the job posted?' one demanded.

" 'I'm just as qualified as she,' said another.

" 'I would like to have interviewed for the position, too,' the third one said. 'And if this promotion goes through, we'll take it to the Human Resources Department!'

"Imagine my chagrin and my boss's surprise at these reactions," Beall continued. "Now bear in mind that I have a very close and excellent relationship with all four members of this team. I felt awful. Not only did I recognize the mistake I had made, but I felt I was being betrayed too! It's like that gut-wrenching feeling you get when you're caught with your hand in the cookie jar—except in this case I wasn't sure whether I'd wronged someone or I'd been wronged."

At this point, Beall thought it wise to stop and reevaluate. He weighed whether he should go forward with the promotion and wait for the furor to subside or rescind the promotion, open up the position, and interview the other women. A third option was to speak with Maria, and, if she agreed, to do away with the new position altogether for the sake of team unity. After agonizing over the choices, he chose the latter. "I felt it would be better to apologize, retreat, lick my wounds, and live to fight another day," he said. "I spoke to Maria and was relieved that she could see the wisdom of the group continuing as before, without a team leader. I know she was disappointed, but her maturity and judgment allowed her to make the right decision."

From Beall's point of view, this solved the problem. He perceived little or no aftermath to this debacle. "The team settled right down, got back to work, and continued overachieving. Today, I still have not created a team leader position, opting instead to have these women as direct reports. They work well enough together to take a group holiday in Las Vegas and leave their husbands behind to house, dog, and baby-sit during their absence. My opinion is that there is no residual rancor."

Well, Beall might have resolved this problem to his own satisfaction, but let's look at a few of the potential costs. At the very least, another woman manager bit the dust—Maria was denied her well-deserved opportunity to join the ranks of WorldCom's team leaders and probably lost a hefty pay raise too. The fracas might have disrupted the office environment for a while. Moreover, Beall informs us that the investigator has moved into a different organization. Fortunately for all involved, the women now enjoy a respectful and professional rapport, but this was a difficult episode in the team's history.

OUR DISCOVERY: THE POWER DEAD-EVEN RULE

It should be evident by now that Maria's co-workers had become engaged in a catfight with her. We know these conflicts are real, even though we don't like to admit it or talk about them. We know they cost everyone financially and emotionally. And we know that women are a huge force: if we learn to be colleagues, we can move mountains; but if we continue with this destructive behavior, we can remain stuck where we are or even diminish our power. But what do we know about *why* this phenomenon exists?

So far, no one has been able to resolve this mystery. But in our research, we have learned that there is one straightforward key to the whole problem: It all boils down to a breakdown in the balance in the Golden Triangle of relationships, power, and self-esteem and thus to a violation of something we call the *Power Dead-Even Rule.*

The Power Dead-Even Rule is a breakthrough in understanding the complex and often baffling love/hate relationships women have with one another. It is a hitherto invisible natural law that operates behind the scenes and helps shape our reactions to other women in our lives. It explains the connection among relationships, power, and self-esteem and why Maria's colleagues reacted so vehemently when she was promoted.

For a positive relationship to be possible between two women, the self-esteem and power of one must be, in the perception of each woman, similar in weight to the self-esteem and power of the other. These essential elements must be kept "dead even." Exceptions might include situations where one woman is older and more experienced than the other, and therefore has more power *a priori.* Another might be a mentoring situation where one woman is actively working toward increasing the power of another.

From our observations, women are somewhat more comfortable with a powerful woman who plays down her importance than one who does not.

In those life situations in which a woman's power is diminished (she loses her job, doesn't receive an expected promotion, or fails publicly), she finds her female co-workers to be extremely supportive. By contrast, when a woman has more power than another woman, behaves as if she has more power, or is perceived as trying to obtain more power, the environment is ripe for conflict. And when, like Maria, she gets a promotion, lands a higher-paying job, or receives public praise from her boss, she is perceived as tipping the balance of the Golden Triangle. Other women believe that she has more power (and perhaps greater self-esteem) than they do, and that can trigger all their hostile reflexes. Simply put, *catfights result when the power and self-esteem among women are not kept in balance—a violation of the Power Dead-Even Rule.*

Most of us have been taught to "be nice" and use indirect forms of aggression when we're upset. So when we sense that the Power Dead-Even Rule has been violated, we may stomp off, gossip, snipe, snub, and withhold friendship instead of confronting a woman we're disturbed by, which would entail mounting a more direct attack. This indirect form of aggression, which is automatic to us, maintains the power and self-esteem of the person who feels angry and powerless.

Ironically, although the Power Dead-Even Rule has a profound impact on all female relationships, *it is invisible to most women.* Perhaps this is because we tend to perceive arguments with other women as personal and unique to the situation. We may believe that "Mary is a bitch" is the source of the problem rather than seeing "Mary violated the Power Dead-Even Rule by getting promoted, and that's why I now perceive her as a bitch," as the culprit.

THE POWER DEAD-EVEN RULE IN ACTION

Following is an illustration of how the Power Dead-Even Rule works in a harmonious relationship between two women, Rose and Amy. In this model, the large outer circles represent the women's power—the tangible external force they wield, which in our society can take the form of position at work, net worth, attractiveness, and so on. The inner circle represents their self-esteem—their sense of inner power and hidden feelings of personal strength and self-worth.

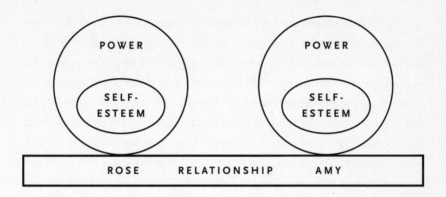

Each double circle represents one woman. Rose's and Amy's power and self-esteem are alike, thus the relationship is balanced. A good, professional friendship can occur within this kind of interpersonal equilibrium.

Now let's look at an example of the Power Dead-Even Rule when the relationship becomes lopsided. If Rose gets promoted to a new position and Amy suddenly becomes her employee, at the very least, Rose vastly increases her external power while Amy's stays the same. (Remember, it is possible for a woman to experience an increase in power without a concomitant boost in self-esteem.) But whatever Rose's internal state, the relationship is no longer balanced, as shown below.

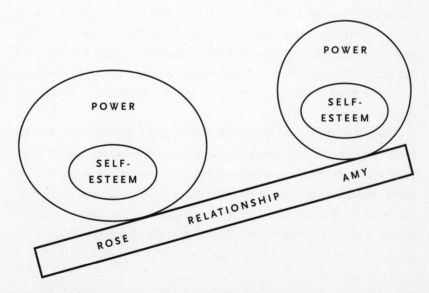

Now the situation has become ripe for trouble. Amy chafes at the fact that Rose seems to have more power than she does—after all, the power among females is supposed to be kept dead even. When Rose, in her new management position, starts giving orders and instructions to Amy, the friction escalates. Not only does the new title increase Rose's power, but also Amy, a former peer but now a subordinate, experiences a decrease in her power. When Rose orders her around, she may perceive that her new boss is trying to belittle her, thus decreasing her self-esteem as well. Rose's promotion may even cause Amy to feel that her former friend has become a "queen bee."

Stung by a "Queen Bee"

Years ago, Pat was on the receiving end of such a transformation. She was working in a large Fortune 500 company and had a great relationship with one of her co-workers. Pat and Marci had shared intimacies, so Pat knew about the difficulties in Marci's marriage, her infertility treatments, the man she almost married, the personal secrets women often share. One day, Marci was promoted to vice president and left on a three-week vacation immediately thereafter.

When she returned, Pat sensed a major sea change in the relationship. Marci's communication was cordial but chilly. They spoke often but only about the business at hand. Around this time, Pat caught a whopper of a cold and decided to spend the day in bed. Although she had worked at this company for a year and a half, this was her first sick day. She called in and asked to speak to her boss, Marci, who was out of the office at a meeting. Finally, not being able to reach her, Pat told Marci's secretary she'd be at home for the day.

Back at work the next day with Kleenex in hand and a big red nose, Pat was summoned into Marci's office first thing. Marci demanded to know where Pat had been the previous day. After receiving the explanation and being told about the phone call, Marci snapped, "If you're not coming in, you must speak to me directly." Pat explained her attempt to do so, but Marci cut her off. Confused and shocked, and still in fog from the cold, Pat said, "Oh," and left.

Profoundly hurt by what felt like an attack from a person she'd considered a friend, Pat spent her lunch hour crying. She decided she couldn't leave the relationship in such a tense state; this had to be addressed. After lunch, she walked back into Marci's office, asked if she could have a few minutes, and closed the door. "After our discussion this morning, I feel like you don't trust me," Pat explained.

"That's your problem," Marci retorted.

Stunned by this response, Pat was speechless (a rarity) and again simply said "Okay" and walked out. End of conversation, end of relationship, end of Pat ever going out of her way to assist Marci.

How could this have happened? Pat and Marci worked in a hierarchical company that was run at the top by attorneys. Marci was one of the most senior women, and for her to succeed, she had to become tough and armor herself to protect herself—from the *men*. Sometimes queen bee behavior entails deliberate attempts to "behave in ways more typical of a man," which, of course, can damage relations with other females. In a recent interview about her book *Sex & Power*, Susan Estrich, a law professor at the University of Southern California (and the first female president of the *Harvard Law Review* as well as Michael Dukakis's 1988 presidential campaign manager), explains how this can happen. "When you talk to women at the very top," she told *Working Woman* magazine, "it becomes clear that part of their success is due to convincing men that they aren't like other women. . . . Denying their status as women becomes a reflex. So when they get high up enough—far from making a difference for the women who come after them—they're still in the business of proving to the guys that they're really *not* one of the girls."[1]

Unfortunately, Pat was on the receiving end of Marci's need to prove herself. This new executive behaved coldly with the other women in her department too, which, paradoxically, significantly undermined her power base. While Marci did need to distance herself a bit in her new role, establishing herself as more of a superior with those who had been her peers, killing the relationship with Pat was not to her advantage, since she would have benefited from Pat's help (and from the goodwill of other similarly alienated former female co-workers).

This behavior of senior women distancing themselves from junior women happens so often that it has been labeled the Queen Bee Syndrome. The following illustration shows why, according to the Power Dead-Even Rule, the friendship between an employee and a Queen Bee cannot be maintained.

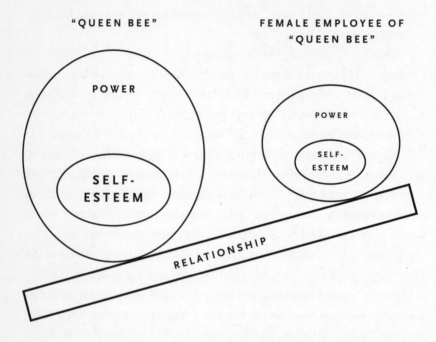

POWER IS IN THE EYE OF THE BEHOLDER

As you can see, the relationship between two women can be irreparably damaged when one person's power and self-esteem grow or shrink in relation to the other's. The balancing act between power and self-esteem is difficult and delicate, especially when changes in status occur. Furthermore, it can depend solely on the individual perceptions of the women involved. Symbols of power can be impressive within a social context and shared value system, but power is always in the eye of the beholder.

Consider, for instance, Carla's situation. Carla had been an entry-level engineer in a large biomedical equipment company. She was preparing to attend her organization's sales meeting in another state—a first for her. Nancy, a marketing assistant, called her one afternoon to ask if she would bring some materials for her, since she wouldn't be attending the meeting. Carla and Nancy were both in their late twenties, but Carla had her own office and didn't work as anyone's assistant. Nancy, on the other hand, was confined to a cubicle and answered her boss's phone. When Carla agreed to carry the materials, Nancy responded, "Great. You can come pick them up whenever you want."

That made Carla see red. "Whatever!" she barked into the phone and hung up.

An hour later, Nancy called again to say, "You still haven't picked up this stuff."

Carla, who had been taking the passive-aggressive route, blurted out, "I guess I assumed that if you wanted me to do you a favor, you would bring those materials to me."

"It started a huge mess," Carla confided to Susan at a workshop several years later. "By the time I got to the sales meeting, I found out that Nancy had called her boss and wildly exaggerated and misspoken about what had happened. She claimed that I had refused to take those items, saying 'I'm more senior than you are.' I ended up getting into trouble for it.

"I guess, based on the Power Dead-Even Rule, both of us had less power than we wanted to have. Nancy was someone's assistant, and I was at the bottom of the barrel among the engineers. On the other hand, she saw me as a threat because even though I was lowest on the prestige ladder I had an office and a title. Still, I thought I was due some respect from her because of my title, which I had earned through hard work. And besides, I think part of the problem was that she had what I thought was unseemly high self-esteem—when, in truth, my friends are always telling me that my low sense of self-esteem is something I should really work on."

Carla made several interesting points. There can be a perception of power that is at odds with reality, and the same can be true of self-esteem. Many women have either more or less power than they think they do. Power does not necessarily correlate with self-esteem, and others often see us as more or less self-confident than we actually feel we are. Far more women than men suffer from low self-esteem, so it's especially difficult on us when a woman comes along who we believe has very high self-esteem, especially when we feel our own self-esteem is low.

In this particular incident, Carla misconstrued Nancy's behavior as emblematic of high self-esteem. Actually, we believe that both women had low self-esteem and were probably trying to outpower each other. Nancy didn't give Carla the power Carla thought she was due, perhaps insisting that Carla come fetch her materials as a way of bolstering her own low self-esteem. An individual with low self-esteem might try to act as if her power is greater than it is or overtly exert what little power she has—as in Nancy's demands that Carla do her bidding—in order to make herself feel better. She might also try to build her power in more covert ways like disparaging another woman behind her back to her superiors. A person with high self-esteem, on the other hand, feels good about herself and often has no need to become involved in such power games to prove how important she is.

Because of the symbols of power attendant upon her position, Carla believed she deserved to be treated by Nancy with a little deference. Unfortunately, this attitude can be problematic in women's relationships, especially since any sort of one-upmanship is a quick violation of the Power Dead-Even Rule. Symbols of power are only valid when people behave toward them as if they are imbued with meaning by being responsive to the "powerful" person's needs and wants. In this case, apparently Nancy was going to show Carla that she wasn't impressed with Carla's office and title. Furthermore, power flows to women through their relationships, not from external symbols. This is the reverse of how power operates in the male world, where such symbols make a positive impression and hold sway. A saleswoman wearing a flashy diamond ring and bracelet might have a hard time closing a deal with another woman because such displays can violate the Power Dead-Even Rule, but a man might be wowed by the saleswoman's apparent affluence and implied success and be eager to work with her.

Sometimes other women don't give us the power we believe we should have. Or they may recognize our power but seek to diminish it in order to amplify their own, using gossip, backbiting, and sniping to give themselves a boost and even the score. Unfortunately, if a woman's self-esteem is quite low, no matter how much power she obtains, she may find it difficult to create solid professional friendships with other women because she will likely feel perpetually out of balance with them.

THE IMPULSE TOWARD HOMEOSTASIS

This leads us to another important component of the Power Dead-Even Rule, which dictates that self-esteem will always seek a level of homeostasis.

Homeostasis is the tendency of a person to maintain a sense of internal stability and balance. If your self-esteem is low in one facet of your life, such as work, you may strive to increase it in another, such as your appearance or your family life. This, of course, can be healthy—you're seeking to compensate for feeling inadequate in one area by shoring up your self-esteem elsewhere. However, sometimes our impulse toward homeostasis can create problems with other women.

Imagine the boss tells you a report you recently slaved over is "junk." You can:

1. Blame the source: "The boss is an idiot" (a particular favorite of men).

2. Seek alternative views, such as asking others their opinion of the report.

3. Blame yourself: "I'm so dumb" (a particular favorite of women).

4. Take it out on someone else. Unfortunately, this is usually someone—such as a female co-worker or a close family member—who is more similar to you than the perpetrator.

Let's look at this last option. Elaine, a working woman in a low-level administrative position, usually feels like a servant by the end of her typical eight-hour, "get me a cup of coffee," "type this by three," "pick up my laundry on the way back from lunch" job. Her self-esteem and the sense of power that she holds in her world are running on empty by the time she drives home after work. In order for her to get back in balance, she must replenish both.

Sadly, much to the chagrin of her family and friends, this balancing act may occur at their expense. Elaine may snap at others. She may refuse to comply with their requests. She may command others to do her bidding. She may also worry her loved ones by spending hours at the gym or endlessly dieting, as a way of increasing her power over her own body, at least, and her self-esteem. ("If I lose five more pounds, I'll be more attractive.") This kind of behavior can make Elaine seem self-centered and "bitchy" or dangerously self-destructive, but she's just trying to survive. She's trying to reach homeostasis.

We often see this dynamic, for example, in administrative assistants who are treated as peons by those around them and then tend to create difficulties for female visitors or even other female co-workers, but not the men who treat them poorly. Many nurses absorb the directives and criticisms of the doctors with whom they work because they have to, but they then pass along the grief to the junior nurses below them. That's why nurses are frequently known for "eating their young." As newly minted RNs start working, they are often treated poorly. You might expect that senior nurses would take the young ones under their wings and show them the ropes. Unfortunately, most often that is not the case. Driven by poor self-esteem or a sense of powerlessness, many women resort to sending an "I'm better than you, and let me show you in how many ways" message that may seem to help them achieve homeostasis but that also hobbles the possibility of attaining power equality in women's relationships.

The Damage Done

A woman's low self-esteem can cause her to damage relationships with other women in a way that is often very difficult for her or her intended victim to understand at the time. Lara described a situation that caused her much pain. "I was working as a customer service representative for an insurance company, and my boss was a woman," she told us. "I was leaving the lunchroom with a co-worker and heading back to my desk. It was a minute before one—the end of my 'lunch hour.' My boss, Melanie, was walking into the lunchroom, and when she saw me, she looked at her watch and said, 'It's time to get back to work.' It felt as if she was treating me like a child, when I'm really a responsible and hardworking employee with more than a 'nine-to-five' mentality.

"I was very hurt, and I retorted, 'I'm aware of the time, and in fact I have another minute before my lunch hour is over.' I couldn't believe she would make an issue over such a petty thing, even if I had been late in returning from lunch. After all, we didn't work in a 'clock-punching' environment. When my boss got back from her lunch, she asked to see me in her office. I followed her in, and she demanded, 'What is your problem?!?'

"I was shocked by this apparent accusation. I told her, 'Prior to your calling me in, I had no problem, but now it appears that *you're* my problem.'"

What Lara didn't have a way of knowing was that Melanie, one of the few women in the company at a senior level, was in a precarious situation. The organization was still unsure it had made the right move in promoting her to her high position. She often found herself excluded from formal activities, such as meetings, and informal gatherings like golf outings. The truth is, if not for potential legal ramifications, she would have been out of a job months ago. All this had resulted in Melanie thinking poorly of herself and sensing a reduction in her external power. Lowered self-esteem and a reduced sense of power equal an imbalance according to the Power Dead-Even Rule—even though Melanie was the boss! Jumping on Lara was Melanie's misguided attempt at achieving some sort of personal, internal homeostasis.

Poor self-esteem can have unanticipated reverberations in women's relationships, when, like Melanie, we find ourselves in power-deficient circumstances. It is our natural inclination to seek homeostasis to buck up our esteem elsewhere. Melanie's criticism of Lara was her unconscious attempt to make herself feel better by exerting what little actual power she still had, since her peers and those above were constantly battering her standing.

BALANCING THE EQUATION

As you can see, an important component of the catfight equation involves how well your female colleagues think of themselves. If a particular colleague acts and believes as if she's extremely important in this world, and you don't have the same perception of yourself, it will bode ill for the relationship. The converse is also true. If your power or self-esteem is inflated compared with hers, that alone will skew your relationship.

But at least there is a remedy for this. To keep a relationship with another woman in balance so as to avoid catfights, you have the option of deliberately building up her self-esteem. You can do so by giving sincere compliments and offering her empathy and support. When you show a woman that you care about her, your caring will enhance how she sees herself. She feels heard and valued, not discounted. We all want to be taken seriously. With positive, supportive energy, a woman will feel she is a worthy person, at least in your eyes.

Even if they know nothing of the Power Dead-Even Rule, many women seem to know instinctively how to keep their self-esteem balanced in their work relationships with other women. Imagine this simple scenario: Sandra has noticed that Martha is wearing a great new suit. "Martha, that's a fabulous outfit," she may say. "Is it new?"

To which Martha might quickly reply, "Oh, this old thing? I got it on sale."

Martha kept the power dead even. With her compliment, Sandra had given her more power and perhaps increased her self-esteem, but Martha wisely decreased her own power (but not necessarily her own self-esteem) by denigrating her chic ensemble. She was careful, however, to do so in a way that didn't belittle Sandra for her compliment. For instance, Martha didn't say, "This old thing? I've always thought it was a little tacky," which would have insulted Sandra's sense of style.

Similarly, Laura may say to Barbara, "I love your new haircut. It really suits you!"

And Barbara would reply, "Thanks, Laura. By the way, I've been meaning to ask you where you got that beautiful necklace you wore yesterday."

Again, Barbara keeps the power dead even. Laura gave her more power by admiring her hair, so Barbara increased Laura's by complimenting her necklace. All four women left their interactions feeling happy—their relationships were intact and rewarding.

Ironically, men who observe these kinds of conversations often conclude that the women have low self-esteem. "Why are they putting themselves down?" the men wonder. "Why can't they just take a compliment?" But many women intuitively know otherwise. Rather than lowering their self-esteem, they actually maintain it because they fulfilled the cardinal goal of protecting and preserving their relationships. Furthermore, some women are embarrassed by power and actively avoid seeming powerful, according to Susan Estrich. "It's hard to find a woman who says, 'I want power,'" Estrich notes. "You find these powerful women forever explaining how they aren't really powerful, or they don't want power, or they don't want *more* power."[2] Could this be their attempt to keep within the confines of the Power Dead-Even Rule?

The balancing of power might have helped resolve the conflict between Pat and Marci, when Pat called in sick but was chastised anyway. If, for instance, Marci had said, "What have I done that looked like I didn't trust you?" or "I didn't hear that you had called in," or "In the future, if you get sick and I'm not here, I'd prefer that you call back again so we can speak directly," then Pat would have believed that Marci cared enough about the relationship to have addressed the issue, and their connection would have gotten back on track. Dismissing another woman's concerns can be perceived as an attack on her power and self-esteem, even if you don't think the concerns are warranted, while a tiny admission of culpability—"I didn't hear that you'd called in"—goes a long way in assuaging an imbalance.

When a Colleague's Self-Esteem Is Low

Consciously adopting power-balancing strategies can be helpful at work. When you know that your self-esteem is greater than a female co-worker's whose relationship you value, your interactions could include compassion and empathy, and reassurance by pointing out what she is good at. This comes from your genuine concern for how the other woman feels and a desire to help her in whatever way you can. Some less secure women may feel envious of your self-confidence and perceive your positive sense of self as too powerful, however. These women may try to "bring you down," so it will behoove you to be careful when focusing on enhancing their self-esteem.

Suppose, for instance, that you and Paula have been at the same level for several years, and you encounter the difficult situation in which you have been promoted over her. You're bound to have problems, but in order to keep the power dead even, you might try several approaches:

- *Decrease your own power in Paula's eyes:* "Yeah, they gave me this new title, but I didn't get a pay increase." Or "I'm not eligible for overtime anymore." Or "The reason I got this is because I've been here longer."

- *Increase Paula's self-esteem:* "Paula, I know you're really qualified. Maybe the next promotion that comes around will be yours." "I think you're an outstanding employee of this company." You're honestly saying what you believe.

- *Increase Paula's power:* If you're in a position to do so, give Paula a plum assignment that would provide her with an opportunity to visibly succeed and demonstrate her skills.

However, don't try to decrease your own self-esteem with statements such as: "I didn't deserve this. I'm an idiot. I don't know why they gave me the job." While this is something women often tend to do, we do not indicate it here as a viable option. Negative self-talk won't help either you or your colleague in the long run.

What If Your Self-Esteem Is Low?

Not only should you be cognizant of your co-workers' self-esteem, but your sense of self-worth comes into play too. If you're feeling low, you may be more reactive to what would normally pass as everyday banter or constructive feedback. You may find yourself taking seemingly small issues personally. Go back to your responses in the self-esteem profile in chapter 1. How did you score? If your self-esteem is relatively low, that could contribute to conflicts with other females.

There are many ways to elevate your self-esteem, including psychotherapy. There are myriad books and other resources you can turn to for help in managing this problem, too. (We've listed some in Appendix A.) One quick method is to pay attention to your self-talk and change it to more positive patterns. In *What to Say When You Talk to Your Self*, psychologist Shad Helmstetter offers the following as examples of negative self-talk:

- It's just no use.

- When will I ever learn?

- I don't have the talent.

- Nothing ever goes right for me.[3]

These are usually indicators of low self-esteem. A writer friend suggested the following technique to deal with these self-defeating messages, which she calls "writing the internal critic." Sit down with pen and paper and put into words all the nasty internal dialogue that stops you from doing what you want with your life—you're not good enough, smart enough, important enough to be doing the work you strive to do or having what you want in life. You may need to do this several times. It can help you visually *see* all the negative messages you're sending yourself so that eventually you can dismiss them as the useless ramblings of a leftover childhood script.

Psychologist Helmstetter suggests you learn to substitute those negative internal messages with more positive self-talk. He suggests the following affirmations:

- I can do anything I believe I can do! I've got it and every day I get more of it. I have talent, skills, and ability.

- I am not afraid of anything or anyone. I have strength, power, conviction, and confidence! I like challenges and meet them head-on, face-to-face—especially today.

- Nothing seems to stop me. I have lots of determination. I turn problems into advantages. I find possibilities in things that other people never give a chance.[4]

A totally different approach is: "Don't look at it; just move." This is based on the theory of self-perception: if you behave differently from how you feel, your behavior will have an impact on how you feel. "I don't feel very confident walking into this meeting and giving this presentation, but I'll act like a confident person. I'll stride in with my head held high, respond with poise, and move around the room with self-assurance. Lo and behold, I begin to feel confident and people treat me like I'm competent."

This is known as the "fake it till you make it" strategy. In physics, there is an equation that defines momentum as mass times velocity. In other words, it's hard to stop an object when it's in motion. Even if you're feeling insecure, get up and get going. Success breeds success.

IN THIS CHAPTER, we have covered how the Power Dead-Even Rule operates among women. But where does it come from? What is it about our nature that makes us want to create equilibrium with other women, no matter what the cost? And why do we strike out with such rancor when the balance between us has been upset? In the next two chapters, we'll examine the biological and social origins of the Power Dead-Even Rule.

THREE

FROM THE XX FILES: THE ORIGINS OF WOMAN-TO-WOMAN CONFLICT

IMAGINE THAT YOU and a female peer have been assigned a coveted project that could lead to great visibility and even a potential promotion. You've worked well with Angela for several years and are happy to share this exciting opportunity with her. But just as the project gets under way, you've been called out of town for a week to troubleshoot an ongoing assignment that suddenly needs your personal guidance. As you pack your materials and prepare to leave, you quickly ask Angela to divvy up the responsibilities. You breeze out of the office, confident that she will do so fairly.

Upon your return, you discover that Angela has indeed parceled out the duties. But contrary to your expectations, she has kept the juicy parts of this new project—the ones that could bring positive attention and visibility—for herself and has left you with the dregs: the hard backstage work that will garner little external reward. You feel hurt, betrayed, and then furious. Distressed and disappointed, you turn to co-workers Irene and Miriam for support and validation, sharing with them the gory details of Angela's treachery. You are in pain, so you need to vent, but you also want to connect with people whom you trust. And when the three of you next encounter Angela in the hall, you all greet her with frosty stares and turn your backs on her.

Viewed from the outside, one might think that you are gossiping or, even worse, fomenting a catfight. After all, this was to be a team effort, and someone has to do the dirty work. But in our research we have discovered that such a visceral response may be hardwired into women's bodies and minds. Our evolutionary heritage, the structure of our uniquely female brains, and the function of our hormones have coalesced to create within us the impulse to form extremely close emotional ties with other women—ties that can quickly devolve into enmity if we feel disappointed or betrayed. As one of the foremost researchers on female aggression, Finnish psychologist Kaj Björkqvist has explained, "Girls tend to form dyadic relationships, with very deep psychological expectations from their best friends. Because their expectations are high, they feel deeply betrayed when the friendship falls apart. They become as antagonistic afterwards as they had been bonded before."[1] When girls grow into women, the dynamics of friendship change little.

Due to our female gifts, we are able to read other women accurately and expect that they will be trustworthy, generous, honest, and caring. Usually, we are not disappointed. However, when another woman violates the Power Dead-Even Rule and sabotages us at work or increases her power (either on her own accord or through a third party), we feel hurt and angry. We may reach out to others for support through gossip, ultimately undermining our new foe's success.

As distasteful as this kind of behavior may seem (especially if we're on the receiving end of it), in evolutionary terms it may have been crucial for our survival. In this chapter we'll examine primate, brain, and hormone research in order to tease out the biological origins of this kind of behavior. We've come to some conclusions that startled us.

Hierarchy and the Male Reproductive Imperative

When it comes to gender, the name of the game for both males and females is progeny: that is, getting our genes into the gene pool. We feel driven to procreate. If you're a male, this may take just a few minutes, and if you're lucky, you can do it many times a day. Unfortunately, your fellow males all have the same agenda, and they're vying for access to the females too. This creates conflict. Males of many species fight with other males for the opportunity to continue their line—some (from animals as tiny as mice to those as mighty as lions) will even eat the young of their rivals in an attempt to ensure their own genetic dominance.[2]

When Pat was a student in Boulder, Colorado, she had firsthand experience with the male reproductive imperative—and it wasn't because of the proximity of hundreds of frat boys. Her university was perched against the Rockies, and every fall the canyons would echo with the terrifying din of male elk up in the mountains running at one another, butting heads, and tangling antlers. Some even died in these violent clashes. Pat was mystified as to why these majestic animals would behave this way. But as time went on, she learned that elk use their annual bloody battles to establish the dominant males—the ones who would mate with the females.

This innate need to compete for position seems brutal, yet it may have a purpose beyond that of reproduction. Many social scientists believe it has led to the creation of hierarchical social structures (an alpha male on top with the other lesser males finding their positions below him in a sort of pyramidal arrangement). Such an order prevents constant bloodshed and anarchy among males. Indeed, one of the advantages of this type of dominance hierarchy is that it eventually engenders security and peacefulness. Every male knows his place and keeps to it until and unless he feels ready to challenge the leader.

SOME LESSONS FROM OUR MALE PRIMATE COUSINS

Although it might be unwise to draw direct links between primates and humans—after all, we have a level of intelligence that they do not—according to psychology professor Shelley E. Taylor and her research associates at the University of California, Los Angeles, "It would be foolish to claim that there is nothing to be learned from primate behavior."[3] Chimpanzees are our nearest living kin, with 99 percent of their genes overlapping our own. (In contrast, only 50 percent of the mouse genome is identical to ours.[4]) If we examine the differences in social order among male and female chimps, we can find some similarities as to how we humans function. We may even uncover there some of the roots of our own female behavior.

Let's look first at the bonds among male chimpanzees. These are ephemeral. Males form coalitions to achieve status: together they establish the alpha male; they join forces to hunt down dinner, to defend against intruders, or to attack the lowest monkey on the totem pole. Frans de Waal, a Dutch-born zoologist and ethologist, and one of the world's leading researchers in primate behavior at the Yerkes Regional Primate Research Center at Emory University, has found from his research that "adult male chimpanzees seem to live in a hierarchical world with . . . a single permanent goal: power."[5] Once the goal is reached, a coalition will dissolve, only to reform with a different combination of players when a new challenge arises.

Males base their relationships on a tit-for-tat strategy: If you help me, I'll help you. If you hurt me, I'll get even. Such male chimp coalitions are difficult to predict, de Waal explains: "The unreliable, Machiavellian nature of male power games implies that every friend is a potential foe and vice versa,"[6] he writes in *Peacemaking Among the Primates.* Indeed, as Deborah Blum, author of *Sex on the Brain,* tells us, male chimps are "constantly plotting coups and negotiating for better allies."[7] Sound familiar?

The male hierarchy among chimps is formal, and members communicate their status to one another frequently. The dominant male shows his superiority by literally making his hair stand on end—this gives the illusion of his being even larger than he actually is. Subordinates will demonstrate their lowliness by grunting and bowing in submission. When this status communication breaks down, fights erupt. According to de Waal, male chimps have twenty times as many aggressive incidents among them as females do. But they also are quick to make up; 47 percent are conciliatory after a conflict.[8] "The formal hierarchy may be seen as a device to maintain cohesion in spite of rivalry," de Waal explains.[9]

Among males, the display of status is helpful. When you don't have to fight constantly about the social order, you automatically understand the limits of your behavior, what you can and cannot do. This sort of solidarity can be important if the males in a troop must close ranks to defend against aggressive rivals in neighboring territories.

In case you think that such struggles for dominance occur only among lesser beasts, social psychologists have documented how human adolescent boys also jockey for position among themselves. In an interesting series of studies conducted over a period of eight years, researcher Ritch Savin-Williams at the University of Chicago investigated the behavior of children between the ages of eleven and seventeen at sleep-away summer camps in

New England, Michigan, and New York. The adolescents were observed when they arose and went to bed, during meals and cabin cleanup, in the course of cabin discussions, and while participating in athletics.

Savin-Williams found that within the first few days (if not hours) of coming together, skirmishes broke out among the boys (more on the girls later). The more dominant boys ordered around the less dominant ones; they ridiculed, bragged, shoved or pushed, verbally threatened, interrupted, or otherwise tried to control their bunkmates. Soon, the most physically mature boys took their positions as the leaders of the group.

But this hostile environment didn't last long. Over time, Savin-Williams explains, "the frequency of dominance acts within a group decreased as the hierarchy became more clearly linear; the expression of one's status also became more overt." That is, once each boy knew his place in the social order, the need to fight for position subsided.[10] The boys settled down and went about the business of being happy campers.

A LITTLE HELP FROM OUR FRIENDS

We females also have the reproductive imperative to move our genes into the gene pool, but of necessity we must proceed differently from males. Once a female has been impregnated, gestation will, depending on the species, physically tax her body for a period of several weeks to several months. During this time, she is vulnerable as she becomes less agile and able to physically protect herself. And once the baby or litter is born, she must now care for her offspring until they are independent enough to fend for themselves.

For the most part, unlike males, females do not need or use conflict to establish a hierarchy to guarantee the continuation of their genes. Rather than competing with other females, they tend to rely on help from their same-gender friends to ensure their offspring's survival. Females don't fight over access to power. Their quarrels usually revolve around access to *resources*—food, protection of the young, males, promotions, coveted assignments.

Raising a baby, whether you are a human or a lower-order mammal, is a time- and energy-intensive activity. To make the best use of both, chimpanzees will often reciprocally care for and nurse one another's infants. But

if a female chimp takes more than her fair share of food or otherwise im-
perils one of the group's babies, the other females will severely ostracize
her. Says de Waal, "While it's uncommon, females do appear sometimes to
completely lose their tempers, fighting to crippling injury or worse." The
chimps even seem to hold a grudge. De Waal describes the females hurt by
the offense as "vindictive and irreconcilable. They're angry for days or even
longer; they slap, they push, and won't come to the ex-friend's aid." Compared with male chimpanzees, "females apparently find it much harder to
forgive a trespass, a failure of a trusted friendship."[11]

In contrast to male conciliatory behavior after conflict, de Waal has
found that only 18 percent of female chimpanzees make peace following a
fight. They have a good reason to take group offenses personally—a transgression of a female friendship can endanger the children, and biologically,
a threat to offspring is high stakes indeed, perhaps necessitating sustained
anger until the threat has been thoroughly eliminated.

OTHER LESSONS FROM OUR PRIMATE SISTERS

Surrounded by other females, female primates demonstrate significant
connectedness, and their relationships tend to be more constant than are
male relationships. Female chimps also have hierarchies, but their structure tends to be rather vague, with only rare status communication. Female
chimpanzee hierarchies are far less oriented toward dominance and power
than the protean male hierarchies. And while the male groups will continuously re-create themselves through conflict, matrilineal social contracts
are unchanged over many years and often generations. Female-female
coalitions typically involve close kin and are usually organized to the exclusion of females and juveniles from other matrilines.[12] De Waal explains that
adult female chimps live in "a horizontal world of social connections,"
whose goal is *security*, not power. It is of paramount importance to keep
good relationships within this small circle of family and friends: although
some females may exert considerable sway, they will not turn against a female friend or relative. But they will let aggression run its destructive course
in the case of a fight with a rival.[13]

The situation changes markedly if a threat comes from an adult male.
If a female wants something from a male such as a banana or for him to stop

pestering her, or if she needs to protect her baby from him, she physically cannot attack him directly. A female primate is often half the size of her male counterpart, and any direct aggression on her part would put her and her offspring at risk. So she learns either to get what she wants in a round-about way (she may sneak behind the male's back and nab the banana when he's not looking) or she creates an alliance with other females in the troop, and together they have more strength and power to reach the goal.

According to primatologist Barbara Smuts, when a threat comes from a male, many different kinds of primates will "form coalitions with females [of the same species] to whom they are not closely related. Such coalitions can mobilize very quickly in response to male aggression, since any females nearby can be recruited."[14] Female primates have been observed to join forces against males when they harass, herd, or scare other females.[15]

In *Good Natured: The Origins of Right and Wrong in Humans and Other Animals,* Frans de Waal provided a fascinating example of how female chimps came to the aid of a female troopmate when she was threatened by Jimoh, the alpha male in the Yerkes Field Station group. Jimoh detected that a mating between this female, one of his favorites, and Socko, an adolescent male, was taking place:

> Socko and the female had wisely disappeared from view, but Jimoh had gone looking for them. Normally, the old male would merely chase off the culprit, but for some reason—perhaps because the female had repeatedly refused to mate with Jimoh himself that day—he this time went full speed after Socko and did not give up. He chased him all around the enclosure. . . .
>
> Before he could accomplish his aim, several females close to the scene began to "woaow" bark. This indignant sound is used in protest against aggressors and intruders. At first the callers looked around to see how the rest of the group was reacting; but when others joined in, particularly the top-ranking female, the intensity of their calls quickly increased until literally everyone's voice was part of a deafening chorus. The scattered beginning almost gave the impression that the group was taking a vote. Once the protest had swelled to a chorus, Jimoh broke off

his attack with a nervous grin on his face; he got the message. Had he failed to respond, there would no doubt have been concerted female action to end the disturbance.[16]

Although we might think that a male's superior "rank," size, and strength would inhibit these defensive attacks, once female monkeys have teamed up, the males have a hard time subduing them. *New York Times* science writer Natalie Angier reminds us that "female alliances keep females free."[17]

After a fight with other females outside their small circle of connections, female chimps have little reason to make up. De Waal found that females, in fact, often have one or two enemies with whom reconciliation is out of the question. "Rather than calling females less conciliatory than males, I prefer to call them more selective," he writes. "The distinction between friend and foe seems infinitely sharper for females."[18] Because male coalitions are ephemeral, their "friendliness" and spirit of cooperation are instrumental—they exist to achieve a certain goal. The relationships among males are not as deep, so the hurt isn't as great if alliances shift. But betrayal among females who have ongoing profound relationships with one another can have significant and long-lasting consequences.

De Waal's conclusion supports the possibility that what we call a violation of the Power Dead-Even Rule, with its powerful and enduring impact on relationships, may actually be a woman's inborn response when she believes that her metaphoric (as well as her actual) gene pool is threatened. And it is perhaps these evolutionary factors that can help us understand why young girls will be inculcated early on to "share" and "play nicely" with one another and ultimately conform to the Power Dead-Even Rule. As Natalie Angier writes in *Woman: An Intimate Geography*:

> In the annals of our primate pasts, females are drawn to other females for strength. . . . The recurring theme is one of coalition and desire, of an aggressive need for female alliance. Here is the possible cradle of the fantasy best friend, and the reason that we care so much about girls and our position in the peerage, and that our female friendships feel like life and death . . .[19]

Going back to Ritch Savin-Williams's research with adolescents at summer camp, his findings indicated that the social structure among girls (even "high-ranking" girls) was much more flexible than that of the boys. The girls in his studies seldom asserted their influence by physical means or by arguing, since they were not seeking power. There was no obvious leader—and sometimes an "alpha" girl would slip to "beta" position and then back to "alpha" during her stay at camp. In fact, often more than one leader would emerge from these groups: one girl who was adept at getting things done while another who was good at helping others with their feelings.

The Female Brain

Imagine that a beloved member of your team has been fired this morning, and you and Ellen, a female colleague, are hashing over the situation because it upset you both. Your male boss watches you "gossip" and wonders why you've chosen to "waste your time" talking about Mary. "She's gone," Justin grumbles dismissively. "Why do you have to belabor the point? Turn the page and move on." He neither understands nor values an activity that you and Ellen find crucial. But emotions and words are closely connected in the female brain; remaining silent about something so deeply meaningful can feel distressing and isolating. Not wishing to stop talking about Mary's bad luck, you and Ellen slip into the ladies' room to continue your postmortem.

This kind of male/female disparity highlights the fact that men's brains are quite different from women's. Since "genes into the gene pool" is a primary motivator, we can only surmise that over the millennia, in chicken-and-egg fashion, our female brains have evolved in unique ways to help us conserve and preserve resources for our own survival and that of our offspring. Researchers have found that women are wired to seek out interaction and do well at it, to be empathetic, and to have great positive and negative verbal facility. (We're adept at using words to calm as well as to attack.) All these attributes help us maintain our connections to others, which is important if we are to live successfully in intense relationships with females who can help us survive.

Up until fairly recently, it was believed that male and female brains were, reproductive necessities aside, more or less identical. Most of us learned in school that the cortex, the outer coating or gray matter of the right hemisphere, is responsible for artistic development, music and nonlanguage sounds, intuitive thought, and visual and spatial relations. It deals with the emotional and the abstract and helps us to see shapes and patterns. The cortex of the left side is engaged in much more linear pursuits. It is said to be responsible for logic, concrete reasoning, and cognitive or analytic skills like language and math. The two hemispheres are connected with a thick bundle of fibers called the *corpus callosum* that allows one side to communicate with the other.

All this may still be true—for men. Most of the early research that documented this lateralization of the brain came from studies of male soldiers who had suffered wartime brain injuries. More recently, however, with the use of sophisticated brain-imaging techniques such as functional PET scans (which show in great and glowing detail what brain structures are utilized when we undertake specific activities), researchers have found that the female brain is not quite so neatly organized. For instance, the centers that control language and emotional responses can be found on *both* sides of the female brain. Moreover, whereas the male brain averages 13 percent more neurons in the cortex, the female brain has 13 percent more neuropil, specialized cells that permit brain cells to communicate with one another.

The corpus callosum is much thicker in women than men, also implying that we experience more communication and cooperation between the two hemispheres. The greater the connections between left and right hemispheres, the more articulate one is. The more intricately wired female brain allows for more information to be exchanged between both sides: emotions are better integrated with our verbal abilities, making us more fluent at expressing our feelings to others.[20] Perhaps this is also why a man will tend to find it more challenging to tell you how he feels than would a woman; the information moves from one part of his brain to the other with more difficulty.

Women also bring in and process information differently than men do. Due to the way female brains have evolved, we see, smell, and sense danger more readily. Even our peripheral vision is broader. Perhaps these heightened senses help female animals become more quickly mobilized in situations that might threaten their offspring. Our split-second reactions also differ from men's. In women, this function is linked to a verbal response—

we call out to allies for help—whereas in men, it is linked to physical action—fighting or fleeing.

Research with newborn babies also helps us understand inborn gender differences before culture and society exert their influence. For instance, research has shown that loud noises and physical discomfort irritate and frighten infant girls more than they do baby boys. Our senses of touch and hearing are also more acute, even as newborns. Baby girls are more adept at picking up social cues; they are more interested in people and faces than newborn boys. In one study of infants who were two to four days old, girls maintained eye contact with silent adults almost twice as long as boys did. When an adult was talking, girls also looked longer. At four months old, most baby girls can distinguish photos of people they know from those of strangers; most boys cannot.[21]

Baby girls are more susceptible to emotional contagion than boys; studies consistently demonstrate that even day-old girls react more intensely to the sound of another baby crying than do boys. (It's not just due to their greater sensitivity to sound, as these babies reacted less intensely to equally loud computer-generated language and animal noises.) It is thought that this more acute response underlies the development of empathy.[22]

Baby girls develop language much earlier than boys do. They're apt to gurgle at people more—boys are just as happy to babble at their toys. They say their first words and learn to speak in short sentences earlier than boys because their brains are more efficiently organized for language acquisition. Consequently, girls are generally more verbally fluent in their preschool years; they read better and are more skillful at manipulating the fundamentals of language like grammar, punctuation, and spelling. They are also more easily comforted by soothing words and songs. At the age of three, 99 percent of girls' verbal language is intelligible. It takes boys, on average, a year to catch up.[23]

Perhaps our verbal advantage explains why sometimes women seem compelled to communicate with one another. In a company where both Pat and Susan worked, two executive secretaries located in the same suite ran into flak from their male bosses who believed the women spent too much time talking to each other. These men did not understand that, because of our unique brain wiring, women are adept at multitasking. Jeanne and

Frances's conversations did not preclude their ability to carry out other functions simultaneously.

Because of their own prejudices (which were honestly based on their own abilities), the male executives asked Jeanne and Frances to cool their conversations. But the women wouldn't—or couldn't. When they continued to talk, their bosses erected a glass partition between their desks to inhibit further verbal interaction. But this didn't stop the pair. They just mouthed words to each other through the glass, despite their bosses' wishes.

Women are much more easily engrossed in emotional responses. Leading Canadian brain researcher Sandra Witleson found, for instance, that women recognize and process emotional content on both sides of the brain, rather than just the right side, as do men.[24] In other experiments, when men and women were asked to think of the saddest images they could muster, PET scans revealed that the area at the front of the limbic system that glowed in response to this request was eight times larger in women than in men.[25]

Women are better at picking up social cues and important nuances of meaning from tone of voice and facial expression; and since we can be so much better than men at reading emotions, we sometimes refer to what we consider an uncanny ability as "women's intuition." We're so attuned to reading these nonverbal signs that we are occasionally prone to misconstruing them, which can get us into trouble and may even lead to a catfight. Such a situation occurred with Lisa, one of Susan's clients. Lisa's boss, Marsha, took her out to dinner to give her some pointed negative feedback about her lack of facial expression. Lisa was caught completely off guard. She didn't perceive that she had a flat affect—this was just her normal relaxed face. But Marsha was offended since she had read into Lisa's neutral expression some sense of negative intent, lack of interest, and even hostility.

Susan advised Lisa that when she was with other women, she should more actively communicate her feelings verbally and also be aware of using more facial expression. "Although you might feel silly doing this at first," Susan continued, "you might try smiling and practicing different expressions in the mirror." By the way, this source of conflict typically doesn't occur in the male culture, since men may be unaware of fine distinctions in expression. In fact, while talking with men, Lisa didn't need to worry about this issue at all. Besides, men might perceive too much smiling as a sign of weakness or powerlessness. At those times, Lisa's relatively "flat affect" would be an advantage.

"Tend and Befriend": The Hormonal Contribution of Oxytocin

A final component of the potential for catfights in our biogenetic heritage may be our hormones. After decades of biomedical research into how hormones influence behavior, we now believe that they affect behavior in rats, monkeys and, yes, humans, too. Hormones are chemical messengers. Once secreted into the bloodstream by specialized cells in the brain, reproductive organs, and elsewhere, they travel to other parts of the body where they produce specific changes. The relationship between our behavior and our hormones is reciprocal: hormones influence how we act, but our actions also influence hormone release.

One of the hormones germane to our understanding of female-to-female relationships is *oxytocin*. Primarily a muscle-contracting hormone, it takes its name from the Greek word meaning "swift birth." Produced at childbirth, it causes the uterus to contract during labor, and it triggers milk ejection when breast-feeding. Oxytocin is present in the bloodstream as a mother first greets her newborn and continues to be released whenever she nurses her infant. According to evolutionary biologist Sarah Blaffer Hrdy and biologist C. Sue Carter, oxytocin is believed to play an important role in creating the mother-infant bond.

In 1968, Joseph Terkel and Jay Rosenblatt of Rutgers University performed an experiment to help them understand the chemical components of maternal-child bonding. These two scientists injected blood from a post-partum rat into a female virgin to see how she would respond to newborn pups. Not nurturing by nature, virgin rats usually ignore other rats' babies, show signs of anxiety around them, or even eat them. But the results of this experiment were dramatic. The injected virgin licked the pups, protected them, and retrieved them when they strayed. It is now believed that oxytocin was among the ingredients that so radically changed the virgin rat's behavior.[26]

Because of these intimacy-enhancing properties (it is also released in men and women during sexual activity and after orgasm), oxytocin has also been called the "love hormone" and has been implicated in the practice of monogamy.[27] It makes people feel better about those around them, and it increases their desire to be next to and connected with others. Researchers have found that people with higher oxytocin levels tend to be calmer, more relaxed and social, and less anxious. This can create a positive feedback loop—people want to be around others who have those attributes.

Oxytocin has an additional role in females. It helps to modulate our responses to threat and danger. This was recently brought to light through the research of psychologist Shelley E. Taylor and her associates at the University of California, Los Angeles. Dr. Taylor was chatting one day with one of her postdoctoral students who had made an offhand comment that most animal studies of stress were conducted using only *male* rats. This intrigued Dr. Taylor, and after a bit of digging, she and her colleagues found that the same was true in human investigations. In fact, only 17 percent of subjects investigated in stress research are women. In an article about Dr. Taylor, *New York Times* health reporter Erica Goode explains, "The notion of a lone warrior locked in combat or surrender mode that emerged from such research did not mesh neatly with evidence from psychological studies, which showed that in stressful situations women often sought out the company and support of others, or coped with stress by nurturing their children."[28]

Given what we now know about our genetic heritage and our brains, that should not be surprising. Indeed, Dr. Taylor along with her colleagues reviewed several hundred studies in a variety of scientific areas including human and animal research on the body's hormonal response to stress. They concluded that whereas the male hormones testosterone and vasopressin mediate men's stress reactions, oxytocin plays a central role in females' response to stress. The effects of oxytocin are strongly modulated by estrogen, which of course circulates at much higher levels in females than in males.[29] In fact, the androgens (especially testosterone and vasopressin) that males possess in abundance have been shown *to inhibit oxytocin release under stressful conditions.*[30]

This is significant. Whereas men, galvanized by surges in their stress hormones, experience the "fight or flight" response when threatened, women may more naturally exhibit oxytocin-induced protective and caring behaviors during those times. Taylor has called this uniquely female phenomenon the impulse to "tend and befriend." Her research suggests that because female animals play the primary role in bringing offspring to maturity, their biological stress responses would have evolved not to jeopardize their health or that of their children, as fighting or running away very easily could. Oxytocin, with its calming properties, may chemically induce a female to engage in "tending" behaviors; that is, quieting and caring for offspring and reaching out to connect with supportive females around her. Here's another instance where alliances with females keep females free.

Taylor cites a fascinating study by social psychologist R. L. Repetti that shows how these chemical differences may express themselves in human families. Investigating the effects of a stressful workday on parenting behaviors, Repetti interviewed fathers, mothers, and their children. He found that when fathers experienced an interpersonally conflictual day at work, they were more apt to be irritable in the evening with their families. Those men whose stressful days involved interpersonal conflicts were more apt to withdraw from their families at home. In contrast, women became more nurturant and caring toward their children when they had had a bad day. On the days when the mothers reported feeling the most stressed, their children described them as being the most loving.[31]

The difference in stress response is noteworthy. As Taylor explains, "Research on human males and females shows that under conditions of stress, the desire to affiliate with others is substantially more marked among females than among males. In fact, it is one of the most robust gender differences in human behavior other than those directly tied to pregnancy and lactation. It is the primary gender difference in adult human behavioral responses to stress."[32]

And perhaps it can help us explain why, in our hypothetical scenario at the opening of this chapter, you might turn to your female colleagues when you believe that another female co-worker sabotaged your progress. It might also help us understand why you would need to talk with a friend about the abrupt dismissal of a colleague, despite your boss's demands to drop the subject and move on. When women are stressed, it's in our nature to turn to other women for support and safety. When the concern and solace we seek is not forthcoming, however, we feel betrayed and hurt. This may also explain why, in chapter 2, Pat felt so shattered by her former friend Marci's cold response to her pleas for understanding.

The Biological Underpinnings of Female Conflicts

From all this research, we can see that our genetic heritage, brain structure, and hormones are linked to our need to establish intimacy with others, and especially other women. We have been wired for empathy, intuition, and connectedness. We have facility with language and emotion that allows us to express our deepest feelings. We look to our female friends for comfort in times of crisis and need. And perhaps because of this, we believe that we understand women and have certain expectations of them and our inter-connectedness with them. Forever bound up in our nonhierarchical net-works of female relationships, we rely on this interdependence to help us and our families get by and in some circumstances even to survive.

Is it any wonder, then, that when we become disappointed due to a will-ful or even an inadvertent violation of the Power Dead-Even Rule—a step toward malelike one-upmanship and hierarchical behavior—we feel hurt and angry? "Who does she think she is?" we might mutter to ourselves in pain or disgust. "Why is she acting as if she's better than I am? How could she do this to me?" Perhaps deep down we are thinking, "Aren't we all in this together?"

As among our chimpanzee cousins, a trespass, a blatant betrayal, a fail-ure of a trusted friendship, or a clandestine or open grab for precious re-sources (such as Angela's) is much harder for us to forgive because it can threaten our livelihood, our children's well-being, and our deepest selves. We thought we knew this person; we thought we could count on her; we thought we were friends, with all that female friendship can imply. And, when suddenly we are shocked to discover that we were mistaken in our as-sessment, we may question our own judgment and feel stricken to the core. We withdraw or we lash out in pain and anger in the only way we know how, and a catfight erupts.

FOUR

LESSONS FROM CHILDHOOD

F ROM THE INFORMATION we presented in the previous chapter, it might seem evident that we have all been genetically,
biologically, and hormonally "preprogrammed" to behave in certain ways—
it's in our nature. While there is a good measure of truth to this—the bio-
behavioral factors we've just described may form a foundation for our
proclivities—it is also true that they are not the *only* factors that influence
who we ultimately become as adults and what we do. We cannot discount the
importance of our society and upbringing in our behavior as females; they
are integral to the development of catfight behaviors, too.

You might think that it all boils down to the age-old nature-versus-
nurture controversy: Are we the way we are because of our genetics or because of the way we have been raised? No one knows the answer. For the
purpose of this book, let's assume that both our biology and our upbringing have an impact on our adult behavior—it's not an either/or proposition,
though these two factors may interact with each other reciprocally: our biological predispositions support the way we are raised, and the way we are
raised is consonant with our biology.

As females, we may have a genetic propensity to connect with other females, so perhaps society has carefully inculcated us to "share" and "play
nicely" with one another (and ultimately conform to the Power Dead-Even
Rule) in order to preserve those all-important alliances and obey our reproductive imperative to protect our progeny. Although no one has been

able to develop a satisfying resolution to the nature/nurture question, biology notwithstanding, it is clear that how we have been raised also plays an important role in how we behave.

WE STOP AT RED LIGHTS

From the moment we were tiny infants, our families (by their modeling behavior and direct intervention) as well as our society (in school, through religious customs and beliefs, from the media, and so on) have taught us to act in certain "acceptable" ways. This is called *social learning* or *socialization.*

We all live with such societally imposed limits on our behavior. Imagine if none of us wanted to stop at red lights or if we decided to take whatever we desired, whether it belonged to us or not. Life would be terribly chaotic and strife ridden. So we abide by certain mutually agreed-upon rules that we have imposed on ourselves for our own good and the good of the community. These rules provide for our safety and well-being.

A family is also a form of community, and every family has its own private standards of behavior. Some are overtly verbalized ("There's a long tradition of going to medical school in the Smith family!" "No child of mine is leaving the house in that kind of outfit!"), but others are simply implied or unconsciously acted upon.

Taken together, these societal and familial rules are what transform us from masses of quivering protoplasm into human beings that function in our society. Limits and rules vary from family to family, region to region, culture to culture, but they exist everywhere that people come into contact with other people. Though they may differ dramatically from one society to the next, all societies and families in the world share the need to establish certain conventions. These conventions primarily concern the following areas:

- Aggression and passivity

- Sexuality and sex role identity

- Dependence and independence

- Emotional development and attachment to others

- Achievement

- Cooperation and competition

- Sense of individuality and community

- Right and wrong

- Concrete living experiences such as eating, excreting, working, cleanliness, attire, pain, birth, death, and so on

DEVELOPING A SEX ROLE IDENTITY

These rules for society can be overt or hidden. For our culture, for instance, it's a clearly accepted tenet that when it comes to mealtime, we eat with a fork, knife, and spoon from a clean plate; we keep our elbows off the table; we chew our food with our mouths closed; we don't slurp our noodles; we sit on chairs at a table instead of squatting on the ground. But other rules and conventions that shape how we behave are more hidden. This is especially true when it comes to the tenets that dictate *sex roles* and *gender identity.* How we act as males and females in the world grows from a combination of the biological determinants we've discussed in chapter 3 and these social imperatives.

Gender identity is an important part of the unchanging core of our personalities, and it develops early. According to psychoanalyst Robert Stoller, it is "with rare exception firmly and irreversibly established for both sexes by the time a child is around three."[1] Children learn how boys and girls "ought to" act from the way their parents, caregivers, and teachers treat them; by observation of adult behavior; and through peer pressure, television, magazines, and movies. These factors leave indelible impressions that we carry with us into adulthood.

Although we live in the same society, males and females are actually raised in unique and distinct cultures. In America we tend to assume that because we coexist in the same country, we must all share the same values. After all, the differences are not as great as if our male counterparts had come from Pakistan or Bali or Nigeria.

Or are they? In this chapter we will explore the divergence in social learning and sex role development that occurs in this country, especially as it relates to female conflicts. Is there a difference in how parents behave around infant boys and girls? What impact do the typical games males and females play have on their gender identity as they grow? How does each gender learn to resolve conflict and competition during these games? What happens to gender identity once boys and girls start school? What do teachers and textbooks convey to young inquiring minds? How do differences in male and female culture influence a child as she grows into adulthood?

Please bear in mind that we will be talking about the childhood environment surrounding *most* females and males. Research is based on a bell-shaped curve—the hitch is that there are two tails to that bell curve, so some areas we explore may seem alien to you. There are always exceptions when it comes to human behavior.

PINK BOWS AND BLUE BOOTIES

Despite the differing neurological endowments of male and female humans—even those subtle ones that have been detected in newborns in laboratory settings—repeated research studies have shown that when babies or young toddlers wearing non-color-coded outfits (green and yellow rompers rather than pink and blue ones) are set in the middle of a room, try as they might, the adults observing them will not be able to ascertain from their behavior which are male and which are female. The adults tend to feel sure that the more aggressive youngsters are boys—but they will be correct only half the time! In *Woman: An Intimate Geography*, Natalie Angier points to other research demonstrating that when people are shown a videotape of a crying baby and told that it's a boy, they will describe the child as looking angry. If they're told it's a girl, they will say she looks scared or miserable.[2] We tend to project our beliefs about children's behavior based on our own gender-specific expectations and prejudices—in these cases that boys are more aggressive than girls, who are more emotionally vulnerable.

The truth is, whether or not male and female infants actually act differently, in our society we treat them quite differently from the moment we wrap them in their little blue or pink receiving blankets right after delivery. Parents will even tape pink bows to the tops of their baby girls' bald heads or put blue booties on their baby boys' feet shortly after they bring them home from the hospital so strangers can be clued in to the child's gender and treat her or him accordingly. Some parents we have observed will adopt different attitudes toward their children in utero, after a prenatal ultrasound shows the child's gender. If the fetus is a boy, every time he starts kicking they'll boast about what a good football player he'll become; if it's a girl, they may gently rub the pregnant abdomen in response to the very same behavior, as if to comfort her.

Social psychologists studying sex role development have found that because of this kind of disparate treatment throughout childhood, American girls are taught to be fragile, dependent, compliant, cooperative, and nurturant; whereas boys learn to be sturdy, independent, active, assertive, aggressive, and unemotional. Dr. Sandra L. Bem, an expert on sex roles, wrote in 1983, "Adults in the child's world rarely notice or remark upon how strong a little girl is or how nurturant a little boy is becoming, despite their readiness to note precisely these attributes in the 'appropriate' sex."[3]

The seeds for a divergence in sex roles are planted very early. Studying play interactions among firstborn four-month-old infants and their parents, Dr. Lori Roggman of the University of Arkansas and Dr. J. Craig Peery of Brigham Young University found that the amount of time parents spent touching and gazing at their infants (and the babies' return gaze) was influenced by the parents' and child's gender. Fathers, they noted, touched their sons more than their daughters. In turn, boy infants gazed at their dads more than their moms. Other researchers have found that mothers talk to and look at their baby girls more often than they interact with their baby boys.[4] Roggman and Peery concluded that parental differences like these "represent the clear potential for differential socialization of males and females by both fathers and mothers in the first few months of life."[5]

Reports of such gender-related differences are legion in social psychology journals. Research has shown that fathers frequently carry their baby boys in one arm (the way a running back might tuck a football into the crook of his arm), while they often hold baby girls more carefully with both hands, caress them closer to the chest, and cuddle them more than boys. Boys are tossed into the air and roughhoused; they are tickled more. We allow them to cry longer before we pick them up, while we often attend to girls as soon as they make the first peep. This may teach girls at a very young age that someone will pay attention, soothe their pain, and try to meet their needs—whereas boys are taught to tough it out.

In one study, researcher Alyson Burns and her colleagues at the University of California, Davis, observed hundreds of families visiting the Sacramento Zoo and found that girl toddlers were more likely to be carried or pushed in a stroller, whereas boy toddlers were more apt to walk, especially with their fathers.[6] In these and countless other nearly imperceptible ways, girls learn dependence while boys learn independence.

We even use language differently with our children. Men and women speak louder to baby boys than they do to baby girls, to whom parents make more cooing sounds. We often tease our boys and give them funny nicknames like Bubba, Pumpkin Head, and Squirt, whereas we call our girls Beautiful, Sweetheart, Princess, and Little Doll. Even parents who believe they are treating their babies in a gender-neutral way can be observed holding and speaking to their infants differently.[7] These linguistic differences persist as our children grow older.

Not only do parents speak differently to their boy children than to their girl children; men and women differ from each other in the way in which they address children in general. Psycholinguists Jean Berko Gleason and Esther Blank Greif have found that most fathers issue commands and use commandlike terms when they speak to their children. Additionally, fathers give more directives to their sons than to their daughters. This may be one reason why many boys are apt to order around their playmates and can be less polite than girls, using expressions such as "Gimme that" or "Get lost."[8] Mothers often use the language of involvement. Instead of commands, they will say, "Let's do . . ." or "Let's go . . ."[9] They are actually modeling for their daughters how to get others to do what they want without being confrontational, and thus reducing the risk of conflict.

CULTURAL INFLUENCES

Children learn about gender roles not just from their parents but from nursery rhymes, fairy tales, cartoons, television shows, movies, stories, video/Internet games, newspapers, magazines, and books as well. When most of us currently in the workforce were growing up, more often than not the underlying theme in these various cultural influences was that the females should be sweet, kind, and good.

In most of the popular stories of our childhood, the strong female characters, those who are active in the world, are portrayed as cruel, spiteful, evil hags. *Cinderella* and *Snow White* teach girls that in order to succeed and win the prince, they must be lovable and unassuming rather than mean and evil like their stepsisters or the wicked queen. In *Alice in Wonderland*, the malevolent Queen of Hearts shouts the violent order "Off with their heads!" Hansel and Gretel fend off a witch who was fixing to eat them, and Dorothy in *The Wizard of Oz* encounters the Wicked Witch of the West, who is bent on her demise (and that of her little dog, too!). All these strong women are disgraced or destroyed in the end.

According to psychologist Dana Crowley Jack, the myth that good women are passive and gentle is reinforced by these kinds of stories:

> The tale of *Beauty and the Beast* lays out the Western mythology of gender, aggression, and sexuality. Man is a beast; woman is an unaggressive beauty. In relation to man, woman possesses "magic" powers either to call forth his aggressive nature, as did the witch who turned the prince into a beast, or to transform him from a beast into a prince, as does Belle.[10]

For girls growing up today, however, the lines are not as clearly drawn as they were for us. Contemporary media are filled with images of good and bad boys and girls. Powerful female role models have seeped into our culture—the influence of Buffy the Vampire Slayer and Xena the Warrior Princess have far exceeded Wonder Woman's legacy. Pokémon characters of both genders have armies and go to war. Movie companies such as Disney, in particular, have based their feature-length cartoons on strong heroines such as Pocahontas and Mulan, a Chinese girl who dresses as a boy and goes to war to defend her country. Television and Internet characters like Sailor Moon and the Powerpuff Girls are incorporated into games aimed at girls. Powerpuff Girls, ironically named Blossom, Bubbles, and Buttercup are, according to their Web site, "preparing to RUMBLE." Gamesters are exhorted to "first choose a training regimen, then select your favorite defender of Townsville for the final challenge. The girls are counting on you, so GET TOUGH!" This is a far cry from the passivity of the Sleeping Beauty of yesteryear.

However, despite this more gender-equal pop-culture bent, if you conducted an informal survey of youngsters' Halloween costumes, you would still find an awful lot of little girls dressed as fairy princesses, ballerinas decked out in tutus, and witches in evidence. Boys still tend to dress as pirates, devils, soldiers, and cowboys. According to Dorothy Clark, a professor of children's literature at California State University, Northridge, "The culture is giving double messages to girls."[11] They are receiving the message that they are indeed power puffs.

TOYING AROUND WITH SEX ROLES

Though our modern toy stores are filled with gender-neutral playthings such as Lego, blocks, puzzles, crayons, paints, clay, Tinkertoys, and robotic doggies, what do you think is the most popular toy among little girls? Yes, Barbie is still holding strong. According to Dana Crowley Jack, "The myth has it that American culture today does not heavily gender-type children. The reality is that toys have hardly changed for decades."[12] Whereas the three elements common to boys' toys are speed, power, and noise—Buzz Lightyear comes to mind—girls' toys still most often revolve around nurturing. Toys reflect the kinds of games youngsters play and the diverse cultures they live in. Boys' toys are often more bellicose (Ninja Turtles, Transformers, G.I. Joe, Pokémon), whereas girls' toys reflect their more cooperative, nurturing roles (My Little Pony, dollhouses, play kitchens, dress-up clothes).

Our society and perhaps even our innate natures do much to ensure that never the twain shall meet. Something called Genderbender toys were introduced at the 1993 American International Toy Fair—but you could hardly call them revolutionary. For girls, there was the Wonder Woman action figure, replete with long hair and Barbie-doll figure. Her crime-fighting weapon was a magic wand that dispensed bubbles. To encourage boys to play with dolls, there were Battle Trolls and Troll Warriors.

Fathers are particularly prone to reinforcing the gender-"appropriate" use of playthings with their children. In one Texas study, researchers brought boys and girls into rooms outfitted with gender-specific toys. They instructed both boys and girls to play with the "girl toys" the way a girl would, and then to play with the "boy toys" as a boy would. Then the researchers invited the parents into the rooms, observing whether they participated and helped their children or reacted negatively by interfering or expressing displeasure. Fathers, it was found, were five times more likely to disapprove of cross-sex play by boys than by girls. The mothers were much more flexible in their interactions.[13] Both parents seem to be more comfortable having a girl who's a "tomboy" than a boy who's a "sissy" (which derives from the word *sister*).

In their efforts to be politically correct, some parents have tried to reverse these trends. The results are sometimes surprising. One mother told us that when she gave her five-year-old son a set of Barbies, he organized his collection into battalions and played "War of the Barbies." Another woman gave her young daughter, Jessica, an assortment of toy trucks. After an hour or so, she checked on Jessica because it had become so quiet in the playroom and found that the little girl was actually "playing house" with her new trucks. She had created a truck family with a daddy truck, mommy truck, and baby trucks.

Jessica's interaction with the truck family is especially interesting because research studies have suggested that nurturing behavior is both a biological process and a learned activity among female primates who must be shown how to be maternal toward their young in order to mother properly. (When researchers deprive female monkeys of contact with their own mothers or other females during the first eight months of life, they may become abusive, even murderous, once their own offspring are born, oxytocin notwithstanding.) According to UCLA psychologist Shelley E. Taylor, nurturing behavior in human females "may be oxytocin based, socially mediated, mediated by higher-order brain functions, or some combination of these three processes."[14] Whatever the source, young Jessica had already assimilated her gender-based role as "Mommy."

The Mattel Toy Company's difficulties in naming one of its new Barbies shows the double bind that can occur in the creation of toys for girls that include the notion of power. Jill Barad, the then CEO of the company, is reported to have said, "At first we called her CEO Barbie, but not a single girl knew what a CEO was . . . then we were going to call her President Barbie, but everyone thought that meant president of the United States. Then it was Boss Barbie, but girls said the name was rude because bosses can be mean. So we struck a deal with *Working Woman* magazine, and we think it is the most kid-friendly title."[15] They named the doll "Working Woman Barbie." Notice Barbie's fall from powerful CEO to a nondescript, undifferentiated function.

SOLIDIFYING SEX ROLE IDENTITY

Carol Nagy Jacklin, a psychology professor at the University of Southern California, points out that young children know more about their own sex-appropriate behavior and attitudes at much earlier ages than we have any reason to believe. Jacklin and Stanford University developmental psychologist Eleanor Maccoby showed in joint studies that as early as thirty-three months of age, children prefer same-sex playmates. After observing one hundred preschoolers on playgrounds, they found that four-and-a-half-year-olds spend three times as much time with same-sex playmates as they do with those of the opposite sex, even when activities are gender neutral like riding Big Wheels, climbing jungle gyms, or using finger paints. By the time youngsters reach the age of six and a half, they spend eleven times as much time with same-sex friends. In another, more recent survey, 36 percent of the preschoolers included said they had playmates of the opposite sex. By kindergarten, only 23 percent did. By the second grade, mixed-gender friendships were almost nonexistent.[16]

This gender segregation occurs because boys and girls have radically different play styles (as we'll explain below), perhaps stemming from biological differences as well as their disparate socialization during infancy and toddlerhood. Moreover, girls have a hard time influencing boys (say, to stop pestering them) by using typically polite suggestions, Maccoby found, whereas boys will change their behavior if other boys (but not girls) order them to do so. It is Maccoby's theory that young girls (just like the rest of us) are reluctant to interact with unresponsive people, and so they soon give up on boys as playmates.

The net effect of highly segregated play groups during middle childhood (between the ages of six and ten) is that they create powerful socializing environments in which boys and girls become differently acculturated. By the time children are six or seven years old, they have clear ideas about gender, and both girls and boys strive to conform to their own sex role stereotypes.[17] Maccoby believes that these segregated play groups lead to boys and girls growing up in essentially different worlds. It is during this period that male and female sex role behaviors become solidified into the distinctive patterns that we recognize in adults.

The Games We Play

In every culture, children are socialized by the games they play and also whom they play them with. The famous Swiss psychologist Jean Piaget described play as the crucible of social development during the school years. Games teach children important lessons about how to behave "appropriately" when they become adults. As such, child's play becomes a laboratory for us to observe how children develop social skills and sex role identities.

It's important to note the difference between "play" and "games." The former is an informal, cooperative interaction that has no particular goals, no rules, no score keeping, no end point, no strategy for winning, and no winners or losers—say, creating a structure out of Tinkertoys or playing with dolls. A game, on the other hand, is a competitive interaction with definite rules, a clear goal, and a predetermined end point (nine innings, four quarters, a particular score). There are always winners in games, and consequently there must be losers. Certain activities, such as bike riding, can be considered play or games depending on how they are organized. If you're just tooling along on a bike with your friends, you're playing, but if you decide to race to the corner and back, it's a game.[18]

In a series of seminal studies in the 1970s, Janet Lever, a social psychologist at Northwestern University, documented exactly how boys' and girls' activities differ. Lever observed and interviewed nearly two hundred fifth-grade children (between the ages of ten and eleven) for one year at Connecticut suburban and urban elementary schools during recess, physical education, and after school. She also collected children's diaries, documenting how they used their leisure time when not in school (what they did, for how long, and with whom), and she interviewed them. She concluded that the children spent 52 percent of their free time playing—but as you might guess, there were distinct differences along gender lines in how the boys and girls organized their activities.

Boys, Lever found, play outdoors far more than girls. Their favorite games—basketball, baseball, football, cowboys and Indians, cops and robbers, and war—must occur outside because they require larger spaces. Ultimately, this allows boys to venture farther from home, encouraging independence. Girls prefer to play with Barbies or board games, which are best played one-on-one indoors. Because of the kinds of games boys engage in, they often play in larger groups. Even when girls played outside, their groups were smaller than boys'. The kinds of games girls played (hopscotch, jump rope, tag) did not require a large number of participants, but even more significant, the girls seemed strongly to prefer playing in pairs—with a best friend whom they got to know intimately. Lever considered girls' indoor activities "private affairs," whereas boys' games were "public" and open to surveillance.

The boys Lever studied also played in more age-heterogeneous groups. Although they may have preferred to play with children their own age, they were more likely to include younger players, using the rationale "You're better off with a little kid in the outfield than no one at all." The younger boys tried to keep up with the older ones and learned to "accept their bruises, stifle their frustrations, or not be invited to play again." The few times that Lever observed the ten-year-old girls playing with younger girls (aged five or six), they treated them as "live dolls," practicing maternal behaviors.

Finally, the girls Lever studied were more likely to play in boys' games than the reverse, probably because there is less social opprobrium for this arrangement. When boys did join the girls' activities, it was usually to interrupt and annoy the girls in the role of a "tease" or "buffoon."

COMPETITION AND TAKING TURNS

Of great interest to us is that the boys Lever observed played far more competitive sports than the girls did. Sixty-five percent of the boys' activities were formal games, compared to only 35 percent of girls' activities. "Girls *played* more than boys and boys *gamed* more than girls," Lever explains.[19] Competitive games are all organized by hierarchies: there are coaches, team captains (often chosen by the children themselves because of their merit), star players, average players, and benchwarmers; and it is clear that the primary way boys interact in such sports is through conflict, striving with their team to come out on top.

University of California anthropologist Alan Dundes writes in an essay entitled "From Game to War" that all sports and games are based on the theme that "involves an all-male preserve in which one male demonstrates his virility, his masculinity, *at the expense of a male opponent.* "[20] Some boys are more powerful and/or skillful than others—this is a given—and boys learn to accept their status in the hierarchy. An executive at AT&T once told us, "As a boy, I always knew my place in the pecking order." He says that gave him the mental space to stop jockeying for position and start playing the game.

Eleanor Maccoby emphasizes the importance of the all-male peer group as the setting in which "boys first discover the requirements of maintaining one's status in the male hierarchy."[21] What goes on during these games? Mostly, boys rehearse being "strong" competitors—perhaps as preparation for their adult lives. In *Staying the Course,* social psychologist Robert Weiss describes how boys learn to maintain hierarchical status in their play environments:

> Peers are the most effective teachers of values. Boys slightly older than kindergartners . . . learn from one another, in playground games and in more or less organized sports, to condemn cheaters and showoffs, the clumsy and the incompetent, the cowardly, the egocentric. They learn in confrontations with other small boys to resist aggression, to conquer fear or at least to mask it, to stand up for themselves. In the world of small boys they learn hardihood. They learn not to cry when their feelings are hurt. . . . They learn not to offer alibis for poor performance, not to ask for help. . . . They learn not to talk about their uncertainties and fears except, perhaps, as a means of overcoming them.[22]

There are no such lessons for girls—quite the contrary. When playing Barbie, there's no star player or coach. In their one-on-one play with a best friend, girls are, in fact, playing "relationship." They prefer intimacy and reciprocity in their play activities: far from hiding their feelings, the sharing of secrets creates a close bond and is a sign of friendship. Girls collaborate on making up games and fantasy play and enjoy deep emotional ties. The divulging of a secret to others can precipitate a breakup, but if a girl gets hurt and cries during a game, she quickly becomes the center of a concerned and supportive group of female playmates.[23] In girls' games, power is shared equally—no one is trying to get the better of anyone else.

Conflict, an inherent element of competition, means we disagree about something. Friendship, on the other hand, means we're in harmony. Since the game of "relationship" is central in the female culture, conflict is to be avoided. It damages friendships. Consequently, when they get into a squabble, girls are repeatedly admonished to "get along and be nice." These are code words for "avoid conflict at all cost." One woman told us that when her daughter orders her friends around, she calls her "Miss Bossy Cow." When asked what she would call her son if he were to display the same behavior, she blanched and then replied, "A natural-born leader, of course." It suddenly dawned on this woman that she had imposed a double standard on her daughter, and it stunned her.

Girls grow up with different rules: the power is always kept dead even. Even when girls play spontaneous competitive games like hopscotch or jump rope, they actually do not compete directly with one another. These are "turn-taking" games in which there's no expressed goal, no strategy for winning, and no defined end to the game. In jump rope, for instance, each girl patiently waits her turn, and when the players are tired or must stop the game, the children compare their achievements. One person's success does not necessarily signify another's failure, as it would in direct competition where there is always a winner and a loser.

Women gravitate toward win-win situations so they can keep relationships intact. This practice in turn taking and indirect competition may come to bear when girls grow into adults in the work world, as we will see.

Among girls, it is more important to be popular than to win. In fact, boasting about prowess almost guarantees that the gloater will become friendless, isolated from others. Because girls place a high value on intimacy with other girls, being ostracized is excruciatingly painful. In the female culture, popularity and intimacy are signs of status—they are more important than success or achievement. In the male culture, having a high position in the hierarchy is what counts most.

Going back to Lever's study, perhaps her most interesting finding is that boys' games last so much longer than girls' do. Seventy-two percent of all the boys' activities that Lever documented spanned an hour or more while only 43 percent of girls' did. She did not watch a single girls' activity, even at recess, that exceeded fifteen minutes. It was common for boys' games to fill the whole twenty-five-minute recess period.

Why should this be so? Lever proposed several answers to this question, some of which are germane to our understanding of workplace conflicts among women. To begin with, competitive boys' games are rule bound, which makes them far more complex than girls' games. Due to the existence of so many rules, boys often become involved in procedural or other disputes with the children on the opposing teams. The boys, Lever found, were able to resolve those disagreements effectively. Although she observed the boys arguing all the time, no game ended because of a fight—the chief goal was to keep the ball in play. In the worst of disputes, the boys would simply agree to repeat the play. A physical education teacher at one of the schools in Lever's study noted that the boys seemed to enjoy these debates as much as they did the actual game, and that older boys would model how to resolve the arguments for the younger ones.

The social learning that occurs during competitive games teaches boys many valuable lessons about resolving conflicts. It encourages the development of the organizational skills necessary to coordinate the activities of several people at once. It provides experience in successfully settling disputes. It may even improve boys' abilities to deal forthrightly with interpersonal competition and conflict.[24] As Lever explains:

> A boy and his best friend often find themselves on opposing teams. They must learn ways to resolve disputes so that the quarrels do not become so heated that they rupture friendships. Boys must learn to "depersonalize the attack." Not only do they learn to compete against friends, they also learn to cooperate with teammates whom they may or may not like personally. Such interpersonal skills have obvious value in organizational milieu.[25]

In the turn-taking games that Lever saw the girls play, however, the children had little experience in settling disputes. When a squabble broke out among them, the game promptly ended, without an attempt at resolution. For most girls, the object of a game like hopscotch is not winning so much as interacting with one another; it's an excuse for talking and sharing feelings. As others have pointed out, if a game stops, there may be tears, threats such as "I won't be your friend anymore," counterthreats, and pouting.[26] Some girls in Lever's study even complained that their friends "couldn't resolve the basic issues of choosing up sides, deciding who is to be captain, which team will start, and sometimes not even what game to play!"[27]

We can surmise from these observations that having far less experience with competition in their play experiences, the girls did not acquire the skills necessary to deal with direct conflict. Lever observed in later research on the complexity of play that "the style of [girls'] competition is indirect, rather than face-to-face, individual rather than team affiliated. Leadership roles are either missing or randomly filled."[28]

Though girls think less in terms of winning and losing than do boys, they have their own unique way of coping with defeat. According to psychologist and marriage expert John Gottman, rather than mask and suppress their emotions as boys do, girls "encourage each other to express their anxieties directly and then take a parental, comforting role, soothing it away with words of love, loyalty and affection."[29] But boys learn that when the game is over, it's over. Because they know how to "depersonalize the attack," after attempting to destroy each other on the playing field, they happily go out for Cokes and hamburgers together after the game.

For little girls, the game is never over. If they have a conflict, it is not readily forgiven and forgotten. In a study of preteens and teenagers at play, anthropologist Marjorie Harness Goodwin found that when girls strongly disapproved of one of their friends' behavior, they exercised the utmost social control by ostracizing her for up to six weeks.[30]

In adulthood, the dynamics change little. Two women condemning each other's ideas in a meeting rarely go to lunch afterward arm in arm; the enmity is retained. But among men accustomed to living in a competitive world, such clashes are soon dismissed as "part of the game." It's just business, they tell themselves.

School

The socialization of girls to "be nice" and "noncompetitive," and to "avoid conflict" begun at home and in the neighborhood continues at school and can have an impact on achievement. In the eighth grade, Susan won a scholarship to a prestigious all-girls high school. This put her in a double bind, however. On the one hand, the scholarship made her and her parents very happy, but on the other, she feared she could lose popularity with the girls at her old school because they would think she was smarter than the rest of them. In order to minimize her appearance as smarter than her friends, intermittently on tests she would intentionally make mistakes so as not get 100 percent on too many of them.

A growing child's sex role identity is further solidified at school, when a teacher's treatment varies from gender to gender. In the school environment, girls will learn lessons about their "proper place." They learn, for example, that if they speak up, if they are assertive—even aggressive—in pursuing information and achievement or in rejecting pat explanations, if they push to get their answers heard, they may be considered "bossy showoffs," "obnoxious," and "unfeminine." Sadly, this has the effect of encouraging girls to hide their abilities and interests and to shun competition.

This kind of gender training can begin as early as kindergarten. A recent *Wall Street Journal* article highlighted kindergarten awards for five-year-old boys and girls at a school in the Midwest. The awards were given in the following categories:

Boys' Awards	Girls' Awards
Very Best Thinker	All-Around Sweetheart
Most Eager Learner	Sweetest Personality
Most Imaginative	Cutest Personality
Most Enthusiastic	Best Sharer
Most Scientific	Best Artist
Best Friend	Biggest Heart

Mr. Personality	Best Manners
Hardest Worker	Best Helper
Best Sense of Humor	Most Creative[31]

It is clear that the girls in this kindergarten were not being rewarded for their thinking, learning, hard work, or scientific minds. Rather, it was their ability to cooperate and care about others that was emphasized—not bad traits, mind you, but also nothing in the way of supporting female professional advancement. In elementary school, girls are often rewarded with attention and praise for nonacademic achievements such as neat penmanship or getting along with others. Teachers and other adults give them the erroneous impression that tidiness or congeniality will stand them in good stead in the world at large: an agreeable person avoids confrontation and doesn't make waves.

A fascinating study of more than one hundred fourth-, fifth-, and sixth-graders in four states and the District of Columbia by researchers Myra and David Sadker found that "at all grade levels, in all communities, and in all subject areas, boys dominated classroom communication." The researchers observed how teachers responded to students calling out answers. When boys answered without teacher permission, their responses were accepted; when girls did the same, they were admonished to raise their hands. According to the Sadkers, the message conveyed to both genders was that "boys should be academically assertive and grab teacher attention; girls should act like ladies and keep quiet."[32] These teachers were promoting our culture's typical female values of girls following rules, waiting their turn, and being polite. Our culture defines typical male values as verbal competitiveness, aggressiveness, and even impoliteness.

A major 1992 study commissioned by the American Association of University Women on gender differences in educational opportunities found that teachers unwittingly but consistently shortchange girls. Teachers would force boys to work out problems they didn't understand, but would tell girls what to do, particularly in subjects such as math or science for which girls traditionally are perceived to have less affinity. (This perception, by the way, has been proved false by many studies.) Teachers also tend to go easier on girls when it comes to discipline. As a result, boys receive more criticism and become more adept at coping with it by the time they reach adulthood (not to mention the intense critiques they receive from a coach while playing a team sport). Boys are given much more pointed feedback than are girls at school. Girls don't become used to criticism, and, not having learned how to manage it or use it productively, they take it personally and feel devastated when they receive negative feedback in adulthood.

Lest you think this double standard ends with childhood, a study conducted at Wheaton College in the early 1990s by Catherine B. Krupnick, a researcher at the Harvard Graduate School of Education, showed through thousands of hours of videotaped classroom discussions that faculty members would take more seriously male contributions to class discussion than they did female contributions. Teachers would allow the men to dominate the classes. Other research has found that college professors are more likely to remember male students' names, call on them in class, and value their answers. These same professors feel free to interrupt women and ask them "lower-order" questions such as the date of an event rather than its significance.[33]

In addition to feedback from teachers, the textbooks that children read also influence how they see themselves in the world. When most of us in the workforce were growing up, not only were there fewer females than males portrayed in our history and reading books, but the males also were most frequently presented in leadership and professional roles. The adult female characters tended to be cast in nurturing, caregiving roles like mother, teacher, and nurse. Researchers believe these books ingrained in us the belief that men lead and women follow, that men are the main decision-makers in the family, and that women primarily act in helping, nonconfrontational roles where they are peacemakers.

The textbooks in today's classrooms are far more balanced than those of our childhoods, portraying a variety of family situations and powerful female role models. It remains to be seen how or whether these books will influence the coming generations.

On both the playground and in the classroom there is a subtle reinforcement of "appropriate" behavior for boys and girls. These different standards enhance a boy's skill in dealing with competition and power but diminish that trait in girls.

POWER

Many research studies have shown that children have definite ideas about how powerful males and females "should" be and also who "should" control interactions between them. In one study, children as young as two or three already understood that "girls don't hit, but boys like to fight" and that "boys will be the boss when they grow up."[34] In another investigation, five-year-olds were aware that "women are supposed to be gentle and affectionate and that men are supposed to be strong, aggressive, and dominant."[35]

Competitive behavior and the direct use of power are not stereotypical social expectations for females. In a study of fifth-graders, social psychologist Dorothea Braginsky asked groups of girls and boys to get a peer to eat several crackers that had been soaked in quinine—a bitter taste. If they were successful, they would be rewarded with a nickel for each cracker their classmate consumed. The successful boys manipulated their peers using lies in a direct and aggressive approach. They were, according to Braginsky, "less concerned with future encounters than with their immediate success," and their methods were "crude." But the successful girls behaved in a more indirect manner, using "a subtle, evasive method of impression management."

Many of the successful girls used a technique Braginsky called a "money-splitting bribe"—they revealed to their classmate what the experimenter had requested of them and offered to share the money if the other girl ate the crackers. Although Braginsky viewed this as a negative manipulation (after all, these successful girls never offered to share in the eating of the noxious crackers and didn't stress that they would keep half the money), we are inclined to believe that the girls had found a nonconfrontational, nonaggressive way to create a win-win situation and preserve their relationships. According to Braginsky, these girls "emerged from the situation having won the confidence and friendship of the TP [the Target Person, i.e., her classmate]."[36] Interestingly, the girls who attempted to convince their classmates to eat the crackers using the boys' more aggressive methods were unsuccessful.

This research implies that females who use coercive power strategies—who order other females around, for instance, or who lie outright—tend to meet with resistance. With women and girls, indirect methods generally garner greater success.

Researcher Diane Carlson Jones has found that "the key difference between boys and girls is the perception of power holders. Boys readily accept the occupants of top-ranking positions while girls reject the powerful." In searching for what might account for these differences, Jones surmised that when boys act aggressively, this corresponds to our sex role expectations of them. But the same cannot be said of girls. Their aggression runs counter to our norms. "For females . . . only the indirect power style is socially sanctioned; the aggressive style is increasingly closed off as an option. Aggression is never reinforced for females, regardless of age, and in fact is punished with affective rejection,"[37] one of the least desired consequences for the relationship-oriented female. No wonder women tend to be afraid of power.

EATING HUMBLE PIE

Because we have been socialized to eschew conflict, competition, and aggression, girls tend to criticize and reject other girls whose behavior seems competitive. Girls whose actions or behavior suggest they are superior or who call attention to their accomplishments and who compete too vigorously against their friends are likely to be rejected.[38] Indeed, in our society, young females are inculcated to "be humble": Deborah Tannen points out in her book *Talking From 9 to 5* that girls quickly learn that sounding too sure of themselves will prove unpopular with their peers. Tannen quotes anthropologist Marjorie Harness Goodwin, who found that groups of girls at play will penalize and even ostracize a girl who seems too confident. They'll use expressions such as "She thinks she's cute" or "She thinks she's something."[39]

This sort of disapproval is not just child based. Adults will also criticize a boastful, seemingly overconfident girl. Tannen tells the story of ten-year-old Heather DeLoach who became a child celebrity by tap-dancing on a pop music video in a bee costume. When interviewed for a magazine, Heather was quoted as saying, "I'm extremely talented. I guess when the director first set eyes on me he liked me. I try my best to be an actress, and I'm just great. I'm the one and only Bee Girl." A disgruntled female reader wrote in response, "Perhaps ten-year-old Heather should stop being a *bumble*bee and start being a *humble*bee."[40]

Girls are expected to be humble; they are taught not to take the spotlight but rather to emphasize the ways in which they are just like everyone else while downplaying what makes them special. This humbling of girls applies to females of all ages and in all circumstances. During the question-and-answer period for the five finalists at a recent teenage beauty contest, two of the female moderators remarked that one of the contestants responded in a way that made her seem "entirely too sure of herself." They said they were surprised because "she certainly hadn't seemed that way earlier in the contest!"

When we're barraged with these kinds of micromessages about female comportment, we learn that acting with self-assurance can hurt us in the long run—ironically even during beauty contests when we are judged on poise, the female way of displaying confidence.

SOCIAL LEARNING AND FEMALE CONFLICTS

In this chapter, you've seen how as girls we have been raised to develop intimate relationships with close friends and to preserve those relationships at all cost. We've been taught to be gentle, loving, and interdependent. We've been encouraged to be empathic and humble, and we've internalized the belief that being powerful means being considered wicked and evil. We've learned to share secrets with our best friends and to expect that they will comfort us when we're upset. We've learned to wait and take turns, whether we're playing or answering a question in the classroom.

We've learned not to fight—but we haven't learned what to do with our stifled angry feelings if we feel slighted; our childhood environment has not taught us how to settle arguments among ourselves. In fact, we've learned not to compete, not to speak up, not to draw attention to ourselves, and most definitely not to act too powerful or other girls won't like us and may even reject us.

Boys have learned different lessons—the lessons of how to survive in a hierarchy. They have become accustomed to experiencing conflict and differing degrees of interpersonal power. They're used to rough-and-tumble aggression, and they're accustomed to, if not exerting power over others, at least jockeying for position among them. Boys have had much practice settling disputes and conflicts, and they are able to distance themselves personally when attacked.

As products of these two different worlds, it is not surprising that boys and girls, men and women, tend to relate to people differently. Men tend to experience friendliness with other men, whereas women develop friendships that are deep and lasting. If women are friends, they're friends everywhere—in their personal and professional lives. The friendliness of men can come and go as needed. At the beginning of a workshop we once asked the men in the room to tell us what they had learned from the team games they played during childhood. One man exclaimed, "Loyalty! Loyalty to the team." When queried how he would react if he were traded to another team, he responded without missing a beat, "Loyalty to the new team."

Profound and pervasive female friendships are a wonderful and enriching part of being a woman. But unfortunately, they also contribute to our having catfights. While a man can become embroiled in a verbal tussle with a male co-worker and then forget about it once it's over, we rarely forget a disharmony or a slight. Relationships are just too important for us.

Men can work out their differences by throwing their power around in an argument, like a couple of male chimpanzees taking each other's measure by stomping around, glaring at each other, chests out, or maybe even taking a swing at the other guy. Once the confrontation is over, both players are back on even ground. But this kind of power play doesn't work around women, who haven't been socialized to do it and aren't used to it. Women take a display of power more personally than men do. A woman who indicates that she's better than another woman or tries to exert power over her quickly damages the relationship. "Power posturing" is all in a day's work for a man, but a woman who puffs out her chest will quickly be labeled a "bitch." And that is exactly what we will be looking at in the next chapter.

FIVE

THE BITCH FACTOR:
INDIRECT AGGRESSION

WHEN ONE WOMAN in a female-to-female friendship ig-
nores or subverts the tenets of the Power Dead-Even
Rule, the other woman may become angry and look for ways to fight back.
Even as she seeks to rebalance the power in the relationship, though, what
does she do with her anger? As girls grow into adulthood, they are trained to
preserve relationships at all costs, avoid conflict, and "be nice." Rarely are
they afforded the opportunity to practice conflict resolution or the de-
personalization of an attack. How are adult women supposed to express
frustration and sense of betrayal when someone has hurt them or otherwise
violated the Power Dead-Even Rule? What are they to do with their naturally occurring anger?

FEMALES AND INDIRECT AGGRESSION

Feelings of anger tend to be expressed through aggressive behavior, which
can be conveyed directly, overtly, and physically such as in bickering,
yelling, swearing, stealing, slapping, punching, kicking, chasing, pushing,
tripping, or other more violent and deadly means. Aggression is not anger,
but it is the behavior most closely associated with and arising from the emo-

tion of anger. Aggression is behaving with the intent to hurt someone physically or emotionally.[1]

Anger can also be expressed through indirect and covert aggressive behavior as when one tells lies and spreads rumors behind another's back, stomps off and sulks, snubs, plants damaging information or insinuations, takes revenge by sabotage and property destruction, shuns or ostracizes a target person from a social group, refuses to make eye contact or otherwise pretends that person doesn't exist, makes faces or derogatory gestures to others about her—all behaviors we've defined as the hallmarks of catfights.

Most of us would assume that women are indirectly aggressive while men are directly aggressive. When we think of gossiping and cliquishness, we tend to conjure up images of females; and when we think of loud swearing and fistfights, we most often imagine males. But is this stereotyping true? And is it true because women are somehow innately less aggressive than men?

For many years, scientists seemed to think so, as they deemed males the more belligerent gender. Eleanor Maccoby and Carol Nagy Jacklin, the social psychologists who studied how sex roles develop and solidify, claimed this to be true in their 1974 book, *The Psychology of Sex Differences,*[2] and other research seems to back up their assertions. For instance, in a 1977 study of children raised on an Israeli kibbutz where sex differences are deliberately played down, it was found that the girls cooperated, shared, and acted affectionately while on the whole the boys were more apt to engage in disobedience, violence, verbal abuse, and conflictual behavior such as taking another child's toy.[3] We've attributed much of the explanation for this to an overabundance of testosterone in males, which has been associated with hostility and aggressive behavior in both human and animal studies.[4] This portrayal of boys is so common, it has become proverbial—little boys are made of snakes and snails and puppy dog tails, while little girls are made of sugar and spice and everything nice.

However, in a cross-cultural comparison of children in Europe, North America, the Middle East, and Asia, researcher Kaj Björkqvist found that both young boys and girls are physically aggressive all over the world. In children under the age of three, there are *no significant differences* between male and female aggression. "Before they have language, they have their bodies," Björkqvist explains. "And through their bodies they can be aggressive, and so that's what they do, that is how they are."[5] Anyone who has parented young children of both genders is aware that little girls are perfectly capable of kicking, biting, hitting, pinching, shoving. Girls as well as boys become physically aggressive when thwarted.

As Natalie Angier noted in *Woman: An Intimate Geography,* "Of course [girls] are aggressive. They're alive, aren't they? They're primates. They're social animals. So yes, girls may like to play with Barbie, but make the wrong move, sister, and ooh, ah, here's your Dentist Barbie in the trash can, stripped, shorn, and with tooth marks on her boobs."[6]

Just as both males and females demonstrate directly aggressive behavior, research has shown that both genders eventually develop the impulse for indirect aggression. We might even consider its advent part of our normal maturation. Lacking verbal skills, Björkqvist points out, young children of both genders are likely to use physical means to express their feelings. Then, as language develops, youngsters utilize name calling, shouting, cursing, and other verbal abuse to get their points across. The refinement of social skills as the children mature further, says Björkqvist, "gives the possibility of developing a third stage of aggressive strategies, indirect aggression, using the social network as a means of bringing harm to the target of one's aggression."[7] By adulthood, domestic and gang violence aside, most men and women adopt this more circuitous approach—and it's a good thing, too, or there would be a lot more bloodshed in our streets, factories, and boardrooms.

THE INFLUENCE OF SOCIALIZATION

In addition to maturing toward indirect rather than directly aggressive behavior, girls in particular are strongly, maybe even aggressively, discouraged from releasing anger in a physical manner. We believe this is a robust testimonial to the power of socialization. Not only are females instructed against offensive fighting, which they are born with the biological capacity to do; they are also rarely instructed in how to fight defensively.[8] The power of socialization is such that, as the research studies we cited in chapter 4 suggest, three-year-olds already believe that girls never hit and boys like to fight. The socialization process has by then taken hold of these young children's belief systems and behavior.

THE TEN GOLDEN RULES OF GIRLHOOD

From girlhood on, most girls are socialized to believe that "bitchy is bad." As you were growing up, how many times did someone remind you of one of these anti-bitch Dos and Don'ts?

- Relationships are critically important, so work to preserve them.

- "Be nice." "Get along." "Look out for each other." "Remember, we're all in this together."

- Avoid conflict at all costs because it hurts relationships.

- Girls need verbal contact to feel close to one another. Secrets are important. Share them with your best friend.

- Never hit or physically hurt anyone.

- Put the needs of others before your own.

- Competition causes conflict, so avoid direct competition.

- Don't take more than your "share" of any resource: candy, attention, A's, cute clothes, beauty, boys.

- Don't be a show-off. Never brag about your accomplishments or positive attributes. Don't act as if you're better than everyone.

- Don't push other girls around. Don't act as if you're in charge.

There is great social disapproval of confrontational females in our culture; relatively aggressive girls tend to be unhappy about their behavioral tendencies and wish they would be less domineering,[9] whereas male aggression has been elevated to the degree that it is perceived as a sign of valor. Our society in general looks upon female aggression as evidence of pathology,[10] and so it is hardly surprising that most girls and women try to conceal their interpersonal aggression as much as possible. In interviews with sixty women from all walks of life and all racial groups, psychologist Dana Crowley Jack found that two primary factors leading women to mask their aggression involve how they were socialized and cultural expectations about feminine nonaggression. Two-thirds of the interviewees said they learned how to avoid aggressive conflict by watching their mothers.[11] Largely as a result of socialization, by the time children reach the third grade, boys are three times as likely as girls to kick or hit someone who makes them mad.

So what do girls do with their aggressiveness? After all, the desire to hit, kick, bite, and punch doesn't evaporate just because it's strongly frowned upon. Says Natalie Angier, in *Woman: An Intimate Geography*, rather than physically act out their hostility, "girls learn to talk hornet talk. Mastering curse words and barbed insults is an essential task of childhood." Girls also do a lot of what we call "face work." They stick out their tongues, roll their eyes, or sneer. These expressions may seem funny to adults, but studies show they can be effective in conveying anger and dislike or in ostracizing an undesirable child.[12] By age eleven, indirect aggression becomes a girl's prevalent style.

Though most adult females don't use "hornet talk" or facial gestures, they are adept at finding other means of attacking their adversaries. Researchers have found that more men than women will attack by inflicting physical pain, but women are just as aggressive in their attempts at vengeance. They simply express it through the infliction of emotional pain instead[13]—through indirect, rather than direct, means.

THE BIOLOGICAL CASE FOR FEMALE INDIRECTION

When people become embroiled in conflict, one of the variables they unconsciously (or consciously) take into account in determining a course of action is what psychologists call the *effect/danger ratio*. An aggressor wants to have a maximum *effect* on her target with minimum *danger* to herself. To both genders, direct aggression can be risky and may subvert a basic instinctual need to survive. After all, the target of one's aggression can strike back with a vengeance. But since males tend to be larger, stronger, and more muscular than females, unequal power relations coupled with a concomitant fear of injury and retaliation can inhibit direct female aggression.[14]

Indirect aggression, by contrast, is a form of social manipulation in which the aggressor stays hidden and anonymous—she attacks her target circuitously—in order to avoid social disapproval and possible reprisals.

Because it is safest from a biological standpoint, most women use indirect aggression to express their anger. Think of it this way: If a female is devoted to her own survival (and the survival of her offspring, if she has any), would she jeopardize her well-being and place herself and perhaps her children at risk by engaging in a perilous physical altercation? Probably not. The costs would be too great when she factors in the *effect/danger ratio*.

Males, on the other hand, may become involved in dangerous physical confrontations because success can provide them with a bigger payoff. Winning a fight may elevate a male's status within the hierarchy. Therefore, males may be more inclined to use direct aggression in power struggles or to defend their territory against intruders or other enemies. Researchers studying the "young male syndrome" have found some young men will take part in seemingly "trivial" altercations that eventually result in homicide in order to save face when challenged by another male.[15] Bloody turf wars often occur in gang-ridden neighborhoods when members of one group purposefully or inadvertently flaunt their "colors" or step within the boundaries of another. Think of the shouts and scuffles that tend to erupt between two men after a minor car accident or when one "steals" another's parking spot.

Though there are increasing reported incidents of female gang activity and "road rage" violence, female physical aggression appears to be confined to more specific, potentially survival-threatening situations rather than to the broader array of threats that males seem to respond to. Competition over scarce vital resources (food, men) can trigger female direct aggression[16] as well as situations requiring defense of oneself or one's vulnerable children. Researchers have found, for instance, that female adult rats are aggressive toward unfamiliar males and females primarily when they are pregnant or nursing, but these behaviors dissipate rapidly as their pups mature.[17] While both human mothers and fathers would rush to the aid of an endangered child, a woman is less likely to get involved in a screaming fight with someone over a purloined parking spot or a dented fender. Women have learned that throwing punches can be an expensive evolutionary behavior, and when it's a question of saving face, they usually come to the conclusion that fighting is just not worth the possible negative consequences.

This behavior might be related to the human female's ancient instinctual need to protect her progeny. Because nursing females provide crucial sustenance during their offspring's most vulnerable early years of development, says Anne Campbell, professor of psychology at England's Durham University, if a woman wants her children to survive, "she must be equally concerned with her own survival. Because of this, we should expect that women would have evolved a psychology in which the costs of physical danger would have been weighted higher than that of a male."[18]

Dr. Campbell proposes that because of the potentially high personal cost of a violent altercation, females experience a greater level of fear than do males when faced with the same kind of face-saving situation. There is no payoff for females in terms of social status and much to be lost if they are disabled or killed. Women are more apt to quickly move into fear because they are highly attuned to the potentially life-threatening aspect of a given event.

Campbell's ideas have been borne out by research findings that aggressive behavior in our primate cousins can be indirect. When female chimps get into conflict, they have been seen to instigate a male to attack an offending female. In his book *Peacemaking Among the Primates*, Frans de Waal describes how this happens: "She will sit next to the male, arm around his shoulder, directing a few high-pitched barks at her rival. When the male obliges by charging at the other female, we may score it as yet another instance of male aggression; but that's only because we use such crude measures. Among humans as well, female competition may be overlooked."[19] This female chimp used social manipulation. She harassed her target circuitously, thereby remaining safely in the background and potentially avoiding counterattack. She got her male friend to do the deed for her!

FEMALE AND MALE STYLES OF INDIRECT AGGRESSION

Because women are both innately reluctant to be directly aggressive and actively discouraged by society from doing so, all they have left to them are indirect avenues. Men, on the other hand, aren't discouraged from either form of aggression. Psychologist Kaj Björkqvist found that although men do exercise more direct, physical aggression than women, both genders engage in indirect aggression equally. Men are, in fact, quite good at it. They tend to use what Björkqvist calls "rational-appearing aggression" to reduce a target individual's opportunities to express himself. The covertly aggressive man may interrupt, criticize another's work unjustly, belittle an individual, or question his sense of judgment as in "You want to do *what?*"

All this is done with the intent to deliberately hurt another man and make him feel bad about himself. (Interruptions and criticism may be a normal part of the work environment, but when used, as Björkqvist says, "systematically as a means of harassment, they may be highly aggressive acts."[20]) The real purpose of such criticism is to damage another individual interpersonally, but the content is presented as being rational and objective—even helpful: "I was just trying to give you some feedback on that project. I've been doing these for ten years, but if you don't want any of my help, that's fine with me . . ."

Although this is a predominantly male style, some women are good at it too. An actress interviewed for a magazine article described how competing actresses seek to undermine her and other performers in this way: "A couple of actresses are notorious . . . They'll . . . come out of the audition and announce that they've got the part—even when they haven't—so the other actors feel like they don't have a chance . . . Or they'll say stuff like 'Are you really going to wear *that* outfit?' before you go in for your audition."[21]

Other women use saccharine sweetness to deliver their venom. A syrupy tone of voice coupled with what could be taken as cutting words can be confusing if you are on the receiving end. For instance, if you've shared an innovative idea at a meeting, an overly nice, rational-appearing attack might be "Oh that's such an interesting, *unique* way to look at this." On paper the words seem innocuous, but the tone is such that you know the other woman is shouting "What an idiot!" about you to the others gathered at the meeting. If you were to address this directly by asking, "Do you have a problem with what I'm saying?" she could hide behind her perfectly acceptable words and respond, "Oh no, it's just the way you see the world is so *different* from the rest of us." You know that you and your ideas have just been tainted, but the poison was delivered in a sugarcoated pill.

If a woman is not highly skilled in this more frontal attack, however, it can be costly for her to use the rational-appearing aggression techniques.

When her intentions are too clear, she risks retaliation. Consequently, rather than utilizing this style, many women are apt to use social manipulation when being indirectly aggressive. They will make insulting comments about a target person's private life to others, for example. Or they will backbite, spread false rumors, drop hints and allegations without making direct accusations, use "insinuative negative glances" such as rolling eyes in disapproval to make their point to others, or use "cold-shoulder," glaring, and other "do-not-speak-to-me" behaviors.[22]

The advantage, however, goes toward the male style. A person exercising rational-appearing aggression manages to camouflage his hostile intentions effectively by invoking seemingly cogent arguments to support his point of view. He reduces his risk of social condemnation, but the intended victim still suffers psychological injury. Social manipulation such as destructive gossip, on the other hand, is a more readily recognized form of indirect aggression and is less advantageous in terms of the effect/danger ratio—the victim of the attack may be able to trace the backbiting to its source.

The way men use indirect aggression is effective, whereas the way women do it often gets them labeled as bitches!

BITCH!

A woman caught in the throes of a catfight is often referred to as being a "bitch." We've all heard this term, and most of us *hate* it. It has a unique antiwoman slant to it, and there's no male counterpart. What derogatory name is a man most often called during an argument? "Son of a bitch." We rest our case.

The dictionary gives the colloquial meaning of the term "bitch" as "a malicious, unpleasant, selfish woman, especially one who stops at nothing to reach her goal." Why do women in conflict earn the dubious reputation of being "malicious, unpleasant, selfish," and manipulative to the point of being Machiavellian? What makes us seem "bitchy" at times, especially in the context of relationships with other women?

Somehow, even though men and women use indirect aggression equally, the deck is stacked against women. When they are indirect, they fall into negative stereotypes of female behavior. They're accused of being "catty" and "gossipy"; they're seen as determined to destroy their foes by spreading lies. The hitch is that because women are strongly discouraged from being physically aggressive, they learn to be indirect, but then they are rebuked as being bitchy for that very indirection. As Dana Crowley Jack explains, "Women's indirect delivery of aggression is culturally prescribed, socialized at home and in schools, yet, at the same time, is culturally condemned and seen as proof that women are more devious and less principled than men."[23] What a double bind!

Perhaps the best way for women to free themselves of this dilemma is to understand why they behave the way they do and to see that what people derogatorily refer to as gossip and cliquishness are really mostly normal female behaviors. If we examine these behaviors, we can see how they are not necessarily the negative actions they are often assumed to be. Rather, these are carefully evolved strategies that often help women obtain the information and resources they need.

In Defense of Gossip

Gossip has gotten a bad rap, maybe because it is seen as reflecting a female way of being. The scorn often inherent in the term points to a patriarchal interpretation of female interactions. Women tend to talk with other women about relationships and feelings, and men call this *gossip*. Men tend to talk about things—cars, the game, a promotion, their new computer gizmo—and men call it *shoptalk*. The goals of women's communication include creating shared communal meaning and the maintenance of relationships. Therefore, gossip serves many valuable functions in women's lives.

But there is a vast difference between talking *about* someone and talking *against* her (what we have termed *destructive gossip* throughout this book). In a positive sense, talking about someone is a way to bring her into a conversation even though she's not there, a process that creates intimacy with the person you're talking to as well as the one you're talking about. A woman can also use discussions about a third party to gauge her interlocutor's attitude and the support she can expect on a particular issue. For instance, if you don't know where Stephanie stands with regard to the new CEO, you might say, "Harriet really thinks Mark is going to be bad for our business." If Stephanie's response is "Really? I'm surprised she said that," you can gain an understanding of her point of view without asking her directly.

Columnist Liz Smith recently sang the praises of gossip as cathartic. "It is useful," she wrote. "It serves a number of purposes. Gossip relaxes you, establishes you, makes you feel better—indeed, I have seen one [research] paper that posits that gossip makes you live longer. Gossip is an enormous way of exchanging information and thereby of exchanging power. There is power in telling something you know or think you know."[24]

Although we can all conjure up negative images when we think of a gossip, actually the word originates from the Old English term for *godparent*— someone whom you trust and love and can speak to openly. At first the word applied to both genders, but over time, *gossip* took on the connotation of a woman's friends who are present at the birth of her child. Around the sixteenth century, the noun evolved to its current meaning of a chattery woman—as Canadian feminist historian Susan Mann Trofimenkoff puts it, "a person, mostly a woman, of light and trifling character, especially one who delights in trifling talk; a newsmonger, a tattler."[25] The verb has come to denote idle talk or rumor, especially about the personal life of someone else.

Although people often use the word *gossip* in a pejorative sense, the act of gossiping has many purposes, not all of them malicious. And not all gossip is idle. What is gossip, if not the simple conveying of information? History is said to be composed of gossip, and Homer is thought to be the first in a long line of gossipy individuals. As Liz Smith rhapsodizes, "Gossip is based on a common impulse—*Let me tell you a story*. This makes it a basic for studies of history, biography, autobiography, memoirs, romans à clef, novels, diaries, letters. Everything is grist for history's mill, even, or perhaps especially, gossip."[26]

Many women feel obligated to keep their friends apprised of the latest happenings in their lives, good or bad, and sometimes that involves sharing secrets about themselves in relation to a third party. Women seek comfort from female friends by lamenting the difficult situations that occur in their lives—"troubles talk." Unfortunately, often those situations arise from how others have wronged them; they talk about the people who have mistreated them. Although others may construe this as gossip, linguist Jennifer Coates explains that women develop topics progressively, building on one another's points: "Yes, that happened to my best friend too." "My sister had that problem with her husband." This helps women relate to one another and strengthens their feelings of intimacy. (Men "gossip" about others too, but usually their talk revolves around strategic relationships such as power brokers, business deals, advancement, and so on. And they tend to take a conversation in a new direction as a way of asserting power.)[27]

Confiding in another woman strengthens female relationships and can promote an acquaintance to a friend. As Deborah Tannen explains, "Not only is telling secrets evidence of friendship; it *creates* a friendship, when the listener responds in the expected way."[28]

Small talk, another function of gossip, helps female friends and relatives maintain a sense of companionship and connection. Women revel in the details of one another's lives—the outlandish dress a cousin wore to the wedding, what you ate there, how your husband or children behaved—because small confidences create intimacy. Such seemingly inconsequential information is so important to women, in fact, that if they forget some incident or person in a friend's life, she could perceive it as a slight and a sign of their lack of caring. Likewise, when women don't have good friends with whom to share their inner thoughts and impressions, they may feel terribly alone.

Because this kind of interaction is so important to females, we often engage in small talk in a business setting (recall the two executive secretaries who would not stop communicating with each other during work, even when their bosses erected a glass barrier between them). Tannen described a similar situation in which members of a counseling center spent 75 percent of their time in personal discussions and then took care of business effectively in the remaining 25 percent. Of course the men on the center's staff felt that the women were wasting an awful lot of time, but the center's director placed great value on a congenial work environment, feeling that, as Tannen reported, "such personal talk contributes to a sense of rapport that makes the women on her staff happy in their jobs and lays a foundation for the working relationship that enables them to conduct business so efficiently."[29]

Gossip can also be perceived as a way to achieve status and build self-esteem. Writes Liz Smith, "If you always say merely 'Hello. You're looking well. Isn't this *lovely weather?*' then you are a social bore. If you say, 'Let me tell you a story you're just not going to believe,' you'll be unforgettable. Gossip makes you interesting and boosts your self-esteem at having it to relate." This plays itself out among females of all ages. According to several anthropologists who studied the friendship patterns of junior- and senior-high-school students, many teenage girls gain status by being friends with those of higher status—the cheerleaders, the pretty ones, and the girls who are popular with boys. Their primary means of proving the depth of their friendship and cashing in on the resulting positive notoriety was to share these girls' secrets with others. Consequently, some of the higher-status girls preferred to limit their friendships to boys, finding the males less likely to seek out sensational details and disseminate them. Gossip is not a burning issue with boys, because they are more apt to derive status through achievements than through friendships.

Finally, gossip performs an important function as social control. The "What will people say?" "Tongues will wag," which in the past kept women from engaging in sexual promiscuity, bearing children out of wedlock, or breaking other social taboos, was in large part the result of fear of gossip. Throughout the millennia, women have used such social controls to police other women and curb their problematic behaviors. Trofimenkoff writes that gossip "defines a code of behavior by women and for women, with very strict sanctions against transgressors. 'What will people say?' is a much more powerful deterrent than any man-made law."

Gossip is so important to all humans that it is integral to the workplace. Teachers of management have even recognized the power of such talk, according to Trofimenkoff. Their textbooks identify gossip as a major information network in large companies where "the analysts prefer to dub the talk 'the grapevine' and the key people along it 'liaison individuals' but gossip it is. And employees who do not engage in it are 'probably maladjusted.'" Accordingly, large businesses will often rely more on hospitality suites at conventions than on formal seminars or even industrial spying to discover what's going on among their competitors. Gossip has its place.

The Uses and Abuses of a Sharp Tongue

That having been said, however, when gossip is used during female conflict to redress an imbalance of power, we move from talking about someone to talking against her, and that's a whole different story. When do we make this transition? Often it depends on with whom we are sharing a story.

Imagine that you've just had a stressful argument with another woman. You may turn to a close female co-worker to assuage some of your discomfort and share with her the story of the conflict. While others may perceive this as gossip, you may in effect be behaving in a hardwired fashion to relieve your stress—remember, women gravitate toward their friends when they feel threatened. If you tell a friend about the incident, you are most likely looking for support. But if you widen your circle of confidantes to include co-workers, supervisors, and staff, you must ask yourself, "Do I want support, or am I just bad-mouthing Marta so she loses power chips with the others?" It's important to be aware of your intentions as well as the damage your gossip might cause. Some of it may be irreparable.

When you talk against a female co-worker, you expose to others her character flaws, failures, and weaknesses. This is done in the hope of diminishing her power. Sometimes women also use gossipy techniques to spread untruths. One of our Web site correspondents described such a difficult situation: "I worked with a woman who acted like a jealous teenager," she wrote. "I think she wanted to be the 'youngest and prettiest girl at the ball,' and she was threatened when I, a younger woman, arrived. She disliked me before I even knew who she was. I thought her attitude would improve with time, but it never did. She would whine to our supervisor about petty things I did, yet would never so much as make eye contact with me when we passed. She started an awful, ridiculous rumor about me—that I was having an affair with one of the married directors, which I was not—and other outrageous, quite creative lies. I vowed not to stoop to her level and tried to ignore her the best I could, but it made it difficult for me to do my job, and it made me very uncomfortable and mad when I heard about the rumors. Luckily, I moved on to bigger and better things in the company, and I don't have to deal with her anymore."

Although we're sure the woman spreading the falsehoods was able to justify her behavior in her own mind—clearly, she was trying to even the score and make the power dead even between herself and our correspondent—what else could we consider her actions to be, if not quintessential bitchiness?

According to another of our correspondents, destructive gossip was so widespread in the human resources department of the insurance company where she worked that it seemed to be part of the corporate culture. "There are about twenty-five women in my department," Melissa wrote, "and *everybody* talks about *everybody else.* If anyone makes the 'least' mistake or slipup (as if we all haven't at one time or another) there is a 'huffing' and 'puffing' and pointing of fingers with enough vehemence to put Cinderella's stepsisters to shame. Rather than working toward solving a problem, coming together as a team to make sure the same thing doesn't happen again, or backing each other up, the whole point is to find the guilty party and string her up with as much righteous indignation as can be mustered.

"And let something go after it has been resolved? Ha, ha, ha. *Never!* Items that were taken care of years ago continue to be brought up—we waste at least a half hour at any meeting flogging those poor old dead horses. Blanket accusations are thrown without any specifics: 'I've had people tell me . . .' or 'The group isn't following through on check requests . . .' Who? What? When? 'Oh, I don't know . . . someone just told me.' How can anything be resolved when we don't have the details? This from professional women."

The trouble in Melissa's workplace was not just about one woman being indirectly aggressive toward another. This was a systemic disruption: the leader and the team members were not working together to create a positive, productive environment, and everyone suffered—including the squabbling employees, the people the human resources department serves, the company, and ultimately its customers. In chapters 10 and 11, we will cover how to change the contentious culture of this group.

CLIQUES

Gossip serves to cement another aspect of bitchiness: the formation of cliques that are brought together by the sharing of secrets, personal details,

121

stories about others. Cliques are a sore point for many women who as adults can still recall with clarity the pain they felt when they were excluded from a clique they aspired to: on the outside looking in and wondering why the other girls were so "mean" to them. Cliquishness develops among girls around the second grade as they cultivate close relationships with other girls—a best friend—and these duos often pair up with other best-friend couples. Once four to six girlfriends coalesce, a clique is born.

Although a clique might not have begun as a way to exclude others, often that is eventually the result. George Homans, a researcher on the Hawthorne Western Electric project in Illinois that studied team productivity in the 1930s, found that as groups become more cohesive internally, their external relationships begin to suffer. Indeed, the closer the relationships within the cliques, the more exclusionary the members' behavior becomes to those outside the group.[30]

The issue of cliques frequently arises among women in business settings. Nurses, for instance, work different shifts, each one of which often becomes a clique unto itself. The night shift can grow to be a tightly knit group because the members are fewer in number, work difficult hours, and believe they have the toughest job of all the shifts. The cafeteria is dark, often other hospital services are closed, and the physicians are sleeping, so this group tends to be more isolated and to interact with one another more frequently and intensively. This dynamic bears out another of Homans's findings: as interactions increase, "liking" increases too.

Not surprisingly, often a big rift develops in hospitals between the night and day nursing shifts. The two groups frequently find fault with each other's work: day shift workers often criticize those on the night shift for misplaced charts, inventory that has not been stocked, and leaving work for them to do. The night shift nurses, for their part, blame the day shift for failing to procure orders for medications or leaving their work incomplete. The nurses in the varying shifts may not know one another—in fact, they often don't—so they have few opportunities to interact or learn to respect and trust one another. They lack empathy for one another's working situations and therefore fail to give one another the benefit of the doubt, which makes for a hostile workplace.

Cliquishness occurs both on an institutional level and a personal level.

In an essay, writer Jenn Shreve described a difficult situation that arose when she moved across two state lines to take a job in a fledgling company:

> Several months out of college, I was struggling to feel at home in a new city and a nine-to-six office environment that was totally foreign to me. Because many of the women in the office were close in age to me, I assumed they'd politely invite me to a party or suggest a few good places to meet new people. No such luck. They'd loudly arrange to have lunch together or grab drinks after work, then neglect to invite me—or worse, invite me only to ignore me once there.
>
> Most frustrating, nothing was overt. A façade of friendliness craftily concealed the cruelty behind my female co-workers' dismissive smiles, so I could never tell if they were really giving me the cold shoulder or if it was just my imagination.
>
> Another woman came aboard—like me, from another state. Other than that, we didn't have much in common. If the clique of women working in my office didn't care for me, they took an active dislike to her. She was, it turned out, unqualified for the job, but instead of taking a professional tack, they stonewalled her—sending her nasty e-mails, then cutting her out of conversation, work related and otherwise. She lived in my neighborhood; so I began driving her home from work. Because of that, I was stonewalled too. The friendly façade dropped, and all that remained were icy stares.[31]

Cliques are an excellent example of how women's relationships can be really good or just plain terrible. They form because women want to be close, but they can be damaging, especially to those who are excluded. What brings women together in such groups are their commonalities, but eventually a feeling of specialness can pervade if others don't share the same history, qualities, abilities, or interests.

THE FALLOUT OF BITCHINESS

The only outlet women have been allowed for their angry feelings, although it is indirect aggression, can create painful and difficult situations. As we write this, both Pat and Susan can recall being through the ordeal of watching four women, partners in two successful businesses, snip and snipe at one another until their hostility led to the demise of their relationships as well as the collapse of their companies. As friends and colleagues of these women, we found the ruptures heartrending to watch, but it was even more difficult to be brought into the disagreement as confidantes. The cost to Susan was anguish, sleepless nights, and pain because she felt empathetic toward both of the warring factions. Furthermore, one of Susan's friends actually forbade her from having any contact with the enemy—her former partner.

Pat felt terribly awkward with her pair of disputing friends, as if she were asked to take sides between a divorcing couple. She kept asking herself, "Do I listen to Fran but not Toni?" Being open to Toni's opinions felt to Pat as if she were being disloyal to Fran, and vice versa. She was especially embarrassed when one would see her with the other—she'd been found out as a "traitor."

Because of women's tendency to bond by sharing intimate details of their lives, they may feel more vulnerable when they have a falling-out. Women know all about one another's marriages, weight problems, sex lives. Keeping secrets is important among girls; it may even be the number-one quality girls look for in a best friend. When these secrets are divulged during a catfight, no matter what the age of the participants, the betrayal can be devastating. We find ourselves saying or thinking things like "We were so close, but now you're leaving me, and all my personal stuff will be spread all over the world. We can never be close again."

When a quarrel occurs in plain view in an office, it can be not just embarrassing or emotionally unnerving but also professionally destructive. Pat worked with two clients in the same firm who constantly fought with each other. Sometimes they needled each other over subtle simmering issues, but at other times their shouting was so loud that everyone in the office could hear it through the walls. Over time, this hostility spilled over to these women's employees, who gradually became less cooperative with one another. Eventually, the division in the department diminished its productivity.

It is easy to be caught in the trap of listening to a dear employee who is having a fight with a counterpart in another department. If you're not careful, though, you might align yourself with her against the other woman and her friends, colleagues, and manager. The confrontation could escalate, and the departments might end up facing off against each other. Business information might be withheld, co-workers and superiors could exhibit hostility, and the whole tenor of the workplace might turn rancorous.

In one coaching situation, Susan worked with a sweetheart of a sales manager, Caroline, who was being undermined by Becky, a marketing director. Shortly after taking her job, Caroline had fired Becky's brother for incompetence, and now Becky was trying to even the score. Unfortunately, when Caroline went to Jill, her manager, and said, "I'm having trouble being effective because Becky is undermining me," Jill simply told her to get tough. But in this instance, toughness was futile. Caroline was being maligned and sabotaged in her work. She was not getting support from Jill, who was overwhelmed with her own workload and avoided involvement in her employees' personal spats. Becky's boss wasn't doing anything about the undermining, either, particularly because Becky was so artful that her boss couldn't detect it.

Although she was one of the company's top salespeople, Caroline would have quit her job if it hadn't been for the fact that she had an ongoing medical problem and needed health coverage. So she was stuck in an untenable situation. Becky was shrinking Caroline's power while increasing her own.

Taking action, Susan met with Jill and explained, "You have to be a safe harbor for Caroline. She's terribly stressed by this conflict, and without your support, she feels vulnerable and alone." That seemed to do the trick. Jill reached out to Caroline more frequently, and when Caroline cried about the situation in her office, instead of trying to stem the tears, Jill listened compassionately. Although Jill couldn't stop Becky's destructive behavior, her support and involvement fortified Caroline so she could better manage it on her own.

. . .

ZOE, A FORTY-EIGHT-YEAR-OLD WOMAN, as a child had been on the receiving end of a whole raft of aggressiveness, both direct and indirect. The bitchiness of her "friends" has had a lifelong impact on how Zoe perceives herself and how she reacts to indirect aggression aimed at her in the workplace.

"When I was little, my closest friend was Alicia," Zoe said. "Her father died recently, and when I called to offer her my condolences, she told me that the day of the funeral, several of the girls from our old Girl Scout troop had been talking, and my name came up. They were wondering what ever happened to me. Then Alicia said, 'It made me think about *that time*, and how sorry I am for what happened.'

" 'What do you mean?' I asked her. 'Which time? What happened?'

" 'Well, you know,' she said, 'you were always the prettiest one, always the straight-A student. You had the best papers, the best everything, and we hated you for it. Everybody gave you a really bad time growing up. One time at Girl Scouts, we rolled you up in a rug, and everybody took turns kicking you. I'm sorry for it.'

"What a great gift this was," Zoe told Pat. "Imagine having this kind of experience when you're so young and powerless and things are out of your control. Her revelation makes so many of my life experiences fall into place now. I'm not mad at anyone; it just helps me understand myself."

Zoe had been carrying around the scars from this old catfight for nearly forty years. In exploring its consequences, she saw how her experiences had led to feelings of victimization. "People always wonder why I put up with abusive behavior," she said. "To me it was normal; it's what I got used to. I ended up staying in a paternalistic company that made my life miserable for many years because it felt ordinary to me. I didn't see it as abusive."

When we thought about this devastating incident, we had to ask ourselves: How different were these girls' intentions from those of the women we first described in the introduction to this book—our co-workers who ganged up on Christine, the company's highest-ranking woman, and gossiped about her relentlessly in their efforts to tear her down? Christine, like Zoe, had violated the Power Dead-Even Rule by being too perfect and too successful. But receiving her comeuppance at such an early age had permanently scarred Zoe.

When she strives to move forward in her career and life, no woman is safe from these kinds of attacks. But by understanding the Golden Triangle of female relationships, the Power Dead-Even Rule, and how indirect aggression works, it's possible to navigate the sometimes rough seas of relationships more securely. In the following section, we will explore how to move from potential bitch pitfalls into managing the world of female-to-female relationships and how to turn bitter conflict into mutually respectful, collegial relationships.

PART II

COLLEAGUES

Finding

Powerful

Allies and

Friends

Among

Women

in the

Workplace

SIX

THE GOAL IS THE RELATIONSHIP

DOLORES, vice president of operations at a small manufacturing concern, was having a great deal of difficulty per-
suading a large space and aeronautics conglomerate to approve her
company as a subcontractor. Her employees in business development—all
males—had been unable to motivate the woman who administered the aerospace contracts at the giant firm to approve Dolores's company for its bid
list. The men tried for eleven months: they called the woman, named Mona;
they wrote letters to her; they phoned her boss and even her boss's boss.
Nothing doing. When they asked, "Where's the contract?" the stock reply
was, "It's on Mona's desk." The men were cursing and muttering at this recalcitrant and elusive Mona because she thwarted their every effort and, in
effect, had held up the potential for their company to bring in millions of
dollars of work.

Seeking guidance, Dolores came to Susan for a consultation. Rather
than have the men try to extract the contract forcibly from Mona, Susan proposed, why didn't Dolores get more directly involved? "Call Mona yourself," she suggested. "Maybe a friendly conversation with her will help
grease the wheels."

After thinking it over for a few days, Dolores decided to call Mona. They
talked about the contract and what Dolores's company could offer Mona's.
But then, as is often the case among women, the conversation veered toward
the personal. Mona fretted that she was going to have to leave work early be-

cause her teenage son was sick with the stomach flu. Dolores shared that she'd just gotten over the bug and was still feeling a bit miserable. A week later, Dolores made a follow-up call, asking Mona how her son was feeling and inviting her to lunch to enhance their budding relationship.

Over seafood salads and iced teas, they talked about their companies a bit, but they spent the rest of the time getting to know each other as businesswomen. Mona revealed that she had come to work for her large company twenty years earlier as a file clerk; she was surprised and delighted that she'd risen to such a pivotal position in her organization. She also poured out her heart about the troubles in her marriage. Dolores shared her own war stories about becoming a vice president in a male-dominated business.

Within two days of their lunch, the signed contracts arrived at Dolores's office. The men in the business-development department were dumb-founded, but Dolores wasn't. Susan had explained to her how important positive working relationships can be among women, and though Dolores had broached her relationship with Mona for strictly a business gain, after their lunch, both women felt they'd made a new friend, colleague, and ally. Both women had honored the Power Dead-Even Rule: when senior executive Dolores lavished time and attention on Mona, she validated the former file clerk as a vital person in her organization. That generous recognition augmented Mona's self-esteem and perhaps even her power. Mona repaid the power chip by giving Dolores the professional win she was looking for.

Friendships are vital and widespread in the workplace, especially among the ranks of middle management where females now fill 45 percent of all positions.[1] And these relationships are important to women. According to a national survey on employee loyalty, women are more likely than men to credit close ties with co-workers as a factor in their success: 62 percent of those interviewed felt that their co-workers improve their own skills.[2] Having a "best friend" at work correlates, apparently, with high job satisfaction, productivity, and retention rates.

In a study of telecommuters in Great Britain, 69 percent were male, but men make up 56 percent of the workforce.[3] It seems that women actually prefer to go to an office. Even in situations in which they are telecommuters or work extensively through e-mail and the Internet, women will deliberately create and strengthen relationships with other women. "I consider ten or so people I work with to be close friends, even though we've never met," a resource planner at IBM explained in a recent *Working Woman* article. "We trade funny stories, e-mails, and call on a regular basis. We know when one of us has a sick child or is having surgery—we're a support group for each other."[4] According to Jean Baker Miller, clinical professor of psychiatry at Boston University, women's connections with one another clearly enhance their inner growth, self-esteem, and power. Women gain actual energy from having a good conversation with a close friend; they feel more empowered to take constructive action in their lives; they gain clarity into their emotions by talking together about fear, guilt, anger, and other complex feelings; and they often gain a heightened sense of self-esteem from feeling confident that someone else thinks they're worth listening to.[5]

THE NUTS AND BOLTS OF RELATIONSHIP BUILDING FOR WOMEN

The fact is, women friends are central in women's lives. But we also know from painful experience that there is a dark side to female interactions. If you become vulnerable with a female co-worker, she can hurt you deeply when there is a falling-out; what starts as nurturing, intimate sharing can become ammunition during a destructive conflict. It's the best of worlds and the worst of worlds when it comes to female relationships, but women's alliances are well worth preserving, and in this chapter we will explore how to develop and keep these alliances strong.

The primary way to do this is through balanced management of power chips. And one of the major ways that women accrue and cash in chips is through their small, everyday interactions. Sociologists and business experts have found that male business interactions often revolve around delivering information. Men focus on getting to the bottom line quickly. But the interactive dance among women involves many more steps. Yes, women communicate to transmit information just as men do, but they also use these conversations to develop rapport.

Linguists tell us that the goal of woman-to-woman conversation is the maintenance of good social relationships.[6] They have found, in fact, that our very words and facial expressions have great impact on how we get along with other females. There are myriad linguistic devices that we unconsciously use in conversations with one another to help keep the power dead even. These verbal expressions are quite functional in female culture, although they may seem odd or even self-defeating to men.

WOMENSPEAK

Consider the Boy Scout and Girl Scout oaths. Boy Scouts begin their pledge with: "On my honor, I will do my best . . ." When we ask female workshop participants who are former Girl Scouts to recite their club's oath, they begin, "On my honor, I will *try* . . ." and then they stop, laugh, and exclaim, "I can't believe it!" Women naturally incorporate such circumspect expressions into their conversations. They have developed specific unconscious verbal devices and expressions that help other women feel comfortable: using disclaimers, hedges, and tag questions; expressions such as "I'm sorry"; an inclination to talk things over rather than get to the bottom line; and a gentle attitude toward interruptions.

When they use such "womenspeak," however, many women have received pointed feedback from male superiors that they come across as unsure of themselves. So they have specifically worked on shifting their communication style toward a brusquer, male mode. But if they don't return to their female habits when conversing with female colleagues, they are in danger of fomenting a catfight. Anita, an attorney, expressed her frustration because her secretaries kept quitting, and she didn't know why. "My male colleagues don't have this turnover problem, and I treat my assistants the same way they do," she complained. A busy woman, Anita's communication with her secretaries was clipped and to the point. When she learned about relationship talk among women, she suddenly realized that her "efficient" communication style was the culprit.

Let's take a closer look at these linguistic devices and how they function to support female relationships and prevent catfights.

DISCLAIMERS, HEDGES, AND TAG QUESTIONS

Disclaimers, hedges, and tag questions are ways for a woman to save face—both her own and the women to whom she is speaking. She may not want to offend the other women by assuming they share the same opinion. Or she may use a hedge to give herself an out when dealing with a touchy subject.[7]

Disclaimers include expressions such as "This might not make a lot of sense, but . . ." or "I'm not sure about this, however . . ." at the beginning of sentence. Men often hear these words as "Get ready for stupidity," but women use them with one another to sound less authoritarian and more humble.

Hedges comprise terms like "sort of," "maybe," "could be," "a little bit," "perhaps," "kind of," "try," as in "When she *kind of* talks like this, she *perhaps* doesn't sound like she knows what she's talking about, *maybe.*" If a man is listening, it may sound to him as if the woman is deeply unsure of herself; but by softening the force of her words, the speaker lets another woman know that she's deferential and that there is room for a second opinion.

Tag questions are inserted at the end of a sentence and include comments like "Okay?" "You know?" "Don't you think?" "Isn't that true?" Men often hear these as meaning "I need your assurance," but women hear these expressions as "I don't see myself as the big authority here," "I'd like your input," or "I need your involvement."

Women use these linguistic devices in order to maintain a flat power structure and observe the Power Dead-Even Rule. If you were to go up to Margaret and say, "We'll be doing this on Tuesday in this way," her response is likely to be "Who does she think she is to tell me what we're doing?" You are more likely to communicate successfully if you flatten the message and say, "I'm not certain about this, but I was thinking we might do this on Tuesday. What do you think?" Here the message linguistically involves Margaret in the process.

Consider the following two memos regarding the same issue that Jessica sent to Bob and Laura:

Bob:
I had some ideas after our meeting yesterday. I think it would be a good plan to do a survey before we make our final decision. A sampling of employees would work. I look forward to hearing from you.
Jessica

(continues)

Hi, Laura:

I had some ideas after our meeting yesterday. I was thinking we *might want to* look at doing a survey before we make our final decision. It *could* keep us from going down the wrong track. *Maybe* we should *consider* a sampling of the employees involved to get a sense of where they stand. *Just an idea. What do you think?*

Best regards,

Jessica

Notice Jessica's more direct manner with Bob versus her use of inclusionary, deferential language in her memo to Laura. Both memos were effectively targeted to the communications needs of their intended recipients.

"WE," NOT "I"

If women exclude an interpersonal twist from their communication with other women, they run the risk of provoking a catfight. A man might bark at an assistant, "I need this typed by three," and he'll probably get what he needs. But if a woman were to employ the same abrupt directive, her typing would be quickly relegated to the bottom of the pile. A better alternative for her would be to focus not only on the task but also on the exchange of chips and her relationship with the assistant. She's more likely to be successful with "Hi, how are you? You got your hair cut! It looks nice. How's your mom feeling? If you could possibly get this done by three P.M., I'd really appreciate it." Notice the difference between "I need this typed" and "If you could possibly get this done."

Women have also learned to shy away from "I" in situations in which they talk about their accomplishments. An editor at a large publishing house once told us that she and her female colleagues have noticed that when they announce acquisition of a new book to the company they'll say, "We just bought," meaning the company did it. Or they'll report, "We have in a project from that powerhouse agent, Andrea Young." A male editor is more apt to say, "I just bought," or "I have in a project . . ." In order to prevent Power Dead-Even Rule violations, women tend to be more comfortable being part of a group when accepting credit for accomplishments, ideas, and opinions.

"I'M SORRY . . ."

The expression *I'm sorry* has many meanings and functions for women other than a genuine expression of apology. Using "I'm sorry" can help equalize power, for example. Imagine you're entering colleague Liz's office, and you see she's hard at work. You might say, "I'm sorry to interrupt you. Could I just have a minute of your time?" You phrase your request in this way because you don't want to communicate to Liz that your time is more important than hers. If this were a male counterpart, however, initiating an interaction with, "I'm sorry," would immediately put you in a one-down position. You would be less likely to succeed in your interaction.

Women also use "I'm sorry . . ." out of empathy. This is the ability to put yourself in the other person's shoes and "feel her pain." Imagine a coworker who has a terrible sore throat. She might begin a conversation with you by saying "I'm sorry I have to whisper like this. I've got laryngitis." You might respond, "I'm sorry to hear that you're not feeling well." What a *sorry* lot, a man who overhears this conversation might think! But this is a perfectly appropriate female communication because the women are expressing concern for and attention to each other.

"I'm sorry" does not necessarily mean "I apologize." For women, the latter may be a much more serious expression of contrition for an offense. It clearly means, "I made a mistake and ask for your forgiveness." Some men may be oblivious to these subtle but all-important distinctions; for them, the expressions can be synonymous.

TALKING IT OVER VERSUS GIVING THE BOTTOM LINE

Imagine that you drop into Harry's office soliciting suggestions on a cost overrun in a project snafu. Even though you're the one seeking suggestions, Harry doesn't want others (including you) to think he needs help providing them—something that might cause him to lose status in the hierarchy.

Consequently he is more likely to pull a discussion of the problem inside himself and sort through the options privately in his mind. This inclination induces him to give you the bottom line without further ado.

You ask: "What should we do?"

Harry's simple response: "Do X."

Thankful for the tip, you say, "Good idea" and depart.

Now imagine you pop into Brenda's office soliciting advice for the same problem and she says, "Do X." You're likely to mentally react, "Hrrumph! She thinks she knows everything!"

Since you and Brenda don't live in a hierarchical world, she is less likely to lose position and, in fact, can enhance your relationship by talking over the problem with you rather than going straight for the bottom line. Therefore, it would be far more effective for Brenda to say, "We could do X, but I'm not sure we have enough money for X, so I'm leaning toward Y. *What do you think?*"

This kind of participatory, process-oriented decision making works for women. It's how they deal with the competing constructs of telling someone what to do (a hierarchical move) and keeping the power dead even. Involvement in decision making allows them simultaneously to solve the problem and to bond with each other. That's why a woman is more likely to give you the process and reasoning of how she reached her decision. And the two of you probably feel you've come up with a better decision because there was more input in making it.

Recently, when we were discussing this book, we ran into a situation that highlights how important it is for women to "process" with each other. Susan had been working all week with groups of men and in order to communicate with them, she had forced herself to bottom-line it as much as possible. Pat called to talk about an issue we had within a chapter. Susan's clipped response: "We shouldn't include that material."

"Wait a minute!" Pat said with a startled laugh. "It's me! I'm a woman. You need to tell me how you got to that decision." We both had a good chuckle over this. With two women who aren't as close or trusting of each other, however, such an interaction could have easily taken a more sinister turn.

DISCUSSING VERSUS INTERRUPTING

Take a moment to watch kids playing at any schoolyard. The boys verbally climb on top of one another; when one speaks, another one talks right over him. There's a lot of shouting going on among them. Now observe the girls. One speaks, then she's quiet; another speaks, then she's quiet; and back to the first one again. Females learn at a very early age to take turns to avoid head-on competition, be it verbal or during a physical game.

In the work setting, this learned behavior can be seen in typically back-and-forth flow of conversation between women colleagues. Women can build on the same topic, taking turns adding suggestions and ideas for as long as thirty minutes,[8] eventually developing a communal meaning among themselves. They use nonintrusive responses such as "Hmm" or "Yeah" or "Ah" to indicate they're paying attention and to encourage the speaker to continue. (Women do occasionally break into conversations legitimately with enthusiastic interruption. It's acceptable to get so excited about a topic that one's two cents must be added.)

Researchers have found that women often construct a discussion, whereas men have a dialogue of position statements. As British linguist Jennifer Coates explains, "In public domains where the norm is that one speaker speaks at a time, and where the goal of participants is to grab speakership, then interruption is a strategy for gaining the floor. In private conversations between equals, on the other hand, where the chief goal of interaction is the maintenance of good social relationships, . . . the goal is not to take the floor *from* another speaker, but to participate in conversation *with* other speakers."[9] This latter form is more typical of female-to-female communication.

Men tend to interrupt other male speakers to change the course of a conversation. They might shoot down an idea and supplant it with their own. But if you were to try that at a meeting with another woman, you would be in gross violation of the Power Dead-Even Rule. An effective way of expressing a divergent point of view is to ask for clarification: "Can you tell a little bit more about your idea, so I understand how it would work here?" It might also be helpful to tie your idea into your colleague's. You could say, "I like your suggestion that we do X. But what if after we do X, we try Y?" Both these statements maintain equality while they allow you to express your dissenting idea.

Women are also watchful that their cohorts are not hurt by a discussion or a change in direction at a meeting. "Is it okay with you if we change the subject for a minute?"a female executive might ask. She may even diminish her own contributions with expressions such as "What was I saying?" or "That was a stupid idea." The comeback might be, "Oh no, no. That was helpful to me in thinking this through." One woman has put herself down—her self-esteem is slightly dented—and the other woman has brought her back up.

Body Language Speaks Volumes

In addition to verbal communication, another way women support their relationships with other women is through a variety of nonverbal cues, such as nods, smiles, body posture, head tilts, and facial expressions. Women will frequently nod their heads during conversations as an indication that they agree, as an encouragement to continue, or simply as an affirmation that they're attending to what the other person is saying. Men, in contrast, usually nod only when they agree with what's being said. Women also smile much more frequently than men do.[10] They have a stronger tendency to communicate relationship with facial expressions that can mimic the feelings others express.

Whereas men tend to stand shoulder to shoulder in conversation and look generally in the same direction as the person who is speaking, women tend to stand face-to-face when interacting. They seem to listen with their whole bodies: they lean forward toward a speaker and increase this movement as they become involved in the conversation. This leaning stance communicates, "Your words are important to me." The "head tilt" is another signal that "I'm attending to you, I care about what you're saying, and you matter to me." Women often tilt their heads to one side during a conversation, a posture that communicates vulnerability (the carotid artery is exposed) and can enhance relationships among women as an indication of power subordinance.

PERSONALITY DIFFERENCES

Understanding the subtlety of verbal and nonverbal cues can help you adapt your communication strategies to fit the needs of your colleagues, both female and male, as Jessica was able to do with her memos to Bob and Laura on pages 135–136. In addition to these more superficial conversational cues, however, interpersonal communication can be affected by underlying personality styles. Men and women tend to have unique approaches toward solving problems, seeking information, making decisions, and communicating everything from ideas to complaints. Understanding the differing mindsets of your colleagues can be a crucial tool to help you balance power. It's particularly necessary to understand differing underlying personality styles of women—because the balance can be so delicate, complex, and easily toppled by miscommunication.

THINKERS VERSUS FEELERS

Among human beings, there is a substantial personality dichotomy between people who prefer to make decisions based on thinking and logic, and people who prefer to make them based on feelings and emotions. The labels "Thinker" and "Feeler" are derived from the work of Katherine Briggs and Isabel Myers, a mother-daughter psychologist team who developed a widely used personality typology based on the theories of Carl Jung. According to analysis of behavioral preferences based on the Myers-Briggs Type Instrument, 65 to 70 percent of women in North America have *feeling* preferences, whereas 60 percent of men have *thinking* preferences.

When making decisions with a thinking preference, one is more likely to:

- Use logical analysis
- Rely on objective and impersonal criteria
- Draw cause-and-effect relationships
- Be firm minded
- Prize logical order
- Be skeptical

"Thinkers" may not readily show their feelings and may be surprised when someone brings an emotional angle into the decision-making process. They tend to make decisions logically, and to a feeler may appear to pay insufficient attention to others' concerns. But they have a strong need to be treated fairly.

Those who prefer making decisions with a feeling preference are more likely to:

- Apply personal priorities

- Weigh human values and motives, their own and others'

- Value warmth in relationships and enjoy pleasing people

- Prize harmony

- Trust others easily

"Feelers" tend to be aware of their own and other people's emotions. Because they need harmony, their efficiency can be disturbed by office feuds. They often allow their decisions to be influenced by their own or others' personal likes and wishes. They hate giving people bad news and tend to be sympathetic.[11]

ARE YOU A THINKER OR A FEELER?

Think back to a difficult decision you've had to make. Now imagine you were explaining to a friend or colleague the process you went through to make your decision. Would you walk your listener through the solution logically— i.e., "When we were deciding to buy this house, first I checked out all the comparable properties for sale in the neighborhood, then we looked at our savings, and finally we visited the school to see if it had the academic standards we were looking for"? If so, you are probably a thinker. If, on the other hand, you would be more likely to tell your listener about how you took into account the impact of your decision on other people—"When we were deciding to buy this house, I thought the kids would really love the big yard. I noticed it's halfway between my mother's house and my sister's, and when we visited the school we found that we really liked the teachers"—then you are probably a feeler. The following exercise can help you determine your preferences.

ARE YOU A THINKER OR A FEELER?

Choose the response that most closely fits your usual style:

1. You are restructuring your department. As you consider the changes you wonder:

    Thinking: If this structure will streamline the workflow.

    Feeling: If Norma will be upset about the changes in her job.

2. Your boss calls you in to give you some positive feedback. Which would you prefer to hear?

    Thinking: That you're logical and intellectual.

    Feeling: That you're loyal and caring.

3. For the third time this month, Brianna has come in late. You told her that the next time she was late, you would write her up. This is her third strike. Which is your response?

    Thinking: She knew the consequences so you write her up.

    Feeling: You know she's having marital problems and her eyes are red, so you pass on it.

4. Unfortunately, you must lay off two employees, and you feel very bad.

    Thinking: You choose to lay off Marjorie and Scott because their core skills are becoming less important to the business.

    Feeling: You choose to lay off Brenda and Tony. You can't lay off Marjorie because she's pregnant, and you can't lay off Scott because he has three kids in college.

(continues)

5. You must decide which printer to hire.

   Thinking: You choose ABC Co. because they are the cheapest.

   Feeling: You choose XYZ Co. because the employees there are so friendly.

6. You are working on a project with several colleagues. Which are you most likely to say?

   Thinking: "I like the way we're making decisions in a thought-out, consistent way, weighing the impact of each suggestion."

   Feeling: "I'm glad that we are getting along so well. Everyone's opinion gets heard and no one is too bossy."

7. While reading some of the human-resource policies for your company, you are more likely to find yourself:

   Thinking: Grateful that there are rules that guide the company to treat everyone fairly and consistently.

   Feeling: Saying that policies are fine as long as you don't take them too literally. There are always exceptions, and we need to treat everyone in a compassionate way since each employee is special.

Because more women are typically feelers while more men are thinkers, we may readily adjust to gender differences in communication, as we expect men and women to behave differently. But problems can quickly arise when thinking and feeling women interact with each other. To a feeling woman, a thinking woman might appear cold and insensitive. She may seem deviant to the feeler, who might denounce the thinker as a "bitch." Conversely, to a woman who prefers the thinking mode, a feeling type can seem overly emotional and illogical.

In the following letter, "thinking" Sarah rails against her "feeling" boss:

Here's a classic example of how Julie deals with things: I had left for a meeting, which she knew about and had approved. When it was time to leave for the seminar, I did not tell her I was leaving because (1) she was in a meeting herself; (2) I had told her about it previously; and (3) she had personally approved my going. In addition, my co-worker, also attending the meeting with me, told me she had told Julie that we would be out of the office. I thought I covered all my bases. When I returned to the office the next day, I found that Julie had left me a voice mail telling me (and I quote EXACTLY), "I know you're in this off-site meeting, but I'm hurt that you didn't tell me you were going." Can you imagine one of my *male* bosses calling me up and telling me he was "hurt" because I didn't stop in personally to tell him I was going to a meeting he had previously sanctioned?

If you're a thinking woman, you may find that you have an easier time working with men, who are predominantly thinkers, than with other women, who are predominantly feelers. The alignment of personality types will take precedence over the alignment of gender. So how do you preserve your relationships with women if you're a thinker working with feelers, or vice versa?

If your colleague's style is the opposite of yours, flex toward her preferences so that she will better hear and understand you. If you have a feeling preference and you're dealing with a thinker, then make a concerted effort to organize your ideas and present them in a logical manner. You might, for instance, list the costs and benefits of a new program you're proposing rather than saying, "Everyone will love it!" If, on the other hand, you have a thinking preference and you're dealing with a feeler, you might include an emotional and personal component in your logical discussion. After you've presented your ideas, you might add, "By the way, Joan and Lilly are all for this idea." Or, "This will boost the morale of the department."

Direct versus Indirect

Another personality clash occurs between people who have a direct style of interaction (they are specific and on point) and people who are more indirect (they tend to be circumspect). Again, women tend to be indirect, while men tend to be direct. But as with thinking types versus feeling types, problems can quickly arise when women with differing styles interact. That's exactly what happened to Barbara, a department director at a large urban hospital. As the chairperson of several committees, Barbara spent a great deal of time in meetings. She prided herself on how well she got along with her male colleagues as well as her ability to balance her workload, leadership responsibilities, and home life.

But one day, Barbara opened a resignation letter from Sandra, the hospital's sales director, who served on her Quality Improvement Committee. "Despite several requests to change the time of the meetings, you refused to accommodate my needs," the letter read. "Therefore I can no longer endure the hardship serving on the committee has caused."

Barbara was perplexed and angry. What was Sandra talking about? As she reflected on recent meetings, she recalled a few occasions when Sandra had muttered, "These seven A.M. meetings always make me drink two extra cups of coffee. I have to get up thirty minutes early. How about you?" Barbara had always smiled and agreed that she too downed extra caffeine on these mornings. Could that be what Sandra was referring to as her "several requests to change the time of the meetings"?

Barbara is a direct person, whereas Sandra prefers an indirect approach. Unfortunately, conflict between the two is highly likely. Direct people mean what they say, say what they mean, lay it on the line, and tell it like it is. Indirect people find the direct approach "too abrasive and abrupt," so they bring up problems by hinting, making suggestions, or asking questions about them. Direct people often find this indirect approach manipulative and dishonest.

ARE YOU DIRECT OR INDIRECT?

What follows are typical direct and indirect responses to uncomfortable situations. Which response would feel more natural to you?

1. It's very hot in the meeting room.

   Indirect: "I wonder what the temperature is in here."

   Direct: "Where's the thermostat? Does anybody mind if I turn on the air conditioning?"

2. You're on a business trip and unexpectedly have to spend a lot of cash on a taxi ride. Much to your surprise, the driver doesn't take credit cards. Once at your destination, you say to a colleague:

    Indirect: "You wouldn't believe how much I had to pay for my cab."

    Direct: "May I borrow fifty dollars?"

3. You're chairing a committee and feel that you're doing the lion's share of the work. To a fellow committee member you say:

    Indirect: "I've had to work on this at home every night this week."

    Direct: "Could you take this part of the project and work on it? I need it by Friday."

4. You're irritated that your co-worker leaves her food to molder in the refrigerator for weeks. You ask:

    Indirect: "Don't you just hate it when people expect their mothers to come in to clean up the kitchen?"

    Direct: "Would you mind throwing away the food you're not going to eat by the end of the week?"

5. A female co-worker interrupts you in mid-sentence during a meeting. Later you meet her in the hallway. You say:

    Indirect: "I don't think everyone got to make her point at the meeting."

    Direct: "You might not even realize that this happened, but when I was trying to make my point at the meeting, you sort of cut me off."

Sometimes the choice of direct or indirect style is modulated by the power of the individual with whom we are talking. A person is much less likely to be direct with someone who has more power and more likely to be direct with a peer (and even more likely with an employee). For instance, if you have to deliver a difficult message to your boss about her faulty idea, you're far less apt to say, "That seems unworkable," than "That's interesting, but I'm wondering how it would work here." Both men and women tend to become indirect at different times: according to Deborah Tannen, women are more evasive when they must tell people what to do (this would be a violation of the Power Dead-Even Rule); men equivocate when they talk about problems, weaknesses, errors, and emotions—issues that can weaken their position in the hierarchy.

Let's get back to Barbara, with her direct style, and her communication problems with more indirect women. Later that day she approached Sherry, a member of management, about a report she'd written requesting a new laser instrument for the hospital. "Did I give you everything you need in that report?" Barbara asked.

Sherry's vague reply—"I wonder if the projected budget numbers should be included"—left Barbara confused and frustrated once more: Are the budget numbers key to the report or not? How will I know if another part of the report is deficient? A more direct person would have responded: "The report is complete except for the budget numbers. It would be helpful to add the projected volume of laser procedures and revenue for the first two years with the new laser. That information will help justify our return on investment. I'd appreciate it if you could get all that to me by five o'clock tomorrow so I'll have it for the management meeting. Do you think you can make the deadline?"

It's dangerous, however, to give such a direct statement to an indirect woman—to whom a pointed command might constitute a violation of the Power Dead-Even Rule. In that case, you might soften your message with a few verbal hedges: *"I was just thinking that the report seems complete except for the budget numbers. Maybe if you add the projected volume of laser procedures and revenue for the first two years, it would help justify our return on investment. What do you think? Anyway, if at all possible, do you think you can get this to me by five o'clock tomorrow? Okay?"*

Both direct and indirect people are doing the best they can within their systems of communication. But their divergent styles can lead to misunderstandings and serious personal conflicts if these differing styles remain invisible to them. Because of the Power Dead-Even Rule, it can be especially useful for women—even direct women—to consciously adopt indirect techniques when it comes to telling other women what to do.

To sidestep potential difficulties, it's helpful to notice whether a person you are dealing with uses direct or indirect communication and, as in the case of thinking versus feeling, flex to her style. If you're direct like Barbara and you're working with someone who is indirect, you'll need to state your needs, problems, and issues in a more indirect manner: *"If you have a few seconds, I'd appreciate any tips you might give me for that laser request."* You'll also need to be on the alert for problems lobbed at you in an indirect way: "Gosh these meetings are awfully early" may very well mean "I don't like it, and at the very least you need to take some note of my displeasure."

If, however, you're an indirect person and you must involve a direct colleague in getting something done, you may need to beef up what you say. Try: *"These early meetings are wreaking havoc with my life. Is it possible to discuss alternatives?"* And when your direct co-worker says, "I've got a problem with the page layout," you must also bear in mind that her intent is not to be unkind but to discuss an issue that is a problem for her.

When two indirect people get embroiled in a conflict, they can read each other's indirect signals even though more direct people might be oblivious to what's going on between them. Imagine, for instance, that you were supposed to have a meeting with Joanne in the morning. You were there at the appointed time, but she never showed up. You run into her in the hallway later and say, "Oh, you're here today."

Although you haven't attacked her for standing you up, Joanne knows she has been caught. She replies, "It's been such a busy day. I didn't anticipate having to put all this extra time in on the Jones project." She indirectly signals that she didn't make the meeting because of a pressing deadline.

"I'm swamped, too," you respond, "especially since I fell an hour behind this morning." Of course, that's your dig that Joanne wasted your time.

You walk off in a huff, ripe for a catfight, especially since Joanne violated the Power Dead-Even Rule by flaking out on you and not calling to let you know in advance that she couldn't make it. That's a power move—her rudeness communicates to you that she believes her concerns are more important than yours. You would like her to apologize for missing the meeting or at the very least provide you with a chip to get the relationship back on track.

To avoid the coming conflict, you might adopt a more direct approach and ask for what you need. You might say, for instance, *"We need to reschedule this meeting for next week. I want to make sure that we set it up for a time when you can make it. If you find yourself getting behind, would you do me a fa-vor and give me a heads-up?"*

"WHY?" VERSUS "HELP ME UNDERSTAND"

A key point of conflict between direct and indirect people is the gathering of information. Direct people will tend to solicit information directly—and what could be more direct than asking "why"? As Barbara's leadership role at the hospital continued to grow, so did her curiosity about why the orga-nization ran the way it did. Being an inquisitive person, she asked lots of questions about procedures, policies, and meetings. "Why does this hap-pen?" "Why are you doing it that way?" While some of her colleagues hap-pily entertained her questions and appreciated her natural sense of curiosity, Barbara noticed that her ubiquitous "Why?" caused others to stiffen, stammer, and act insulted and even defensive.

"Why?" helps direct people like Barbara better understand the world. As a girl she would wonder, "Why is the sky blue?" "Why do birds fly?" Now she's asking, "Why is the board meeting held on Tuesdays?" "Why aren't these reports distributed?" She is just trying to understand how the world operates. But indirect people use the word *why* to signal a problem. When addressed to them, this simple question can offend indirect people because they hear it as impugning their intentions and questioning the validity of their work or their actions.

If you, a direct person, ask a colleague, "Why did you go to that meet-ing?" you may be curious about what spurred her to attend, but if she is in-direct, she may hear the question as your suggestion that she should not have gone. That's because an indirect person would have used the very same question to obliquely signal that you should have stayed home. "Why?" can cause her to come up with excuses and justifications for what she did, and that can put her on the defensive. Suddenly, she is in a one-down position, and the power is no longer dead even between you. The direct per-son wouldn't hear implied criticism. She would simply reply with an ex-planation.

When Barbara asked "Why?" to better understand how the hospital functions, her indirect colleagues saw her as criticizing them, pointing out mistakes, and saying that something is wrong with the way they do their jobs. Conflict and misunderstandings are bound to grow out of such mis-construed interactions.

We have found that an easy way to prevent misinterpretations of "Why?" is for the direct person to substitute with "Help me understand," as in "Can you help me understand the decision to hold board meetings on Tuesdays?" This expression decreases the indirect person's defensiveness while it opens the door for the direct person to get at the information she wants. Rather than being accusatory, the direct person is asking for help without upsetting the power balance between colleagues.

Managing Your Chips

Until this point, many of the relationship-building strategies we have suggested relate to your keeping the power dead even with female colleagues. On some level, this could be understood as careful power chip management. You're more likely to gain chips with a female colleague if you flex your style to communicate with her in a manner that works for her rather than one that works for you.

In chapter 1 we introduced this Chip Theory, which is based on a sense of equity: each of us is endowed with a certain number of power chips—positive attributes or actions—that we constantly exchange with others. Chips work well among women because mutuality is an essential of female friendship: I listen to you and you listen to me; I give to you and you give to me. It's this sense of reciprocity, the positive exchange of chips, that keeps the power dead even among us—Dolores befriends Mona and takes her to lunch, and Mona reciprocates by signing the long-shelved contract.

The chips women exchange need not be material. In interviews with 204 girls and women between the ages of eight and ninety for her book, *Connecting: The Enduring Power of Female Friendship*, journalist Sandy Sheehy found that "reciprocity of time and attention mattered far more to the women . . . than reciprocity of the material sort."[12] Women tend to be moved by relational chips such as compliments on their business acumen or attire. They want other women to ask them whether the people in their lives are well and happy. This sort of attention helps them feel cared about and flattered by the knowledge that another busy woman remembers the particulars of their lives. A particularly chip-savvy woman might even note in her address files the names of a female colleague's family members or assistant, recent personal events like a marriage or death, or a business success so she can quickly call up these all-important details while in conversation.

Women more than men tend to solicit and proffer positive feedback, and they want to know the specifics—not just that you liked the presentation but which aspects of it were effective and why: "You really caught the board's attention from the outset when you listed those stunning numbers . . ." Women want to know what they did well so they can do it again. This helps them build self-confidence, and it enhances their self-esteem.

Chips can be little gifts like a note card thanking a woman for a great interview or the help she gave you in a crisis or something thoughtful she said about you to a higher-up. Susan recently received a brief e-mail that could be construed as a chip from a woman she'd just met at a conference: *"Enjoyed meeting you. Always a plus when you sit by someone who is enjoyable to talk with. Call or e-mail, and we'll get together."* Simple communications like these lubricate relationships. Words of encouragement also count. So do raises and promotions—in a big way—as well as opportunities to give a person visibility with the powers that be.

Sharing something personal about yourself with another woman can also be a chip. Talking about painful events is even more significant than giving good news. To reveal that you're getting a divorce can be a chip because you're revealing intimacies; it's a sign of trust to bare one's soul. In essence, you're saying, "I'm telling you this because I believe you'll treat me in a way that's in my best interest." Allowing yourself to be vulnerable is a great compliment to your confidante.

There are four keys to managing and administering your chips:

Key #1: Remember that everyone is an accountant. Your co-worker may be a nurse, an engineer, or a secretary, but she is also an expert scorekeeper. Know that your female colleagues are constantly keeping track of how many chips you owe them and/or how many they owe you. Although people don't usually keep conscious track of favors given and received, we do have an internal sense of the balance of relationships. And we frequently hold our female colleagues to a higher standard than the men: at a recent seminar in Michigan, when we asked a group of female nurses why they criticized the female doctors in their medical group for leaving behind empty coffee cups, the nurses said, "Because they should know better!"

Key #2: Adhere to the rules of supply and demand. Different people prize different kinds of chips, and it's important to understand and honor the distinctions. In the early years of her career, Pat went from working in a female-dominated university department to an environment populated by statisticians. She soon learned that if she threw a lot of interaction at these co-workers, rather than increase her chip account, it would *cost* her chips. The statisticians resented as intrusive the chitchat that had made the women in her previous job so happy.

To learn who values which kind of chips, carefully observe and talk to co-workers. Watch interaction styles. If you try to engage a colleague with chatty interactions but she responds more brusquely, you'll gain more chips by keeping your comments brief and by withholding what she might consider fluff than by going on and on.

You also gain chips by appealing to your co-workers' interests. Inquire with sincerity about their weekend activities. If they respond enthusiastically with tales about their tennis game or garden, this gives you clues about their interests and values. If a co-worker has lots of cat pictures in her cubicle, you can bet that cats are worth a lot of chips to her. When you ask how her feline friends are doing, you're bound to earn some chips with her.

Key #3: Create a chip surplus. The best boss you ever had probably had a chip surplus with you—meaning that over time, he or she had created many situations to enhance goodwill by giving you opportunities to be creative, to be in the limelight, or to earn bonuses. Your boss could also amass a chip surplus by giving you positive feedback that felt good because of its sincerity or visibility in front of others. With this surplus in place, chances are the minute your boss needed something done, you did it—fast—whether or not you had any enthusiasm for it or the time.

It's important that you actively do favors for those who are important in your life, based on what they individually value. And we don't mean only people who are powerful in the traditional sense (the boss or higher-ups). Try to develop a chip surplus with administrative assistants and support staff, too. Assistants can make your life easy or difficult, depending on how you interact with them. And well-treated facilities people may be willing to tend to your needs first when the air conditioning is on the fritz.

If a woman colleague didn't get an expected promotion, you might say, "Sorry you missed out this time; you really deserved it." Such a statement gives you power because you have helped this woman raise her self-esteem and you have accorded her some recognition. If she respects the Power Dead-Even Rule, when called upon in the future, she may very well do what she can to help you.

In your efforts to create a chip surplus, you should, however, only give chips that are genuine. Never lavish false praise; your true feelings are bound to leak out verbally or nonverbally, and people hate feeling manipulated. Proper chip management is neither calculating nor insincere.

Key #4: Avoid a chip deficit. Even the blandest individual can become a creative genius when it comes time to even the chip score. She can withhold information, "forget" to tell you that the big cheese called, lose documents you need, ignore your crises, or do literally *exactly* what you asked—the very complaints we've heard from hundreds of women about their subordinates. (We heard a great story about this last tactic concerning a ship captain who was in heavy chip deficit with his crew. Unhappy with an unsightly mess on the deck created by ship mechanics repairing a broken propeller, the captain yelled, "Get rid of it." He meant that they should take the damaged propeller below, but they did *exactly* what he asked. They heaved the propeller overboard.)

As we've seen, there aren't just gender differences in the workplace; there are also interpersonal differences within the genders. You may actually have to be conscious of your behavior—not just acting one way with a man and another way with a woman, but one way with a thinking or a direct woman and another way with a feeling and an indirect woman. This Catch-22 is emblematic of the tricky double binds women can find themselves coping with as they make their way through an organization.

Though you may use all the strategies we've suggested in this chapter—womenspeak, body language, awareness of personality differences, chip management—you still can run the risk of becoming embroiled in a catfight.

That's because there is an additional layer of complexity that bedevils women's relationships with one another: the many double binds that arise from inadvertent or deliberate violations of the Power Dead-Even Rule as we attempt to move forward in our careers. We will be looking at those more carefully, and especially the commotion over promotion, in the following chapter.

SEVEN

LOOSENING POWER
DEAD-EVEN DOUBLE BINDS

DONNA WAS STUNNED. She thought this was going to be her proudest professional moment as well as a major milestone for the women in her organization. Instead, it turned into a nightmare for her. How did she go from being on top of the world to feeling so miserable? What caused this change?

Strangely enough, she got promoted.

Shortly after she became the first woman to reach the highest executive level in her company, the rumors began to fly! Some said she didn't really deserve the promotion. Others said someone else was more qualified. Donna soon was labeled a snob—too good for her old buddies. And the most mortifying comment was that she had "slept her way to the top." She knew she had landed the vice presidency through gallons of blood, sweat, and tears, and it seemed to her that this should have been obvious to everyone. It wasn't. Instead of jubilation, Donna nose-dived into anger and depression. And the most searing aspect of the vicious attacks was that most of them came from other women, her co-workers whom she had considered to be her friends.

How could this have happened?

Easy. Donna violated the Power Dead-Even Rule—big-time. When a woman is singled out for a promotion, the reaction among her female co-workers is rarely neutral. As we have seen, the kind of public endorsement inherent in a career advance has the potential to evoke feelings of betrayal, jealousy, resentment, anger, and revenge among the women left behind. In an effort to make themselves feel better and keep their self-esteem intact, those not selected may brag, gossip, sabotage, use slander, or form a clique to isolate and target the promoted woman—all forms of indirect aggression aimed at tearing her down.

Promotions are among the most glaring examples of what we call *double binds*—inadvertent violations of the Power Dead-Even Rule in which you're damned if you do and damned if you don't. Actually, we've discerned two major categories of double binds. The first arise from women competing with one another. You might encounter these as you advance in your career since they involve how you handle promotions or other positive achievements. Double binds such as these can result when you receive an award or other public accolades, when a key project goes to you at the expense of another woman, or when you garner an all-important promotion. Ostensibly innocent behaviors on your part like tooting your own horn, taking credit for your successes, and accepting praise can all put you in catfight territory even though they stem from seemingly positive situations.

The second category of double binds arises, ironically, from the female impulse toward friendships and interrelatedness. Women are self-driven to have intimate relationships, but these can be fraught with problems in the workplace. This second type of double bind can include situations you face if you have close friends at work with whom you have shared many secrets, instances in which you are required to "play the game" and must maintain confidentiality, the tendency to be sucked into a pal's conflict with another woman, or the ire you can evoke among female co-workers if you relate well to men.

In this chapter we explore what these predicaments entail, when they occur, and what you can do about them in order to short-circuit the trouble they might provoke. First, let's look at the double binds that arise from female competitiveness. We will list the dilemmas, offer useful tips on how to sidestep them, and then delve a bit deeper into how to avoid backbiting and gossip if you're about to promote a woman and if you've been hired into a company from the outside.

The Commotion over Promotions

Here's what Peggy, one of our correspondents, wrote to us about her "big" week:

> I'm a corporate paralegal working in an international firm. I recently had a problem with a co-worker whom I considered my friend. Maryann came to our department as a secretary after her boss was fired. I stuck my neck out for her and convinced my boss to hire her because I heard she was good at what she did. We worked together for more than two years and got along great. But then I was promoted from an hourly position to a salaried one. This came totally out of the blue, as I never requested it, nor did I have prior knowledge of it.
>
> Right after I got the exciting news on Friday, I shared it with Maryann. I thought she'd be happy for me. She seemed to be—she even joked that from now on I could pick up our lunches and run errands so she wouldn't lose any money coming back late from lunch. But the following Monday morning, she came into work and told me never to speak to her again. She also went around the office telling others I looked down on her. When I went to the supply room, she followed me back into my office tossing files on my desk. She told me that was her area, and I should stay out, even though the copier is there. I decided to defuse the situation and sit down to talk with her. I began by saying, "If I did anything to hurt you, I'm deeply sorry. In no way was it intentional." She then informed me in a very loud voice that she would not speak to me without a witness present, as I was being "mean." Both of our bosses must have heard this, but stayed in their offices with their heads down and never said a word.
>
> Maryann has since transferred to another department, but she still bad-mouths me.

Like so many women with whom we've interacted, Peggy was dinged by an inadvertent violation of the Power Dead-Even Rule. Her upward mobility exerted decidedly downward pressure on her friendship with Maryann. But her troubles may not have ended there. Unfortunately, many newly promoted women must not only fend off attacks like these from those below them, but soon they may sense that support from above is eroding too. All this, while taking on a new job with greater responsibilities. When a first woman is promoted to a senior executive position in an organization, often the man who selected her will hear the negative comments about her. One CEO told us his new female executive had, according to his other female employees, suddenly become "drunk with power," and he assumed that either he had chosen the wrong person or she had truly metamorphosed into a demon.

Using the Power Dead-Even Rule as a touchstone, you can see how your sudden rise upsets the balance that had previously existed between you and your female co-workers. Whether subtly or dramatically, your power increases with a promotion, and that's enough to tip the scales. Transition is the culprit here. In the eyes of your former peers, you ostensibly move from a lower degree of power and self-esteem to a higher echelon. That change, although seemingly positive for you, is what triggers hostility and aggressive behavior in the other women—the very people with whom you need to interact to feel good about yourself—thereby placing you in a double bind.

However, the story does not end there. If you put the shoe on the other foot, you can easily imagine how you might feel after you'd been passed over for a promotion in favor of a friend and co-worker. Recently newspaper psychologist Joyce Brothers received the following letter from such an aggrieved reader:

> Dear Dr. Brothers: My best friend got a job that I wanted badly and I just can't cope with it. I didn't even know that she had applied. Still, I feel betrayed. We used to see each other at least once a week. Now, I can't do that anymore, and I can't tell her why. I hate her. What can I say, and what can I do not to feel as I do?—W.A.[1]

Who hasn't felt the pain of being rejected? Certainly we have. Within two months of Pat's being hired at the large company, two other women joined the organization at the same level. All three of them held the same sort of position, although they lived and worked in different states. After about two years on the job, the other women were promoted to assistant vice president, but Pat was not. If these two colleagues hadn't existed and Pat had missed the promotion, it wouldn't have bothered her, but this seemed to be a loud announcement that they were "good" and she wasn't. Pat felt angry, hurt, and disappointed, but being catfight savvy, she never acted on these emotions. Even though it was extraordinarily painful, she called her former peers the next day and congratulated them.

Still, under these circumstances the impulse to engage in hurtful behavior is strong and can leave you frustrated and dissatisfied if ignored.

TOOTING YOUR OWN HORN

As women we're often "sisters in sorrow"—we listen to one another's troubles talk and provide support when times are hard. We may even prefer to hear one another's problems because it gives us the opportunity to be comforting, nurturing, and intimate. In fact, when we share bad news, we expect that our female friends won't abandon us. But what happens when something good happens? Unfortunately, if we flaunt the good news as openly and forthrightly as men do, we can run afoul of the Power Dead-Even Rule.

To avoid violations, sometimes we diminish our own good fortune. One of our friends, a freelance business journalist, recently landed a job with a major metropolitan newspaper. Not only did she "forget" to call us when an important piece of her work covered the whole front page of the business section—articles, sidebars, and all—but when we phoned to congratulate her, she said with great modesty, "Oh that! It was no big deal."

Sometimes our failure to toot our own horns can be detrimental to female advancement in general. Susan was speaking to a group of executive women one day about the Power Dead-Even Rule when suddenly one of the participants said, "Now I understand why I did what I did last week." It turns out that Paula, the president of one of the largest shoe companies in the country, was vacationing with her family at a dude ranch. Paula likes to work with the horses. One morning she was mucking out the stables with Nicole, a young woman who was also vacationing there, when Nicole asked, "What do you do for a living?"

"Oh, I'm in apparel," Paula answered casually.

"Are you a salesperson?"

"Well, no," Paula replied, "I don't sell."

"Do you design?" Nicole continued, apparently intrigued by Paula's evasiveness.

"No, I don't design," Paula responded and let the matter drop.

"You know," she told Susan, "I couldn't figure out why I was so reluctant to reveal to Nicole that I was the president of a shoe company. Now that I think of it, maybe one of the best things I could have done was to serve as a role model and tell her what I do for a living. I could have talked with her about what it's like to have that kind of a job so she'd have a role model of a woman in a position like that." It was a loss for both women.

On the other hand, if we're not careful about how we exult in a bit of good fortune, other women—even good friends—may take offense. Marla, a successful stockbroker, called her oldest and dearest friend, Penny, to share her good news about a huge year-end bonus. "I can't believe it," Marla blurted. "I'm going to take my vacation in Tahiti this year!" Penny, a social worker, seemed excited on the phone. But shortly thereafter, the two former grade-school chums had a major falling-out. Penny was upset that Marla didn't return her phone calls in what she considered a timely manner. Suddenly she felt unimportant in Marla's life, even though Marla, wealthy or not, still felt very attached to her childhood friend and had no intention of dropping her. The bad feelings were resolved only after much late-night soul-searching and many tearful phone calls.

TAKING CREDIT FOR ACHIEVEMENTS

Recently, Pat was shopping at one of those cavernous office supply warehouses that have sprung up around the country. While she was checking out, she noticed the usual array of personnel photos on the store's front wall. Pictures of the service, merchandise, furniture, copy center, and office supply managers—all men—were posted. But there was a blank space where the service manager's picture should have hung above the name Alyssa Meyers. Curious about the obvious disparity, Pat asked the woman ringing up her sale, "What happened to Alyssa Meyers's picture? It's not up there with the rest of them."

The salesclerk replied, "Oh, Alyssa didn't want it there." Pat could only imagine the trouble Alyssa might have encountered if she so demonstrably displayed her power. And yet by downplaying our power, women can and do become invisible. This double bind also plays out in how we impart our accomplishments.

For instance, the one-upmanship inherent in talking well of yourself can work against you when interviewing for a job or promotion—the only situation where you may feel justified and comfortable extolling your many accomplishments and talents. Unfortunately, when women come across as being confident in a job interview, even if they're extremely competent, they run the risk of violating the Power Dead-Even Rule with the interviewer. It's another double bind! The very information you need to convey to land a job may, in the end, prevent you from getting it!

This has been substantiated by research. In one study that relied on simulated job interviews, when a woman spoke well of herself and had the ability to enhance a male interviewer's position, he was more likely to "hire" her. But if she couldn't help him advance no matter how competent she was, he was more likely to hire a woman who appeared modest. The situation was even more punishing when the interviewers were female. If an interviewee spoke well of herself to a female interviewer, whether or not it could enhance the interviewer's position, she was less likely to be "hired." Psychologist Laurie A. Rudman of Rutgers University concluded from these findings that "women were more punitive toward the self-promoting women than were the men." And self-effacing women won points with both genders.[2]

Women pay a price for violating the Power Dead-Even Rule even if it's an unwitting trespass. But what do you do if you must interview with a woman? Do you humble yourself before her? Do you offend her with your many accomplishments? How do you get that job without explaining how good you are at what you do?

ACCEPTING PRAISE

Imagine, too, the trouble you can get into when you are on the receiving end of kudos. The CEO at a senior staff meeting applauded a project that Rebecca had chaired for several years. She was flattered that he'd mentioned her favorite assignment at all and elated that he'd complimented her so broadly in such a public setting.

We imagine the men were sitting around the conference table thinking about what they would have to do to get the CEO to praise them that way. They probably cared very little about Rebecca or her achievements, but they would want to get the same attention. She needn't worry about them all that much. But this big moment for Rebecca could, unfortunately, bring her much grief from other women in the room. At least some of them must have bristled at the praise bestowed on her.

When we asked Rebecca how her female colleagues responded, she said, "Funny you should mention it. I had just gotten a haircut and Lola, one of my employees who is having a performance problem, said to me, 'Your hair is very nice. I hope *you* like it.' I heard that as a backhanded slap. While the CEO was talking about me, Lola sat across from me with a stony expression on her face, like all the life had drained out of her."

Uh-oh.

How to Unravel
Promotion/Achievement-Related Double Binds

In truth, new bosses of both genders are frequently tested. Male bosses may be assessed for competence and whether they will hold employees accountable, especially for parts of their jobs they dislike. New female bosses must deal with two dimensions: They focus on the job, as the men do, but they also have to pay attention to their relationships with other women.

If you are aware that your successes are about to or have already ruffled the feathers of the women around you, it will be your responsibility to help set them at ease. For instance, if you know a promotion or other honor is coming your way, most likely you're planning for the exciting responsibilities that lie before you as well as how you will deal with your new reality. That can be fine for men, but because you're a woman, you can't just accept your achievements and blithely leave everyone else behind—because they might be *right behind you*, ready to plunge daggers into your back. You'd better have a plan. It may not be fair; men don't have to bother with this when they are successful. But that's the price we have to pay for the strong alliances we make with other women.

It is possible to head off destructive situations by preparing for them. Let's look at some of the preemptive and protective actions you can take to safeguard yourself if you expect hostility from your female co-workers because of double binds induced by inadvertent success-oriented violations of the Power Dead-Even Rule.

1. ASSESS THE SITUATION

It's important to be hyperconscious of your behavior. Are you acting in ways that could be construed as violations of the Power Dead-Even Rule? One of the senior executive women whom Carol Gallagher interviewed for *Going to the Top* described a phenomenon that really bothered her: what she called the "Bride of Dracula" syndrome. "Women whose talents I've been hoping would be recognized finally do get promoted and turn into witches overnight—power-mad with smoke coming out of their ears. I just want to smack them and say, 'What happened to those talented team players that I so wanted to get promoted?'"[3]

It's one thing for others to spitefully complain that you're a "power-mad witch" when it's just not true. But it's an entirely different proposition if you're throwing your weight around and parading your good fortune. Examine your behavior and attitude. Is there any truth to these accusations?

Now refer back to your scores in the power and self-esteem profiles in chapter 1 while you visualize the inner and outer circles of the Power Dead-Even model. Has your own power or self-esteem been augmented as a result of the change in your status? What about those who might feel their power and self-esteem have been eroded because of your success? How out of balance are you with these other women? Of course, you don't want to reduce your power or self-esteem to put the relationships back on track (and you certainly don't want to retreat from your new position), but there are some steps you can take to ease the transition.

2. FLATTEN THE INTERACTIONS

Being savvy about female interpersonal dynamics can work to your advantage. You want credit for your accomplishments but hate the Power Dead-Even grief that can accompany them. Sometimes for the sake of your own peace of mind, it's quite useful to play down your power when you're with other women.

It's important to flatten your conversations with your current female colleagues, especially if you're anticipating a promotion or other accolades. If, for instance, a co-worker says to you, "You must be excited about your new appointment," a response such as "I hope it's just the first of many for women who work here" will win you points. "Thanks. I'm looking forward to jumping in with both feet" may go over with the guys, but such a statement can sound too self-serving for a woman who is under close scrutiny for violations of the Power Dead-Even Rule.

Perhaps the best solution to the tooting-your-own-horn dilemma is to rely on female-style body language and the many linguistic devices that comprise womenspeak (see chapter 6). During a job interview, for instance, you might say, "This really wasn't a big deal but . . ." and then go on to describe the very big deal that you accomplished. You could also add, "I didn't do this alone. I was very fortunate to head up a great, highly motivated team."

These kinds of deferential hedges prevent you from coming across as if you're too enthusiastically patting yourself on the back. Before you even talk about your success on a project, you linguistically signal "But I don't think too much of myself because of what I'm going to tell you . . ." Your résumé can speak loudly and clearly about your achievements even though in the interview you can be more circumspect and unpretentious in terms of how you present yourself. (Of course it would be unwise to be so self-effacing with a male interviewer, as that could have the opposite effect.)

3. Manage Your Chips Early in the Game

If you have some time before an honor or promotion will be announced, it's wise to go into heavy chip management, particularly with those women who you expect to attack or undermine you. You'll have to do double duty beefing up those relationships by creating a chip surplus with them as soon as possible. Offer them assistance, include them in activities you think they might like to be informed about, and find skills or achievements about which you can sincerely compliment them.

You may feel more harried than ever, but taking the time to sincerely ask questions about your female colleagues' families and to notice and comment on recent successes like their ability to handle difficult customers will pay off. Often upwardly mobile women complain to us, "I don't have time for all this chitchat anymore." Our response: You can pay now by doing the relationship work, or you can pay later by dealing with the sabotage. It's not a question of if you will pay, but when.

4. Symbolically Minimize Your Position

If you suddenly have more power than the women around you, one of the best ways to avoid a catfight is to put your subordinates at ease by symbolically minimizing your superior position. This can be accomplished in small ways. For instance, whereas you might have asked someone to copy a document or pick up a fax for you in the past, it may now be helpful to get up and do it yourself, for the first few weeks at least, or until reality settles in and everyone is relieved to know that you didn't turn into the "Bride of Dracula."

5. Gently but Firmly Assert Your Authority

A great way to extricate yourself from the new promotion bind is to organize career-planning sessions with your new direct reports. Ask them about their goals and where they want to go in the organization. Begin identifying ways that you can assist them in moving toward those objectives and then quickly implement some of those strategies. For instance, if Megan needs more exposure to senior management and there's an opportunity for her to give a presentation to them, you can tell her, "We've spoken about your getting more exposure. Here's our chance. Why don't we get you ready so you can knock their socks off?" Or if Heather says, "I'm weak in budgeting," find a one-day seminar on the subject. Make sure she goes and that your department pays for it.

You've moved from talking about supporting these women to demonstrating with proactive behaviors that you're willing to follow through. This is a great way to establish rapport and show your employees that you care about them. It also lets them know they're important, which naturally builds self-esteem. That can help to even the power imbalance among you. When you give your employees what they ask for and need related to their professional development, you show them that you respect and believe in them and that you're all on the same side.

Besides, this kind of career planning is one of the best ways for you to assert your authority gently as the new manager without overt displays of power. You're showing interest in your employees' well-being and career progress, but it's still clear that you're the person in charge because you're the one who is doling out the perks. If you can pull this off and manage your relationships well, we guarantee that your female employees will be devoted to and supportive of you and your goals. If your employees feel that you genuinely care about them—because you really do—the benefits will redound tenfold to you.

That having been said, you also need to hold your employees accountable for their responsibilities. We all want to be liked, but productivity and accountability cannot suffer while you are taking over the reins of your new position. Oftentimes you must make a choice between being the "most popular" and being the leader—the person who can articulate clear goals and vision.

6. Stay Professional and Positive in Your Interactions

What can you do if, despite your best efforts, you become the target of indirect aggression from females in the organization? For starters, once the sniping begins, don't let on that it's getting to you. Unfortunately, if you bleed publicly, it will encourage and reinforce further attacks. You must ignore the backbiting and remain professional. This can be hard work, especially if you feel former friends have wounded you. But when you don't allow yourself to be dragged into the emotional tumult, you, as the leader, can focus on your department's business goals and vision and bring everyone else along with you.

When Susan was only twenty-two, she had an opportunity to learn this difficult lesson. Fresh out of college with a bachelor's degree (in those days, most nurses didn't have one), she was hired to supervise an intensive-care unit at a large hospital—her first real job. Most of the nurses in the unit were respectful and professional, except for Lois. She had no B.S. and seemed constantly irritated about Susan's position over her, especially because they were the same age. Not surprisingly, Lois tried to diminish Susan's power at every turn: she gossiped about her to anyone who would listen; she ignored her, making no eye contact or other acknowledgment of her existence; she hid clinical information about patients; she disregarded Susan's role as supervisor and would not communicate anything about doctors or patients to her.

For the sake of the patients in the ICU, it was critical that Susan be kept apprised of this information. Rather than striking back, she decided she would focus her communications with Lois on the patients. She managed her demeanor by holding her head high, taking a deep breath before approaching Lois, and keeping the discussion on a professional level: "Did Dr. White call about changing Mr. Jones's medication?" "Did Mrs. Sampson's temperature come down?" She received curt, one-word responses, but at least she was able to assert her role as leader. And on a daily basis Susan reiterated the department's role in delivering top-quality patient care by saying, "The whole reason we're here is for the patients and their families and to help the doctors get the best information about them so they can better prescribe medical care."

The more Susan focused on the mission of ICU nurses, the more everyone else could get on with the job at hand. In fact, Susan was careful not to complain about Lois to the other nurses in the unit, which was tempting because she felt so isolated and demeaned by her behavior. Even subtle facial expressions during meetings can communicate feelings, so Susan was careful to manage those. In fact, she praised Lois's nursing skills to the other nurses and gave her positive feedback directly.

Intuitively, Susan recognized that it's helpful to give the person who is attacking you truthful, positive feedback. It disarms them. It's difficult to continue condemning someone who tells you what a competent and skilled employee you are. Also, it subtly reinforces that you're the boss—after all, you're the one who is empowered to pass judgment on an employee's performance.

7. CONFRONT THE OFFENDING PARTY

Looking back on the experience today, Susan believes it would have been better for her and the department if she had confronted Lois directly about her insubordination. Citing specific incidents, she might have said, "This has got to stop. I've given you time, I've praised your positive contributions to the department, but we need to talk about the ways I see you undermining my authority and the role that I play here. It's interfering with teamwork and the department's delivery of top-quality care. We have to come up with a plan for how your behavior is going to change." By saying this, Susan might have stopped this destructive behavior sooner. In chapter 9, you will find suggestions on how to successfully deal with difficult people.

8. ENLIST THE HELP OF YOUR SUPERIOR

If, after all this, you still come under attack from female co-workers, you might also consider asking the person who selected you for the job to explain to your co-workers why you were the one chosen for the promotion. Request that your superior speak one-on-one with the employees who applied for the position to clarify why they didn't get it and what they need to do to be considered the next time. You might also enlist the support of your human resources department or an organizational consultant.

IF YOU'VE BEEN PROMOTED FROM WITHIN YOUR ORGANIZATION:

- Anticipate some commotion and realize that it's not about you personally, even though it may feel like it. It's a question of the Power Dead-Even Rule.

- Create a chip surplus before you take the new position.

- Make sure that you flatten your behavior even more immediately after the promotion; i.e., get your own coffee and faxes.

(continues)

- Don't change your relationship behavior. If you asked co-workers about their kids before you were promoted, be sure to keep asking those same questions now that you're managing them.

- Hold one-on-one meetings with your team members to discuss goals, expectations, career aspirations, and team behavior.

- If attacked, don't let your attackers know their barbs are getting to you.

- Remain professional with those who attack you and give them positive feedback for their performance.

- You may need to confront the offending party directly about her behavior.

- If the attack becomes intolerable, consider soliciting help from your supervisor, human resources department, or an organizational consultant.

I'm About to Promote a Woman. Now What?

While consulting with the executives of a one-hundred-year-old manufacturing company, Pat was told by the president that although there had never been a senior woman on the executive team, he intended to promote three to those ranks in the next four years. "That first woman will be attacked," Pat warned the group. "You will hear that she has become 'power hungry' and that she's 'a bitch,' especially from the other women. I want you to know this is going to happen in advance. Let's do some planning about how you will manage this situation and support her."

Pat advised the president to be skeptical if he heard such complaints. "Don't automatically believe them," she told him. She also suggested he query the complainer about the "offensive" behavior and point out that men act this way all the time. She further advised the executive team to close ranks to protect their new female members; they should anticipate the attacks and be wary of them because of the underlying influence of the Power Dead-Even Rule.

As you have the power to free yourself from Power Dead-Even double binds when you receive a promotion or are honored with accolades, so should you actively seek to prevent other women from falling victim to them. One of the areas where you can have the greatest influence is in how you treat the promotion of a female co-worker. Again, there are certain pre-emptive actions you can take if you want to head off the destructive fallout that's sure to follow the promotion of a woman.

The first point to remember is that you're putting a female who comes from a world where relationships and equality are critical into a hierarchical environment that rewards competitiveness and one-upmanship. Given that she will be working in a foreign culture, it's not at all surprising that she will have some problems.

In private, congratulate Amy that she got the job. Then explain to her that she might encounter some sabotage from her female co-workers. You could say, "This promotion might change your relationship with peers you've been working with for years, and they could be upset about it. I expect they may attack you. It doesn't mean that these are bad people—it just happens. I want you to know that if they try to make an end run around you and complain to me, I'll send them back to you. But you have to be open to talking to them. I'd encourage you to have one-on-one meetings with your team."

Next, confer privately with each of the other unsuccessful applicants. You might say, "Amy has the position. I know you'll probably be disappointed about this, but I really want your support." Then hold a meeting with the whole department including Amy and talk about why you promoted her. You could say, "You're such a great team. I really didn't want to go outside to hire someone to be your new manager, so I made the decision to choose among you to fill this opening. Boy, was it tough! In the end, I decided to promote Amy, and I expect her to be your leader now. This department has always been one of the most professional in our division, and I anticipate that to be the case in the future."

Don't expect that this will head off all your problems; there's still a good chance of sabotage. One of your first challenges may be another woman complaining about Amy's power grab. Make sure to address complaints about behavior. If Leslie says to you, "I don't like Amy; she's acting like a bitch," you need to ask, "What is it that Amy is doing that makes you think that?" Here's a possible scenario of how this conversation might go:

"She's bitchy because she's bossing me around."

"What is she doing that feels like she's bossing you around?"

"She keeps telling me what to do."

"Do you mean she's giving you assignments?"

"Well, I guess."

"That's her job. Amy's new position means that she's got new responsibilities and goals. And part of her work is to make assignments and ensure that they're completed. It may take a little getting used to, but I'm sure you'll adjust."

However, if Leslie hasn't aired her gripes with Amy first, it's important that you cut her off quickly and send her back to speak to Amy. You want to signal that she can't go around Amy, and that Amy is the boss. Also check a few days later with Leslie to see if she has followed through. If she hasn't, you can ask her when she will. If she says "It's not such a big deal anymore," don't believe her. Probably she has already complained to everyone else. In that case you might say, "I'm a little confused because this issue seemed so very important to you when you first told me about it. Help me understand why it's insignificant now."

Depending on Leslie's response, you could still encourage her to speak with Amy within a predetermined time frame. You could say, "I'd appreciate it if you would talk with her by the end of the week. Afterwards let me know how it went." If you don't hear from Leslie, continue to follow up. This may seem like a lot of work—and it can be, especially if several of your female employees are disgruntled. However, look at it as an investment in a peaceful and well-functioning department later. Resentments can build to a feverish pitch and erupt in enormous conflagrations if you don't resolve them early.

Furthermore, unlike the boss of our paralegal correspondent who kept his head down while she was being assailed verbally, it's imprudent to avoid the problem and let the women work it out for themselves. Sometimes they can't do it without intervention, in which case the hostility can escalate to unbearable and destructive levels. As Amy's manager, you can get a sense from her nonverbal communication and tone of voice that there are strains. We recommend meeting with Amy and asking her about how it's going. If she recognizes that tension is settling in, ask why that might be happening. You can explain how the Power Dead-Even Rule is driving the discomfort.

You might say, for instance, "With this promotion, we've given you more power than the women you're working with who have been your friends for many years. I'm hoping this won't cause a problem, and it may not. It's important that you maintain your power to get the job done, but we also need to make sure that the people who work with you accept you as their leader. We've got two things going on. I need to support you and make it clear that you're the boss of this department. And you have to help your female employees feel better about their power and self-esteem. If you try to exert too much power by acting as if 'I am the boss here,' it will only make the situation worse. Let's plan how you and I can maneuver through this potentially rough patch."

Through all of this, it's important for Amy to feel that you are on her side rather than sense an attitude of "What, you've got a performance problem already?" (Even if Amy has a performance problem, deal with it with her behind closed doors—you need to present a united front to her employees.) Be sure all your behavior and comments are supportive toward her. If jealous employees see a crack in her support system, they will try to widen it. It's where she's vulnerable. For instance, if Leslie complains to you, "Amy doesn't know anything about budget reports; she's never done one. I can't go to her for help with it," and you respond, "You're right. That was one of my concerns when I put her in that position," you've just handed Leslie the ammunition she needs to attack Amy further. At lunch, Leslie may gripe to Gina, "The boss is concerned that Amy doesn't know anything about budgets. I don't know why she got promoted. If you're going to be the manager, you need to have those skills!"

Look at the potential problem this creates: At the next departmental meeting, when Amy asks, "How's the budget going?" Leslie might respond, "Well, if I had someone around here who knew how to do one, I'd be a lot further ahead." Gina, Frank, and Robin nod in assent, and Amy blushes. Now the employees all recognize Amy's Achilles' heel and are apt to attack with greater alacrity as time goes on.

Instead, it would be better to respond to Leslie's complaint with a statement like: "Amy hasn't done many budgets before, but she's a quick study, and I'm sure she will learn how to do one in no time." You might then talk to Amy about getting up to speed on budgets and arrange for her to get extra training from the finance department or from an outside course.

Remember, If You're Promoting a Woman

- Expect some commotion from her former peers.

- Realize that the behavior you're anticipating is normal.

- Inform others of the reason that she's being promoted, and that you expect support for her.

- If others on the team applied for the position, meet with them individually. Tell them why they didn't get the job and how they can advance.

- Prepare the promoted employee for what may be coming.

- If you get a complaint, don't allow end runs. Be sure to send the disgruntled employee back to her boss.

- If complaints continue, ask for an explanation of the behavior and help the employee see the conflict in context of the Power Dead-Even Rule.

- Demonstrate constant, unwavering support. Present a united front.

Hired from Outside

Most of the situations we've outlined so far have involved violations of the Power Dead-Even Rule when women advance within an organization. There is a reason for that. It's probably easier to take a new position of power if you're hired into a company from the outside. The other women may not have the mental set of your having been a peer. They've essentially only known you as the "boss," and although you may have more power than you did in a previous position, your status is unchanged in the eyes of your new female employees. Remember, it's a transition in the level of power that can cause relationships to turn ugly.

When you're interviewing for the job, ask to meet with key team members you will be managing, but make sure you spend time with all the women in this process, even if it's just on the phone. In part, you want to get to know them before you walk in as the new boss. While you're just a candidate, you don't have the increased power that might unsettle a female relationship. It would be easier to make those initial connections with the women when the power dynamic is dormant. If peers and employees meet and approve of you, they're more likely to support your success. You also want to give them the opportunity to learn about you.

When you begin your new position, be sure to call a meeting with everyone to talk about your vision and excitement at being part of this team. Then set up individual meetings for career planning, as we recommended above. Be sure your new employees are clear on your expectations and goals and the kind of department you envision. Also, get to know your employees informally; they will probably be expecting more nurturing and support from you because you're female. You might ask what you can do to help them be more effective in their jobs.

It's also wise to meet the other managers at your level; you'll need their support. If they don't come to you, approach them directly, since they are your new peer group. One of the dangerous mistakes female managers make is to believe that their employees are their peers; they often want to be "friends" even though the power is uneven. In your new position, you need to be a leader, setting expectations, giving feedback, and granting (or denying) salary increases or bonuses for your employees. It's virtually impossible to do that with intimate friends.

And that brings us to the second category of double binds: those that arise from the female impulse for interrelatedness.

THE FEMALE TIES THAT DOUBLE BIND

As we all know, it is possible to have wonderful connections with female colleagues, but there are also many potential pitfalls including the risks you run in divulging secrets, the feelings you can hurt if you maintain a level of privacy about your personal life, and the possibility of confusing a professional relationship with friendship. All these come from our impulse to maintain intimate ties with other females.

HAVING CLOSE FRIENDS AT WORK

Let's start with the dilemma of sharing secrets. Although confiding can bring you closer to another woman (and you need to open your heart to create intimacy), the potential for a catfight can make this behavior problematic. You can get caught in the world of secrets in such a way that you pay big-time. If the power shifts in your favor and a friend feels miffed at your violation of the Power Dead-Even Rule, you are vulnerable. She can expose your entire private life, to ill effect. Think of Monica Lewinsky divulging the details of her love life to co-worker Linda Tripp. What a mistake that was!

Women in very visible positions are at greater risk when establishing close relationships with other women. Diana, Princess of Wales, for instance, couldn't confide in anyone without their potentially making millions by later selling her confidences to the tabloids. Hillary Clinton must have suffered terribly during the period when her husband's infidelity was exposed. Of course most women would have been deeply humiliated to have their spouse's unfaithfulness so publicly discussed and dissected. But we also are able to bond with other women through troubles talk. Whom could Hillary turn to in her time of need?

As women move higher and higher into corporate executive positions, they have more and more difficulty revealing personal parts of their lives. In the case of Diana, it became a financial issue to others, and for Hillary it was a question of political suicide. But for the rest of us, there is also some danger in having friends at work when we advance into the upper echelons.

Given that you spend most of your waking hours at work and feel limited in the rest of the time you have—the household, nurturing your children, or caring for your elderly parents can eat up all your leisure time—sometimes your pool of potential friends can be restricted to either women at the office or no one at all. However, the higher you go in the organization, the more difficult it may be to make friends at work. It can be lonely at the top, especially if you are vulnerable to sabotage or having secrets revealed.

Yet withholding intimacies can generate hurt feelings and even a destructive conflict, especially if you move up in the organization and must become more discreet with women who had been your friends. We're constantly redefining our level of friendship: *"I thought Anne was a good friend, but she didn't tell me that she got a promotion/a new boyfriend/a hysterectomy.*

Maybe our friendship isn't as strong as I thought it was." Information is power, and by keeping confidential what friends and co-workers consider important personal data, it is possible to violate the Power Dead-Even Rule.

Moreover, because the Power Dead-Even Rule asks you to behave as if you have equal power with someone who reports directly to you even if you have more, the subordinate can feel surprised and hurt when you maintain what feels to you like a safe level of privacy. When Pat was a doctoral student, she worked closely with Connie, a thirty-year-old female professor who had warm relationships with the female graduate students in the department. Connie was invited to their potluck parties and Sunday brunches. The women also knew her husband well; Don was included in the general socializing among the grad students.

One day, Pat was sitting in Connie's office, talking about a course-related issue when she realized Connie wasn't wearing her wedding ring. Curious about this, Pat gently inquired about its absence.

"I'm very sad to say that Don and I are getting divorced," Connie replied.

Although this was probably bad news for Connie, it was Pat who felt a pang of pain! She had been excluded from an important life-changing event in Connie's world. It brought into sharp focus the fact that Connie didn't feel as close to Pat (or as able to share intimacies with her) as Pat felt to Connie. In hindsight, Pat understood very clearly that Connie didn't owe her an explanation of her marital status, but from then on Pat felt more distant.

Finally, women can react negatively to the feeling that someone has taken the female inclination toward developing friendships and turned it into an opportunity for self-promotion and business development. As journalist Sandy Sheehy explains, "Far from being examples of friendship activities, networking and related business-success strategies have confused and corrupted the notion of friendship."[4] There is a tendency to misperceive attempts to curry favor as an impulse toward friendship and vice versa.

For instance, if you're the male CEO of an organization and you receive a call from a fellow who runs a company that wants to do business with yours, there is no question in your mind that when he invites you to play a round of golf, he hopes a lucrative deal will come of it. Most men are comfortable with an "I-scratch-your-back-you-scratch-mine" mentality because they experience friendliness at work, rather than the deep friendships that characterize women's relationships. Everybody knows this is how the game is played, and business development budgets are set up for just this kind of entertainment of potential clients.

But if Samantha were to call you to invite you to play golf or to spend a day at a health spa with her, it can seem more complicated; women have different rules about what feels right in a relationship. You might wonder if this were an overture for friendship. Or you might feel resentful that she is using fancy perks to "bribe" you for your business—especially with big-ticket items like a day at a spa. It might feel as if she's showing off, thus unbalancing the power. This can also become a chip management issue, and you might start calculating whether Samantha is spending more money on you than you're spending on her. Is she expecting something from it? Is this a one-way proposition? Is she trying to buy your friendship? And from Samantha's point of view, would your coolness to her genuine invitation be construed as a power move meant to diminish her? Would it stand in the way of her success?

PLAYING THE GAME

Authenticity is critical in female relationships, and yet it often gives rise to another double bind. When we sense a difference of opinion, we may withhold our feelings in an effort to preserve the relationship. Unfortunately, this can have the converse effect of damaging the bond; through our non-verbal cues (which female radar picks up very well) our colleague will sense that we're being insincere with her. As journalist Sandy Sheehy explains in *Connecting: The Enduring Power of Female Friendship*, "If we alter our true selves or hold back our feelings in an effort to preserve a valued friendship, we may inadvertently destroy the valuable connection that makes it so worthwhile."[5]

This can create a double bind for us at work. Generally, men don't expect other men to be authentic. Rather, they assume that they'll have their own agendas. Business can be like playing poker to men: they know it's a game, and they'd be stupid to tip their hand. But women often don't see work as a game; rather, they can view it as a network of connections. Think of it this way: If another woman bluffs or hides the truth, you may wonder about your relationship with her: Can you trust her? Is she on your side? Does she care about you? Women have rather high expectations of one another, and when we sense that another woman's words don't come from her heart, we begin to doubt her integrity and our rapport with her, even if she is required to "play the game" in order to protect her job or company.

Problems can also occur when it comes to keeping company secrets. Imagine that as the director of human resources, you have privileged information about the laying off of certain employees. Suppose one of those about to be let go is a close friend. How do you withhold such an important piece of news from her? And how do you actually dismiss her without destroying the friendship?

The double bind of craving female relationships at work and yet being forced to play the game is truly a dilemma. You may applaud total honesty, but you must be cognizant, especially as you become more powerful and are required to maintain confidentiality, that there is an associated potential price. Are you willing to pay it?

GETTING SUCKED INTO A CATFIGHT

It's difficult enough coping with your own dilemmas, but since women often turn to those close to them when they're hurting, it's easy to see how you could become embroiled in a friend's attempts at covert aggression. Imagine, for instance, that Allison has finally gotten promoted onto the executive committee—she's the first woman in your company to make it. You run into Phyllis, a good pal from another department, in the hallway, and she says with a sly grin, "With all the difficulty Allison had doing that last project, it's amazing that she got this promotion, don't you think?" This isn't a frontal attack like "Isn't Allison a bitch?" But you sense where this conversation is heading, and ultimately it won't bode well for Allison. How do you respond?

Unfortunately, you can't say, "Phyllis, stop belittling Allison. Just because she got promoted doesn't give you the right to undermine her." That could damage your friendship with Phyllis and turn her against you, too. But her behavior must stop for everyone's sake, including Phyllis's (after all, she would be vulnerable to the same kind of attack if she were the one with the big promotion). What to do?

GETTING ALONG WELL WITH MEN

Power Dead-Even Rule double binds are not solely the province of female-to-female interactions. Ironically, when a woman works well with the men in her office, her female cohorts can act as if and believe that she has violated the Power Dead-Even Rule. One of our correspondents described this dilemma well:

> Although I very much enjoy working with women, the most difficult thing I have come across is that many of them are threatened by my ability (or willingness) to adapt to the male social environment. I have often felt like a traitor to women when I'm able to fit in with the guys. I don't mean I sit around and shoot the shit about sports in the lunchroom, but rather have found common ground on which to bond. It seems to be a threat to women that I even have common ground. I constantly struggle with a balance because I really value the support system that working women provide (particularly in the field of computer engineering, which is made up almost entirely of men).

It's wonderful when a woman can fit in and feel comfortable with the guys, but she must also realize that her behavior puts her at the risk of violating the Power Dead-Even Rule.

MANAGING FRIENDSHIP-RELATED DOUBLE BINDS

Women value openness with one another, so the more authenticity you can bring to an interaction, the more successful you will be with a female colleague. However, there are limits, and the higher you rise in an organization, the more advisable it is to keep your own counsel. It's a sad fact of life that you may even need to maintain professional relationships with other women at work rather than true friendships. The following are some strategies that you may find helpful in getting you out of friendship-related double binds.

1. Be Careful about Divulging Secrets

People talk; you can expect that if you share a confidence with one woman, others will be privy to it too. They may not gossip out of spitefulness—perhaps, like the teenage girls we discussed in chapter 5, they just want to heighten their own aura of power by sharing the secrets of highly placed women. Still, you must sense whether a person is safe to share with, so be careful about whom you chose as a confidante. Keep in mind the Power Dead-Even Rule. Assess who has more to gain or lose by exposing information about you.

Deborah, one of Susan's clients, encountered a difficult situation involving secrets that she carefully and successfully tiptoed around. She and her husband were out to dinner with his boss, Cecilia, and her husband. The evening went wonderfully until Cecilia pulled Deborah aside and whispered conspiratorially, "Why don't we girls go out together sometime and talk about what our husbands are *really* like."

Deborah felt frightened and surprised at this sudden show of friendliness and responded with a vague "Sure, maybe we can get together sometime." When she asked Susan's advice, Susan responded, "Your instincts were great. Although you might feel flattered by Cecilia's attention and seeming desire to be close, I would suggest that you stay miles away from any such lunch." This turned out to be excellent guidance. Within a year, Cecilia determined that Deborah's husband was getting too much attention from the bigwigs, thereby threatening her position. She decided to "get" him by bad-mouthing him throughout the organization. Fortunately, Deborah had not provided Cecilia with any personal information about her husband that could have damaged him. The slander campaign failed.

2. Separate Your Personal and Professional Lives

In *Going to the Top*, organizational psychologist Carol Gallagher explains that most of the two hundred senior executive women she studied, while exceptionally good at forming strong professional relationships, didn't mix their professional and personal lives. On a scale of one to ten, with ten meaning one could confide one's deepest and darkest secrets to an individual and one meaning the other person didn't know anything about them, her interviewees reported that only 10 percent of their relationships fell above a six. "These women play their cards relatively close to their vests," Gallagher writes.[6] Indeed, one interviewee, Gale Duff Bloom, president of company communications and corporate image at JCPenney, explained:

> I just don't bring too many personal things to work. I never have.
> I'm married; they know that. They all know my husband. But I
> don't talk too much about my personal life. I love the others, and
> I used to be out there in the field. I had much closer relation-
> ships with many of the managers when I was on district staff and
> then with the district managers when I was on regional staff. But
> the higher up you go, the tougher it is to manage the informa-
> tion you share with those close professional relationships. Then
> you move much further toward nondisclosure. It's a whole dif-
> ferent feeling—not quite as relaxed.[7]

Like the other senior executive women, Bloom became more reticent as her career progressed.

3. MAKE YOUR INTENTIONS CLEAR

The personal/professional boundaries can become muddled when you pursue another woman's business by offering her fancy perks. If you're expected to lavish entertainment on a woman to befriend her and solicit her business, it's best to make your intentions quite clear at the outset. When extending the invitation, be sure to couch it in terms like: "Let's get together on Friday. We can become better acquainted with each other, and maybe in the process we'll find some mutual benefit for our companies. *I want to introduce you to our new product.*" This issue can become bigger the higher you advance in your organization as the pressure may build on you to bring in more business in ways that are traditionally expected of men.

If you're on the receiving end of such an invitation and have no problem accepting it, then go for it. But if you feel uncomfortable in this situation, the easiest solution would be to decline graciously and perhaps suggest a venue that feels more appropriate and less power laden and confusing to you. You might say, for instance, "Oh, what a great invitation. I'd love to go, but I'm just too busy to take the whole day off. Why don't we have lunch?"

4. GENTLY CUT OFF DESTRUCTIVE BEHAVIOR

We believe it's critical that when you hear a friend attacking someone who has gotten an opportunity to move ahead, you immediately respond in a positive way to let her know this is unacceptable. (Besides, if a friend is spreading destructive gossip to you about another woman, there's a high probability that she'll target you in the future.) Essentially, you want to model the behavior you hope she and other women use in the future. The best approach is to change the direction of the conversation to show that you refuse to get caught up in destructive gossip. Be supportive of the successful woman.

Suppose that Tricia now supervises her former co-workers. Nina, Tricia's "former friend," might turn to Denise and say, "Can you believe she got promoted over us? She doesn't even have a college degree!"

If Denise were catty, she might respond, "I always wondered about her education . . . I'd heard a rumor about it, but I really didn't believe it . . . and I'm not surprised." But since Denise is savvy about the Power Dead-Even Rule, she replies instead, "Given Tricia's fifteen years of experience, she really is the most qualified one here. I'm pleased they finally promoted someone based on performance rather than the letters after her name. Sort of gives all of us a little hope, huh? Besides, she understands what we're going through in this department. I think I'd have a harder time if they'd brought in someone from the outside."

Don't get pulled into a friend's quarrel with another woman. We believe that it's our responsibility to take the high road when other women are successful—and to bring those who are interested in starting catfights along with us. We're all in this together.

5. Pay Close Attention to Your Female Relationships

If you are lucky enough to work well with the men in your department, your female co-workers may perceive this as a power move on your part. In that case, you would be wise to manage your relationships with them carefully. Don't exclude the women from your circle of relationships. Be sure to support your interactions with them using chips, womenspeak, and appropriate female body language.

6. Be Generous of Spirit

Many of us, sadly, see the world as a zero-sum game: there's only so much good to go around—someone else nabbed the one plum assignment, promotion, or bonus, so we feel justified in attacking her. If that's your perception, it's important to consider flipping the frame of reference. You will be much better off if you view the situation as: "If she became a vice president, then there's hope for me too." Such an optimistic attitude allows you to be truly happy with someone else's success. Rather than feeling it's her gain and your loss, it's better to view the situation as her gain and inspiration for you.

Consider the double bind in which you might find yourself when passed over for a promotion in favor of a close friend. While we've said that it's the responsibility of the promoted person to tend the relationship, sometimes the person who is passed over can make the first move. With an understanding of the Power Dead-Even Rule and its origins, you can see where some of your discomfort and irritation comes from. Support your self-esteem by remembering your own achievements and the other good parts of your life. And also consider engaging in a frank conversation with your newly promoted friend rather than ambushing her with sabotage and sniping.

Susan found herself in this situation with Kelly, who had been a close friend for more than ten years. Susan had been downsized from a corporate job before she was able to line up a new situation. She had applied for a position that she soon discovered was also on Kelly's agenda. This upset Susan because Kelly still had her old job, while Susan was single and newly unemployed. Kelly knew Susan was competing with her for the job, but she was unaware of how much Susan needed it. And in her anxiety, Susan believed Kelly should have backed away, found another position, or helped her find another position.

As luck would have it, Kelly was chosen as the final candidate, and the company's search committee began checking her references. Ironically, Kelly had listed Susan as one of her references before she realized her friend was also vying for the job. When called upon for her assessment, Susan recommended Kelly glowingly and also phoned the CEO to congratulate him on his excellent choice.

Susan didn't hate Kelly for getting the job and she really valued the friendship, but she wanted Kelly to know the situation was eating her up inside. If she let it pass, the resentment would build and leak out in other ways. So she called Kelly and said, "I just want you to know what I'm feeling. I respect our friendship tremendously, but I didn't like the competition between us. I feel hurt and misunderstood because you didn't get it that I needed that job more than you did. I'm unemployed, and I'm feeling pretty scared right now." Kelly felt terrible about the situation and sent Susan a dozen roses with a note saying, "I'm sorry. I didn't realize how bad things were for you. I'm so glad you were able to be honest with me. Your friendship means everything to me."

The relationship was preserved and probably strengthened; the resolution of this conflict drew Susan and Kelly even closer together. In fact, a few months later, Kelly, in her new position as vice president of human resources, offered Susan a job, which it turned out she didn't need because she had already launched her successful consulting practice.

By sharing a painful truth with a friend rather than lashing out with injurious behavior, you can preserve and protect a threatened relationship. Your friend is likely to trust and believe you in the future, and you will feel closer to each other.

OF COURSE, double binds aren't the only tricky situations we must handle in the workplace. In addition to resolving conflicts unique to women—those arising from seemingly beneficial situations such as a promotion, an award, or a close friendship—we must also learn how to resolve conflicts that crop up naturally in the workplace. Conflict management is one of the most important tools in career building for men and women. But because we are relatively inexperienced in dealing with direct conflict, we must pay special attention to conflict resolution strategies. The following two chapters outline helpful techniques for engaging in productive conflicts with other women.

EIGHT

How to Have Healthy Conflict with Another Woman

W ow, these expenses are really out of whack," Gail exclaimed as she stood in the middle of her office suite,
poring over her department's most recent operating costs. "Overtime is up
ten percent, and telephone and supply costs have jumped twenty percent."

Immediately Jan stiffened. "Whoa, that's not my fault," she protested
loudly to her boss. "Why are you on my case about those numbers? I've been
working as hard as I can." Heads all around the office began swiveling to see
what all the commotion was about.

Gail was taken aback. Focusing on a business problem, she needed help
with how to bring down overhead costs. But Jan had heard her complaints
as a personal attack. She immediately became defensive. "You never support me," she cried. "You always bitch at me, no matter how hard I try.
Maybe if you were a better manager, this wouldn't happen . . ."

"That's just not true," Gail interrupted, feeling the blood rise in her
cheeks. "Besides, who do you think you are, talking to me like that?"

Gail turned on her heel abruptly, and Jan stormed out of her presence,
muttering about how no one appreciates her. For days she sulked around
the office. She began to enlist the help of her peers to conspire against
"Gail-the-bitch," planting the seeds for a major catfight that would ensue.

Within three weeks, the department was flooded with incorrect invoices, disheveled files, bloated inventory. Jan began to divulge departmental business to anyone who would listen. And she spread harmful falsehoods about Gail and her family: that Gail had a wayward daughter (she actually has no children), that Gail had inherited lots of money from her mother's estate (her mother was still alive), that Gail's husband was freeloading (he worked at two jobs).

Poor Gail was not only saddled with cost overruns, but now her department was in disarray and she was personally impugned. She was left to wonder what had gone wrong with her most trusted employees.

A conflict between two women can sometimes turn as nasty as the situation between Gail and Jan. But conflicts aren't always rip-your-throat-out-I'll-never-speak-to-you-again quarrels. If executed and resolved more constructively, they can provide an opportunity for you and the person with whom you disagree to walk out of a room in support of a consensus you've hammered out together. Despite our deeply held beliefs to the contrary, conflict is not necessarily bad. In fact, it's essential to the maintenance of cohesive relationships. As in marriage, it's not an argument itself but how we deal with it that's important.

Productive Conflict and Cooperation

Conflicts are most often caused by lack of communication, differing perceptions, opposing values, disparate perceived outcomes, and, among women, violations of the Power Dead-Even Rule. But not all conflicts are the same. We've identified two major categories—destructive ones, such as Gail and Jan's, and productive conflicts that end in growth and resolution. The former damage relationships and often make it more difficult for the warring parties to move forward. A productive conflict, by contrast, resolves the problem at hand while preserving relationships.

Imagine yourself approaching a female colleague and saying, "I'd like to talk to you about that meeting yesterday. I have a different perspective on where I think we should be headed with this, and I'd like to discuss it with you." Nothing scary about that, right? This is an example of seeing a conflict or disagreement as an alternative way to reach a goal. This sort of direct, substantive encounter can produce growth and strengthen relationships.

If you talk to your colleague about the problem and resolve it, you'll feel closer to her because you've worked out the issue together.

To achieve healthy, productive conflict, you need to master the art of cooperation. And cooperation hinges on:

- Respecting the opposition

- Valuing the relationship with those of the opposing viewpoint

- Recognizing that you need the opposition to implement the desired outcome

- Supporting your opponent's self-esteem and sense of power

- Supporting your own self-esteem and sense of power

Unfortunately, this kind of productive conflict is unfamiliar territory to many of us. We may find any confrontation uncomfortable. Because we're insecure in our ability to navigate a disagreement, we'll often go to great lengths to circumvent it. One workshop participant told Susan, "I'm really bad at this conflict stuff, so I stay away from it altogether."

Susan's response to this woman was, "Of course we all dodge things we don't know how to do well, but evasion is not the best answer. That's why it's so important to learn productive conflict techniques."

Another reason to manage conflict well centers on the fact that you cannot really be close to someone unless you are able to talk with her about all your feelings—including those with which she might be in disagreement. Think of your best friend in the world, the person to whom you can say anything. She won't necessarily agree with you, but at least she'll try to understand issues from your perspective. To have an open rapport, you have to have conflict—and conflict resolution. Conflict doesn't mean you tear each other down; sometimes you just see things differently.

Besides, if you don't know how to resolve arguments productively, festering unresolved resentments might explode later. Other than the obvious negative effects of long simmering bitterness, engaging in healthy conflict can be good for your organization. Sometimes you need it to escape stagnation; if no one is coming forward with new, potentially risky ideas that engender discussion and disagreement, there is no progress.

Catfights are a learned behavior. We have all been taught how to be indirectly aggressive when we disagree with another woman, but we can also learn to behave more productively for the sake of our careers and also to maintain our alliances with other women. In this chapter and the next, we will present many tools to help you reframe and resolve the female-to-female conflicts that can arise in the workplace so that you know how to turn a catfight into a collegial relationship. One of the most effective techniques is to recognize the difference between a content conflict and a relationship conflict. We will also show you how to turn disagreements into productive encounters by avoiding defensiveness in yourself and in the woman with whom you're having a disagreement, as well as how to structure the environment of your conflicts in order to have the most favorable outcomes for everyone. Let's start by analyzing what was really going on between Gail and Jan.

CONTENT CONFLICT VERSUS RELATIONSHIP CONFLICT

Was Gail an incompetent manager? Was Jan responsible for the cost overruns? Actually, these two women were having two distinct conflicts, but they didn't know it. One of the most common reasons that female disagreements evolve into major blow-ups is that we confuse conflicts over actual *content*—a real issue—with conflicts having to do with the relationship between the two people in disagreement.

Gail's problem was factual and specific. She was concerned about her department's rising expenses—a content issue. A content conflict involves a disagreement about something tangible—a specific and measurable fact like the distance from one city to another, the number of ounces in a pound, or the percentage the phone bill was hiked. Gail's complaint had nothing whatsoever to do with Jan's competence.

However, Jan did not hear Gail's words as a factual discussion. Rather, she understood that Gail thought she had fallen down on the job. Jan felt discounted and unappreciated by Gail. This is a relationship issue, one in which the problem centers on what's occurring between two people on an interpersonal level—their feelings, emotions, and perceptions. Relationship conflicts occur when someone believes another is sabotaging her, taking advantage of her, or disregarding her.

This confusion between content conflict and relationship conflict often wreaks havoc with communication among women. Over 60 percent of women prefer to rely more on feelings, harmony, and human values when making decisions rather than on logic and principles. This causes many women to hear that a conflict involves a relationship issue when in reality what was intended was a content discussion. And when they do so, they end up feeling sabotaged, undermined, and insulted. Perhaps this is why men often complain that women take problems so personally. If we interpret a content conflict to be about a relationship, it is only natural that we would feel personally hurt.

Because workplace disagreements most often have to do with content issues like conflicting goals, limited resources, and differing viewpoints about quality—rather than revolving around relationships—it's critical for you first to determine the subject of a conflict in working to resolve the problem properly.

Two women caught in a content rather than a relationship conflict will have difficulty turning their discussion into productive problem solving until they start communicating on the same level—that is, until they're both dealing with either the content or the relationship. In order to do this, at least one of them must grasp the nature of the confusion.

Imagine, for instance, that Gail recognizes that Jan has reacted to her from a relational point of view rather than the content perspective that she intended. After Jan's emotional response, Gail can back up and say, "Hang on a minute. I didn't mean to sound like I was attacking you. I really just want to get your input in fixing this budget snafu. You're so good at problem solving." In this way, Gail reassures Jan that all is well in the relationship—thus defusing some of Jan's defensiveness—and she reiterates her request for content-oriented help.

We recently ran into this type of conflict ourselves with a client. Once someone schedules work with us, we send out a simple one-page contract to make sure we're all expecting the same work, on the same day, in the same city. We hadn't received our contract back from Lori, and someone else requested our services for the day she had reserved. When Holly, who worked with us, asked Lori about whether she had received the contract, she responded in clipped tone, "Yes, we did."

"Well, we haven't received it back yet," Holly continued. "Do you still want that date?"

"Why would you think we wouldn't?" Lori's voice was chilly.

"Since we didn't get the contract and we had someone else who wanted that date, I was checking." Silence. "When do you think you might send it?"

"I'm not sure."

Holly was at a loss, but she could tell something was wrong so she didn't push it. After several strained phone calls, she figured it out. We hadn't worked with Lori in a couple of years, and back then, when our business was less complex, we weren't in the habit of sending out contracts. So, when Lori received her contract from us, she must have felt insulted. She believed we were "friends." Why did we need a contract? Wasn't her word enough? She trusted us. Didn't we trust her?

Just as in the case of Gail and Jan, we were experiencing content rather than relationship conflict. Our issue was pretty cut-and-dried: it was the business procedure of signing contracts with clients. Lori's, however, was a relationship issue—she believed we no longer trusted her, and from her point of view, that sabotaged the friendship. We still send contracts to Lori when she books our time so that there's a written record of the details of our agreement, but we don't press her if she doesn't return them.

When a conflict revolves around content for one woman and relationship for other, it's best to deal with the relationship issue first. Otherwise any solutions that arise won't be optimal, because one party may remain hurt, distrustful, or resentful. If you're familiar with both content and relationship conflicts, one of you can say, "Hold it. Are we disagreeing over something that's between us or an actual issue that's on the table?" If you've been discussing a content issue and discover that it's really a relationship issue, then deal with the relationship at that point.

Even if only one of you has an awareness of the difference in types of conflict, you still can resolve the disagreement productively if you use that knowledge in your discussion. For instance, imagine you approach Francine at lunch and say, "I disagree with what you recommended in that meeting yesterday. I believe it will cost too much and take too long. I don't think we can afford to do it."

Suppose that Francine responds, "Are you angry with me? Why are you attacking me?" You have presented Francine with a content conflict, and she flipped it into a relationship issue. It would be your job to remove the relationship-related discomfort and put the discussion back to the content level by saying something like "I really value you as a colleague and because I trust you so much, I want to talk to you about your proposal." You must reassure Francine about the importance of your connection to her. Without that, she will find it difficult to overcome her initial feeling of defensiveness—that instinctive reaction many of us have when we feel we are coming under attack—to work through the content of your disagreement.

HOW DO YOU APPROACH CONFLICTS?

It's important for you to understand how you instinctively view conflicts. If a problem arises, do you automatically look for a relational issue as its source or a concrete issue? Take a look at the ten situations below. In each scenario, response A reflects a relationship point of view, and response B reflects a content point of view. Which thought pattern are you more likely to choose?

1. A co-worker tells you that she believes your suggestion about holding a company picnic will be too expensive and distracting during this crunch time when productivity is critical. You:

    a. Wonder why she would say something like that. You don't understand why she's so thoughtless of everyone's need for a little R&R during this tough time.

    b. Take her words as "input" and rethink your suggestion to see if her ideas have merit.

2. Your female boss, who knows you've been having problems at home, informs you that an important client has requested you meet with him next week about a major project he wants to give your firm. This means you must be out of town for three days. You:

    a. Wonder why she would ask you to do such a thing. After all, she knows about your difficulties at home. You don't understand because you thought she was your friend.

    b. Book your flight with the understanding that this client could put your firm on the map.

(continues)

3. A female friend working at another company is supposed to meet you for lunch at noon today. It is 12:20, and she has not arrived. You:

   a. Are upset that she would treat you like this. You thought she would have the decency to show up on time.

   b. Decide to call her office to ensure that the date and time are correct. Once confirmed, you have a cup of coffee and plan to order lunch for yourself if she hasn't arrived by 12:30. She obviously has gotten detained in traffic or something else came up which is out of her control. You hope she's okay.

4. You worked hard on a presentation to the city council in hopes of having a stop sign put up by the elementary school. You ask your closest friend to let you practice your speech in front of her. After hearing you out, Joline tells you it would be more persuasive if you changed the order of some of the sections and added more punch to the ending. You:

   a. Feel hurt that she doesn't appreciate the time and effort you put into this speech. You really aren't looking for input from her; you just wanted to practice your presentation. You wonder why she's so critical.

   b. Are grateful that she thinks this stop sign is a good idea too. You listen to what she has to say and take her ideas into consideration. She has never steered you wrong before!

5. You invited one of your best friends to the symphony on several occasions, but she has not been able to attend due to her busy travel schedule. You called Rita again today to see if she is available next Wednesday. Once more, she says she'll be out of town. You:

   a. Wonder if Rita is trying to send you a signal about your relationship.

   b. Feel bad for her because her job is preventing her from participating in so many of the activities she enjoys. You tell Rita you'll buy her a tape of the performance and bring it by on your lunch break someday soon.

6. Your boss informs you that she believes the blouse you're wearing is too sexy and is decreasing your male co-workers' inclination to take you seriously. You:

   a. Are furious. How dare she speak to you like this, after all the times you've supported her when others criticized her management abilities.

   b. Realize that she has always tried to serve as a mentor to you. Perhaps she has a point.

7. You received some critical feedback from your boss today. She said your work hasn't been up to par lately. You:

   a. Wonder if the comment you made the other day about her son offended her.

   b. Take a critical look at your performance to see if her comment has any merit.

8. Kristin keeps resisting your recommendation. When you ask what's behind her balkiness, her responses don't make sense to you. You:

   a. Begin to wonder if you've done something to offend her.

   b. Take a hard look at the facts and your assessment of the situation.

9. You depend on Katie to provide you with data for your weekly reports. Lately you have had to ask repeatedly for the information, and it is slow in coming. You:

   a. Ask her if there is something wrong between you.

   b. Ask if she is having problems getting her work done.

10. Carla told you this morning that she hates it when co-workers use all the paper in the copier and don't refill it. You:

    a. Wonder if she thinks you are the culprit.

    b. Agree. It drives you nuts too.

(continues)

> If you've chosen A in the majority of these scenarios, then it's likely that you view conflicts from a relational rather than a content vantage point. If you've chosen B most often, you see conflicts through the lens of content. Whichever choices you made, however, be careful not to misread a conflict just because you're accustomed to approaching it from a habitual vantage point.

MANAGING YOUR OWN DEFENSIVENESS

Defensiveness—your own and that of the person with whom you are having a disagreement—cuts off productive discussion and underlies many female-to-female conflicts. If you don't diminish defensiveness, no matter whose it is, you may spend 90 percent of your time trying to get around it rather than dealing with the substantive issues that require resolution.

Imagine that you're working away at your desk when Flo barges in and declares in a fevered, accusatory tone, "You promised you would have that information to me by three o'clock. You didn't get it to me. I had to go to the meeting without it, and everyone there jumped all over my case." You had fully intended to get the information to Flo, but your boss gave you a red-hot assignment at the last moment, and you couldn't do both. The information for Flo was the one piece of work that had slipped.

How do you typically react when someone comes at you like this? Humans do things for reasons that make sense to us. Our natural inclination when someone jumps on us is to explain our behavior. We become defensive. But this creates a vicious cycle. Flo attacks, so you defend; so she attacks even harder, and you feel you have to defend even more. Rather than mollifying Flo, your defensive explanation actually exacerbates the conflict.

Our ability to solve problems effectively is greatly diminished when we become defensive. But most of us will still actively defend ourselves when someone tries to damage our self-esteem. In fact, one of the keys to managing conflict is to learn how to control our tendency toward defensiveness and the defensiveness of the person with whom we're dealing. If we can disarm the defensiveness, we may not have solved the conflict, but we will have fundamentally changed the tone of the interaction for the better. The following steps will help:

1. Become Aware

We are often unaware of our own defensive reactions until someone points them out to us. "I wasn't being defensive," we sputter (defensively). "I was just correcting some incorrect facts." Unfortunately, this lack of awareness can cause extensive, long-lasting harm with co-workers. Ask yourself what happens mentally, physically, and emotionally when you feel on the defensive. First, you may realize that you stop listening to the other person. Instead, you may engage in an internal dialogue aimed at making yourself feel better. Your defensive thoughts might include: "I did the best I could; you don't understand." Or, "You're not so hot yourself; I caught you making much bigger mistakes than this." You may also recognize the physical components of a stress response: your heartbeat and breathing rates increase; you become tense and hot all over; your mouth goes dry; and so on. You may find yourself crossing your arms or legs. You also feel hurt, angry, misunderstood, and disrespected.

By becoming more aware of your own responses when someone attacks you, you can turn your insight into strategic action in terms of managing the conflict. Rather than its being a question of your feeling hurt, you can say to yourself, "What am I going to do to maneuver through this problem?"

2. Relax

Communication expert Albert Mehrabian estimates that only 7 percent of the emotional impact of a message comes from your words; 93 percent derives from body language and intonation.[1] Even if you say "I'm fine" but you're not, unconscious nonverbal cues will probably betray you. To disarm yourself, it's best to relax. Start taking deeper, slower breaths. Check your facial muscles to see if your jaw is tight. If so, slacken it. Pay attention to your posture and body language: Are your arms or legs crossed? If so, uncross them. If you've made a fist, open your hand. Listen to your tone of voice: Is it clipped? Angry? High-pitched? Make an effort to modulate your speech so that it sounds more like your normal speaking voice.

3. SHIFT YOUR FOCUS

Defensiveness is all about focusing exclusively on what's happening to you rather than listening to what the person with whom you're in conflict is saying. One of the best ways to release yourself from defensiveness is to concentrate on her words and gestures. (An anagram for *listen* is *silent*; you need to silence your internal dialogue to really hear the other person.) Make a conscious effort to stop your self-talk and pay attention to her complaints. This may be difficult, particularly when she's telling you how terrible you are. Our natural human reaction is to justify why we did what we did because we did it for reasons that made sense to us at the time. But instead of sticking up for your actions, you must get behind the other person's eyeballs and figure out how the world looks to her—not why you were right, not why it made all the sense in the world to you to do what you did, not why she's unjustified in her criticisms—but what the problem is from her point of view. You can't grasp her reality unless you zip your lip and listen.

4. LET HER HAVE HER SAY

It's especially important not to interrupt someone as she's pouring out her complaint. Most likely she has rehearsed her statement from A to Z, and when you stop her at H, she may feel compelled to go back to A all over again because she believes you haven't been paying attention to her. In fact, she may now feel obliged to speak slower and louder. Focus on listening calmly. Remind yourself that you will have a chance to speak once your colleague has spoken her mind.

5. USE ACTIVE LISTENING TECHNIQUES

After your co-worker has excoriated you about all your terrible transgressions and how angry she is about them, your next step is to paraphrase her perspective. For instance, you might say to Flo, whom you have so sorely disappointed: "So you're saying that because you had to go to the meeting without the data, everyone attacked you, and you felt like a fool."

Paraphrasing is your way of proving to Flo that you've heard what she said. If your response to her complaint is a dismissive or patronizing statement such as "I know, I know," or "It can't be all that bad, can it?" your colleague won't trust that you really grasp the depths of her problem. Even an honest "I'm sorry" may be inadequate because she is concerned that you may do this again and she'll end up with the same egg on her face. Until she feels secure in the knowledge that you understand the issue she is raising, she may feel justified to tell you over and over again how much you've ruined her life. When you paraphrase, you prove that you've listened and that you understand.

6. LEGITIMIZE HER FEELINGS

Your next statement should be something in the order of "If I were in your shoes, I'd probably feel the same way." Keep in mind that you're not telling the other woman she was right and you were wrong, and that you're not giving in. You're simply empathizing—you understand her feelings. You're saying if the world looked the same way to you as it does to her, you'd most probably have the same reaction.

7. SIDESTEP OFFENSIVE LANGUAGE

In the midst of an argument, your co-worker pulls out certain expressions that you find offensive, such as "bitch," "goddammit," "screw you." The use of these incendiary expressions can feel like a frontal attack and can easily provoke your defensiveness. What do you do? You must make a choice at this point. You can either address the provocative words, or you can continue with the conflict at hand. You cannot deal with both at the same time.

Usually we choose to ignore the invectives and strive toward resolving the conflict. We would rather put a disagreement to bed than get embroiled in a shouting match about obscenities and name-calling. Besides, you can go back to the person the next day after you've both cooled off and say, "If we ever have a conflict like that again, I would appreciate it if you wouldn't use that language with me."

If you do try to deal with words during a disagreement, you run the risk of reinforcing their use. It's just like the five-year-old who brings her first four-letter word home and plants it in the middle of the dinner table. She blurts out, "Damn!" and her parents' reaction is so extreme that she thinks,

"I must remember this word. It's the most powerful one I've come across so far." The same is true in adult conflicts. If the other woman utters an invective to which you react, she will most likely keep pushing that button because it puts her in control. Conversely, if you ignore the word, she might try it a few times, but if she doesn't get the response she's looking for, she'll probably give up and leave the offensive language behind.

Bear in mind that this is our value choice. It may not be the right choice for you.

ACCEPTING CRITICISM

The single most effective provocateur of defensive behavior is criticism. Being criticized naturally makes us want to defend ourselves—especially when it catches us by surprise. Criticism is sometimes warranted, and great personal and professional growth can emanate from valid feedback. But it's your right to evaluate the criticism to see if it is legitimate or unfounded and to assert yourself if you believe you've been unjustly attacked.

Here are some guidelines for accepting criticism without flinching or reacting to being stung. These suggestions can help you control your defensiveness when you're feeling out of control. When you are presented with criticism:

- Ask for a specific example of what is being criticized.

- Decide for yourself whether the criticism is fair. Is it true? Is the situation something you are able or willing to correct?

- If the criticism is fair, don't make excuses. Instead, think of how you can rectify the situation. Ask: "What can I do to correct this problem?"

- If the criticism is unfair, use "I" statements such as "I feel misunderstood," or "I don't think I can meet your goals." Don't use "you" statements that accuse or insult such as "You've completely misread the situation," or "You're being unreasonable," or "How dare you bring this up! You have no clue what you're talking about."

- Criticism may trigger a retaliatory response in you. Temper that impulse. If you feel as if you're going to lose control, take a break.

Reschedule the conversation for a time when you're composed and can process the information with more objectivity.

- Thank your critic. If she has a conflict with you in the future, she will be much more likely to bring it to you with the hope that it will get resolved. Whether or not the criticism is valid, you are more likely to avoid destructive conflicts and sustain a healthy working environment if your colleagues feel they can calmly discuss their differences with you.

- When receiving criticism, make sure you stand or sit with an upright and open posture. If you believe the criticism is unwarranted, this communicates nonverbally that you feel unshakable. If you feel the criticism is valid, this communicates that you are not going to lash out defensively at your critic.

- If you are attacked while presenting at a meeting, walk with an open posture toward the attacker. That almost always shuts down the confrontation because you're essentially saying, "This isn't getting to me, and I'm going to get you." This may be the opposite of what you feel like doing, which may be turning tail and running out of the room, but it is effective in halting an attack.

How to Prevent the Other Woman
from Becoming Defensive

You may find yourself in a situation where you evoke defensiveness in another woman. You bring up a problem you're having on a joint project, and instead Melinda hears you saying she's not doing her part correctly. Again, it's useful to analyze whether this is a content rather than a relationship conflict. If in your colleague's mind there is a relationship problem, you need to reassure her that your relationship is fine but that you'd like to attack a content problem with her.

Melinda's nonverbal signals will help you recognize whether she is becoming defensive: she may physically pull away, turn sideways, and/or cross her arms and/or legs. She may break eye contact. She could develop a set expression—narrowed eyes, pursed lips—as if she were wearing a mask. Her eyebrows may shoot up. Of course, her language will give her away too. She may actively defend herself with statements such as "You don't understand . . ." "I was going to do that, but . . ." "Why didn't you call me to tell me . . ." And her voice may change, becoming shrill or clipped. None of these cues means anything in itself, but if the minute you broach a topic with another person, she blocks you physically or verbally, this is a tip-off that you've touched on a sensitive issue for her.

When you recognize that your co-worker is becoming defensive, it's wise to stop your discussion and make an effort to lessen her tension. Because your basic strategy is to disarm defensiveness, anything you do to make the conversation easier is critical in conflict resolution. Here are some techniques that will help you communicate with a defensive colleague:

1. DESCRIBE RATHER THAN EVALUATE HER BEHAVIOR

The evaluation of someone's behavior (rather than merely a description of it) can create defensiveness. For instance, if you make a judgmental statement such as "You're lazy" or "You have a bad attitude," not only will your co-worker feel personally attacked, but she will also have no idea what she can change in order to please you. She doesn't know what specific behaviors or incidents you envision as evidence of these, and therefore she has no way to remedy the situation. Her natural tendency, then, would be to defend herself.

It's more effective to describe her behavior: "I thought you were going to have this report ready for me by Friday at five P.M. It's now Tuesday, and you still haven't turned it in. Because of this, I don't have adequate time to review it, and that reflects badly on our department." Now she knows what upset you.

Pat encountered a situation where the description of behavior quickly helped resolve what could have been a major problem between two female colleagues. The president of an insurance company called Pat to help him with Claudia and Maggie; both reported to him and were jointly responsible for pulling off a major project. Unfortunately, these two were in constant conflict, and the project was going nowhere. Pat met with each of the women individually and talked about conflict strategies. Then she brought them together, turned to Claudia, and asked: "Please tell Maggie what the problem is from your perspective."

Claudia simply said, "You don't support me." Despite all the work Pat had done with her beforehand, Claudia still made an evaluative statement.

But Maggie got the message. "What am I doing that looks to you like I don't support you?" she asked. Wonderful, Pat thought. Maggie received a defensiveness-inducing evaluation but asked instead for a description of her "problematic" behavior.

Claudia replied, "I'll tell you what you do. When we're in meetings together and I bring up ideas, you act like a dummy. You never say anything in my defense."

"Oh my God," Maggie explained. "That's why we're such a great team. You're the idea person, and I'm the implementer. When you're generating one idea after another, I sit there thinking, 'How would I implement this one? How would I implement that one?'"

A lightbulb went on in Claudia's head at the recognition of their dynamic. Right then and there, the conflict evaporated.

Alternatively, if rather than asking for a description when Claudia complained, "You don't support me," Maggie had just defended herself, the conversation could have looked like this:

"Yes I do support you."

"No you don't support me."

"Yes I do . . ." And on and on. There's no way to resolve the conflict if you stay with evaluative terms.

2. Look for Win-Win Solutions

Win-win solutions come more naturally to women than to men because most of us have been brought up to look for them, whereas most men are trained in a win-lose competitive model. In a win-win solution, both of you get at least part of what you want. It maintains the self-esteem and power of both women, while a win-lose outcome would most likely diminish the losing party's feelings of self-worth or power. And losers have long memories: "You done me in, and I'm gonna get back at you!"

With a win-win solution, you preserve power chips with your colleagues. Win-win helps you avoid catfights; it's part of being collaborative, and it protects your relationships. Most women use win-win solutions without even thinking about it because the Power Dead-Even Rule underlies their actions.

How do win-win/win-lose solutions work? Karen, the chief of operations at a large company, depended heavily on Natalie, a valued vice president, to help her get her job done. But Natalie was juggling a long commute to work, her job, and two young children. She decided she needed to break the frame because her life was becoming far too stressful. She approached Karen to request a flexible schedule—she wanted to work at home two days a week. But Karen felt she needed Natalie at the office, and wouldn't let her change her routine. Natalie's solution? She quit. This was clearly a win-lose solution. Karen won the battle, but lost the war.

All Karen needed to do was entertain some of Natalie's suggestions. She could have said, "I need you here for our weekly budget and production meetings. You'll have to spend time with everyone on the team during the week, and you'll still need to run your weekly departmental meetings. If an unanticipated problem arises, you'll also probably have to be here to manage it. Can we fit all that into your flex-time schedule?" If Natalie had been able to accommodate her boss's needs, they would both have come out of this conflict with what they wanted—a true win-win solution.

3. Use "I" Statements

Whenever *you* is the first word out of your mouth during a conflict, the other person will build a mental barrier to protect herself from incoming accusations. "You aren't listening to me!" is likely to make her defensive. Besides, you can't really know whether or not she's listening to you. Because you want to avoid defensiveness whenever possible, it's better to use "I" statements to express your reality, as in "I feel . . ." "I think . . ." "I believe . . ." The statement "I feel as though I'm not being heard" is true and less likely to make the other person defensive. You're speaking your reality rather than telling the other woman what her reality is.

4. Avoid the Words *Always* and *Never*

Does the following conflict sound familiar to you?

"You never come to meetings on time."

"Last Tuesday I was on time for the three P.M. meeting."

"That was the first time all month."

"That's just not true! I was on time for the eight-o'clock meeting on Thursday."

It is a rare person who "always" does anything. As a result, when you accuse someone of always being late or always interrupting, because it's not true, it shifts her from dealing with the real issue to proving the untruth of your generalization. The same is true of "never," as in "You never speak up in my defense." Rather than "always" or "never," you might say: *"I noticed you were late for the meeting again today. It seems to me that this has become a pattern. It's critical that we all be present when we start so we don't have to repeat ourselves when people come in late. How can we deal with whatever is causing your lateness?"*

5. Avoid Piling It On

Nothing can raise a person's defenses faster than a statement like "And another thing . . ." If you have several issues with a co-worker, it's best to deal with them one problem at a time. Put the first conflict to bed before you go on to the next, even if that means spreading your discussion over several meetings. If you pile on the criticism in one meeting, you're at risk for creating a jumble of an argument that can actually inflame the conflict and leave both of you angrier and more frustrated.

For instance, you start off complaining to Samantha about issue A: "I wrote the report all by myself, but you got your name on it too!" But then you remember an earlier offense. "And another thing, I got up early Monday morning to meet at seven-thirty, and you didn't saunter in till eight A.M." And while you're at it, you heap on additional transgressions: "And are you aware of how much perfume you wear and that it makes me wheeze?" In the end, none of the issues gets dealt with effectively because Samantha, feeling overwhelmed in a no-win situation, may become defensive.

Resolve one topic before you move on to the next one.

6. Use Humor

Humor, as long as it's not sarcastic or biting and is directed at yourself or the situation and not the person with whom you're in conflict, is one of the most effective ways of de-escalating conflicts, reducing tension, disarming defensiveness, and creating rapport. In *What Mona Lisa Knew,* management psychologist Barbara Mackoff describes how one supervisor arrived at a meeting of indignant employees with a bull's-eye fastened on his chest as a way to open the discussion of worker grievances.

Self-deprecating humor can diffuse the heat of battle. Once, when two women we worked with were quite angry at each other, one turned to the other and said, "I won! I'm madder than you are!" She laughed at herself and defused the conflict so successfully that both women were able to get into problem solving shortly thereafter.

7. Watch Your Nonverbal Cues

We all use gestures—what we call "comfort cues"—to make ourselves feel better in times of stress. These consist of rubbing, patting, and scratching ourselves. Some women twirl their hair. You may say, "Oh, I never do that in public," but you'll be surprised to learn that you probably do it repeatedly. The next time you're stuck in a traffic jam, just look in the cars around you, and you'll see this sort of self-comforting behavior everywhere.

If you're in a conflict with someone, notice if she's calming herself in this way. You can use this information to get a sense of whether she's distressed and likely to be defensive. You can also modify your own display of these cues because you may not want the person with whom you're having this discussion to know how difficult it is for you.

Be conscious of pointing. Waving your finger under someone's nose can aggravate a conflict. A nurse once told Pat, "I was talking to Dr. Brown, and I told him this, and I told him that . . ." While she spoke to Pat, she was wagging her finger. Pat's response was, "I hope that finger wasn't out, because it would have made Dr. Brown angrier." Pointing out of enthusiasm or excitement when you're talking about a fabulous vacation does not offend. It's the accusatory, shaming tone of your conversation coupled with the gesture that's considered a power move in our culture.

Facial expressions can also exacerbate a conflict. Rolling eyes, smirky smiles or grimaces, and deep frowning all convey contempt or disdain and certainly can heighten defensiveness and worsen any conflict. Sometimes you may not want a colleague to know that she is getting to you. You can communicate power with an expressionless countenance—what we call the "stone face"—that seems to communicate a lack of empathy. Women in powerful positions often adopt this expression because they must convey power in this way among men. Using a stone face with other women, however, can lead to defensiveness, because women expect one another to be empathetic.

Conversely, genial facial expressions can soothe hurt feelings. Because women are so good at communicating with nonverbal cues, we can use our demeanor to tell someone we care about what happened, and that we're sorry about her situation. Good eye contact coupled with a sympathetic expression help a colleague feel heard and understood.

8. FOCUS ON THE FUTURE

Although the past is dead and gone, many people love to focus on it. We often bring up old grievances and have difficulty turning the page and moving on. But if we keep regurgitating the past, we can't push forward in our lives.

Rehashing the past is a sure way to make people defensive. How would you react if someone said, "You let me down last year, and it's screwed up my life ever since. I'm really ticked off. You shouldn't have done that."

If you're being berated for a past offense, it's wise to shift to the future and formulate some agreement about what you (or your attacker) will do differently. If, for instance, you didn't get Flo the information she needed and she keeps telling you how embarrassed she was, you could say, "My boss gave me a hot item at the last minute, and I couldn't do both. But I'd like to make a commitment to you that if this happens in the future, I promise to call you within five minutes of getting a conflicting assignment so we can strategize what to do. Would that be okay with you?" Flo may be worried whether another similar lapse will ambush her in the future. By coming up with an agreement about what you will do differently from now on, she now is more likely to feel reassured and may be more willing to back off her attack.

7 STEPS TO HEALTHY CONFLICT RESOLUTION

1. Determine whether you're dealing with a content conflict or relationship conflict. Respond on the appropriate level.

2. Watch your colleagues and determine who is direct and indirect. Flex to her style.

3. Keep a close eye on your colleague's facial expressions and tone of voice when there is disagreement. If you notice her crossing her arms, try to draw her out. If you notice that her voice is becoming shrill, make your voice more calming and caring.

4. Reduce defensiveness (yours and hers) by using "I feel . . ." statements rather than "You are . . ." statements.

5. Use good communication skills such as active listening, paraphrasing, and validation of your colleague's feelings. In place of "Why did you?" use "Help me understand . . ."

6. Keep your sense of humor. Take your job responsibilities very seriously and yourself half as seriously! Laugh with your female cohorts about the female culture.

7. When disagreements have been resolved and the game is over, shake hands, congratulate each other, and move on to the next challenge.

THE SAFETY ZONE

Preventing defensiveness in yourself and in your colleagues is key to managing productive conflict. It can also help if you create a safety zone—a contained environment—for productive conflict. By creating such as safe space, you eliminate a potential source of conflict escalation while you enhance your co-worker's sense of trust and willingness to be open. Here are ways to clear the decks around you so you can focus on a conflict and on resolving it constructively:

1. TAKE A TIME-OUT

There are many instances when the proverbial strategy of counting to ten can come in handy. In some conflicts, you may be so angry you could exacerbate the situation if you confront your co-worker directly at this time. Or you may be unable to discuss a conflict at the moment when she presents it to you because you are on a pressing deadline and can't deal with other distractions. Or she might raise the subject in a public place, and you don't want to bring others in on the argument. Or you are so surprised about what she says, you have no ready response. These are all valid reasons to take a time-out.

To do this, say clearly that you would like to discuss the problem, not now but at another time. Communicate *to the minute* exactly when you will resume the conflict. You might say, for instance, "Beth, can we talk about this problem in fifteen minutes? I need to get this done right now." Or "Why don't we meet in my office at one-thirty so we can resolve this issue?" Be sure to keep your appointment.

Try to avoid the typical vague response of "I can't talk right now. We'll have to deal with this later." Your colleague will likely hear this as a power move, the subtext being "I will determine when we will and will not talk." Because she may perceive your comment as a violation of the Power Dead-Even Rule, she'll only come at you harder and faster, not only now but later, too. If Beth knows exactly when she will have the conversation with you, she's much more likely to back off.

2. MAINTAIN PRIVACY

By airing your grievances in private rather than in public, you can avoid disrupting your office and complicating the issues between you and a colleague by drawing in other people. If you argue in public, you will have an audience, and suddenly it becomes a question of winning or losing face, and neither party is likely to move toward reconciliation.

A public argument can escalate a problem far beyond its original boundaries. In one instance, a long-simmering conflict between two women in the marketing department of a manufacturing company escalated to vicious personal attacks in the middle of the office. One day Robbie, unable to contain her contempt, screamed at her co-worker and cubicle neighbor, Lynne, "The reason your husband is always out of work is because he's a fat, lazy slob."

And Lynne retorted, "Well you're so immature, you still live with your mother!"

All the surrounding staff witnessed this unbridled explosion. Some took sides, and the argument eventually polarized and paralyzed the whole department. Susan, called to mediate, began by lecturing the manager, since Sarah should have intervened before the tension between Robbie and Lynne reached such a fevered pitch. If she was unable to find a collaborative way of making the relationship work, she should have separated the warring parties.

If you begin feeling the heat of an argument building between you and another woman, ask her to come with you to an enclosed space. Look for a room with a door but without an internal window. It's important to conduct an emotion-laden discussion without an audience.

3. NEVER CONDUCT CONFLICT IN WRITING

If you are talking face-to-face with a female colleague about a difficult situation and she begins to react in a negative way, you will likely recognize her nonverbal cues and make an effort to maneuver the conversation into safer waters. You might say, "I'm sorry. I didn't mean for you to take it that way. That sounded more negative than I intended." Even if you're on the phone, you can often hear in a colleague's voice that she responded more negatively than you meant.

But if you communicate a disagreement with a colleague in writing, she can take the conflict in a direction you never imagined. Written communication lacks the nuance of verbal or visual communication. Without subtle signals of tone or facial expression, it's easy to misread a person's true intent. It is therefore imperative to avoid conducting your conflict in writing— and that includes high-tech forms of written communication such as e-mail.

While expediting the exchange of ideas, use of the Internet has also added an extra layer of complexity to conflict resolution, making what was once private quite public. Most of us have had the experience of sending an innocuous e-mail to someone who, unfortunately, takes offense in a way that was never intended. She may counter with a stinging response, copying numerous individuals in the process. People who didn't have to be involved are dragged into the fray. If you reply via e-mail, the conflict can morph into a huge mess.

If you have a bone to pick with someone, you must resist the urge to dash off a quick e-mail stating your complaint. It's difficult because this is just the kind of seemingly direct but actually indirect (you never have to face the person to whom you send the e-mail) communication that women often tend toward and that gets us in trouble. Similarly, if someone sends you an e-mail that pushes your buttons or hits you the wrong way, do *not* dash off a stinging reply. If you feel the need to address the issue, pick up the phone or walk to the office of the person who sent you the e-mail. You might say something like "It sounds as if you're angry about the situation. Is that what you meant? And if so, let's talk about it."

IN THIS CHAPTER we've covered many ways that you can have healthy conflicts with other women—conflicts that don't devolve into catfights—by identifying the kind of conflict you are engaged in, by reducing defensiveness, and by creating a safe, contained environment. In chapter 9, we will continue our discussion of conflicts, this time focusing on conflict styles— the very different ways in which people with different personalities approach dealing with problems. Based on that discussion, we will show you how to deal with certain difficult women—the ones who often cause woman-to-woman catfights.

NINE

HANDLING CONFLICT
WITH STYLE

ONFLICT OCCURS when the needs or concerns of two individuals (including their values, opinions, goals, and behaviors) appear to be incompatible.[1] We often conduct our conflicts using a certain favorite style, one we rely on most of the time and with which we feel the most comfortable, based on our temperament, social skills, and personal predispositions. Some of us tend to collaborate to solve problems and disagreements. Others are more competitive in their conflict resolution. Some of us even acquiesce and/or withdraw when faced with a clash of needs or goals.

Our instinctive style can either help us or hurt us in resolving conflicts, depending on the type of conflict and the style of the person with whom we are in discord. Each way of approaching conflict has its usefulness as well as its limitations. An attitude appropriate for resolving a conflict with your partner might not be as productive when you're at odds with your boss or co-worker. And you'd most likely conduct a conflict with your superior differently than you would with an employee. Because relationships among women in the workplace are especially complex, conflicts can be a breeding ground for sabotage and backbiting.

Fortunately, we're all capable of using different styles at will. So we should be able to change our approach as the situation demands. For instance, if you were a physician, you would likely find yourself gleaning the most successful results in your practice if you were able to use a collaborative style with your patients but a competitive style when demanding services from your patients' HMOs.

Once you understand your own style preferences as well as those of your teammates, and the times these styles would be most effective, your relationships will improve and you may decrease the likelihood of engaging in destructive behavior. In this chapter, you'll determine your preference for conflict style and then take a look at what you can do to maximize its effectiveness or even choose an alternative, more appropriate conflict style depending on the situation and person with whom you are having the disagreement.

Without knowing what the various conflict styles are, answer the following Conflict Styles Questionnaire. This will enable you to comment honestly but also without any foreknowledge that might influence your response.

CONFLICT STYLES QUESTIONNAIRE

Described below are ten workplace situations that could easily instigate a nasty quarrel with another woman. Read each scenario and then decide which of the five options provided best describes how you would normally handle the situation. There are five possible options provided for each incident. Distribute seven points among the five options with your top choice receiving at least four points. Place a circle around the option receiving the most points. (Those options you would never consider will receive no points.)

Example:

The person in the next cubicle speaks too loudly on the phone and drives you batty. You:

_____ a. Don't mention it. After all, she has the right to speak any way she wants.

__1__ b. Avoid being in the area when she is on the phone.

_____ c. Tell her in no uncertain terms to pipe down.

(continues)

__2__ d. Promise to help her on her assignments or do her some other favor if she lowers her voice.

(4) e. Brainstorm with her about what you can both do about the acoustics.

. . .

1. Your job requires that you and others in your department work every other weekend. You were on last weekend. Although you don't have any activities scheduled for the coming weekend, you are looking forward to having the time off. Cynthia, your co-worker, has just approached you and asked if you would work for her next weekend so she can spend time with her new boyfriend. In the past, Cynthia has always been willing to trade shifts with you when you've asked her to cover for you. You:

_____ a. Tell her you'll think about it and then duck whenever she comes around.

_____ b. Agree to change with her even though you really don't want to.

_____ c. Tell her, "Sorry, can't do it. I was looking forward to having next weekend off."

_____ d. Tell her, "I was looking forward to the weekend off, but I'll trade one of the two days with you."

_____ e. Suggest the department get together to develop a system whereby employees who don't mind exchanging weekends can be the first ones approached for swapping. During that meeting, you can bring up Cynthia's dilemma and conjure up weekend coverage for her.

2. You are applying for a job that seems to be perfect. Trouble is, you just found out one of your closest friends has also applied for it. You:

_____ a. Don't mention it to your friend and hope the topic doesn't come up.

_____ b. Talk with her about the situation and try to figure out a way for both of you to get a great job like this.

_____ c. Tell your friend that if she wants you to pull out as a candidate, you will.

_____ d. Agree to pull out of the competition if she will.

_____ e. Expect she'll try to compete for the job just as you will.

3. You and your co-worker, Abby, have just finished a successful project and now must write a report for your joint boss. This report is of secondary importance because your boss has been involved every step of the way. You disagree about how to do this report because you grasp information best if it is laid out in graphics while Abby prefers to process information in narrative form. You:

_____ a. Go ahead with the narrative approach. The report isn't that important.

_____ b. Hang in there and insist on the graphics.

_____ c. Don't talk with her about it.

_____ d. Meet with Abby to see if you can come up with a third way that works for both of you.

_____ e. Suggest that she use narrative form for the part she is doing, while you use graphics for your part.

4. Your boss has just created a new incentive program in your office. For the next month, when customers call in for support services, they will be rating you and your colleagues. The employee with the highest rating will get a free weekend at a luxurious resort. You feel awkward competing with co-workers whom you consider dear friends. You:

_____ a. Keep mum on the issue.

_____ b. Agree to participate but make it clear up-front you won't take the award if you win.

_____ c. Go for it! You'd really enjoy the weekend.

(continues)

_____ d. Talk with your boss about the negative impact you see this having on the team and try to change his mind.

_____ e. Go through the motions but don't put your heart into it.

5. Your boss wants to meet with you to discuss sections she believes you need to add to the report you have written requesting new office equipment. You think this is overkill. You:

_____ a. Do what she tells you to do.

_____ b. Hide from her in hopes she may forget all about it.

_____ c. Meet wtih her to find out why she thinks the added information is necessary and explain your perspective.

_____ d. Let her know that this is wasting your time and ask her to rethink the request.

_____ e. Do as much as she makes you do but not any more than you have to.

6. Cheryl is responsible for coordinating the agenda for a monthly meeting related to a major computer conversion. You have noticed you are always the last to report on what's going on in your area. By then, some members have left the room, and the rest are bored to death and anxious to leave. As a result, your area always gets short shrift. You have heard Cheryl is taking a job with another company in a month. You:

_____ a. Don't bring up the agenda with her.

_____ b. Sit down with her to see if you can come up with another option that meets both your needs.

_____ c. Tell her you are fed up with being last on the agenda and expect this to end.

_____ d. See if you can get her to agree to put you in the first half of the meeting half of the time.

_____ e. Ride it out for the next month.

7. You are working on a project with Felicia. She is quite junior to you and has much less experience but is creative and knowledgeable about the topic. She keeps telling you how the project should be done. Even though it looks very good so far, you are increasingly uncomfortable with Felicia's assertive behavior. You:

_____ a. Allow her to take the lead in the project.

_____ b. Conceal that her approach is bugging you, keep your head down, and hope to get through the project.

_____ c. Divide the project in half, and let her do her part the way she wants.

_____ d. Make it clear you are the senior person and will be calling the shots.

_____ e. Tell her that you value her creativity and knowledge and that you would like to brainstorm ways for both of you to have a positive impact on the project.

8. You know it's not a big deal, but it bugs you that Catherine, a critical member of your support system, who also orders the soft drinks and coffee for the office kitchen, always buys Coke instead of Pepsi. She defiantly states that Coke is superior, but you're a Pepsi fan. When you've talked with her about buying both Coke and Pepsi, she makes lame excuses like "I'd have to go to two sources." You:

_____ a. Don't talk with her about it. It's not worth getting her hackles up.

_____ b. Bring your own Pepsi.

_____ c. Tell her you'll bring up the issue with the office manager if she doesn't address your request.

_____ d. Call a meeting in the department to discuss how supplies are ordered.

_____ e. See if she'll buy Pepsi half the time and Coke half the time.

(continues)

9. You and another manager are sending some employees to a conference. Eileen thinks you should split the cost because your department has a larger training budget. You think she should pay more than you because she's sending more people. You:

_____ a. Let her know that you will not pay for her employees.

_____ b. Sit down with her and brainstorm a variety of approaches for finding additional funding.

_____ c. Agree to split the costs as she wishes.

_____ d. Suggest that your joint boss decide and agree to abide by her decision.

_____ e. You don't mention it, hoping the finance manager will charge her budget for Eileen's employees' attendance.

10. Your department and another are working on a big project. You are all absolutely swamped and up against a tight deadline. There are a lot of thankless tasks associated with the project, and unfortunately the other department is trying to get your department to be responsible for them. You:

_____ a. Propose that your department take on the menial tasks every other week.

_____ b. Don't mention it; it will cause too much conflict.

_____ c. Be the bigger person and take on the work.

_____ d. Clearly state that you will not do the other department's "junk work."

_____ e. Call the employees of both departments together to brainstorm the best solution.

EVALUATING YOUR RESULTS

To determine your conflict style preferences, record the numerical values that you distributed among the five choices for each of the scenarios in the following columns. Some spaces will have zeros. None of the scenarios will equal more than seven points when added horizontally. Circle the response to which you gave the highest score for each scenario. (You'll need this later.) Once you've filled in all the columns, add the numbers vertically in each column and write the total in the area indicated at the bottom.

Example:

The person in the next cubicle speaks too loudly on the phone and drives you batty. You:

_____ a. Don't mention it. After all, she has the right to speak any way she wants.

__1__ b. Avoid being in the area when she is on the phone.

_____ c. Tell her in no uncertain terms to pipe down.

__2__ d. Promise to help her on her assignments or do her some other favor if she lowers her voice.

(4) e. Brainstorm with her what you can both do about the acoustics.

COMPETING	COLLABORATING	AVOIDING	ACCOMMODATING	COMPROMISING
c = 0	e = 4	b = 1	a = 0	d = 2

CONFLICT STYLES SCORECARD

	COMPETING	COLLABORATING	AVOIDING	ACCOMMODATING	COMPROMISING
1.	c =	e =	a =	b =	d =
2.	e =	b =	a =	c =	d =
3.	b =	d =	c =	a =	e =
4.	c =	d =	a =	e =	b =
5.	d =	c =	b =	a =	e =
6.	c =	b =	a =	e =	d =

(continues)

7.	d =	e =	b =	a =	c =
8.	c =	d =	a =	b =	e =
9.	a =	b =	e =	c =	d =
10.	d =	e =	b =	c =	a =

Totals

_____ _____ _____ _____ _____
Competing   Collaborating   Avoiding   Accommodating Compromising

The highest totals represent your preferred styles for managing conflict situations. If you score 20 or above in any one of the styles, this may indicate a problem as you may tend to use this one style in most situations, including some in which it would not be the most functional. If you scored low on a style (10 or less), you may be avoiding this style and not using it when it would be most effective. If you scored rather evenly across all the styles, you tend to vary your approach.

THE FIVE CONFLICT STYLES

As you have noticed from answering the questionnaire, the options listed for each scenario fall into one of the five categories of conflict style: competing, collaborating, avoiding, accommodating, and compromising. These categories were identified by Kenneth W. Thomas, professor of management at the Naval Postgraduate School in Monterey, California, and Ralph H. Kilmann, professor of organization and management at the University of Pittsburgh.

Let's look at these styles and their applications more closely.

COMPETING: "MIGHT MAKES RIGHT"

Competing is an assertive and uncooperative conflict style. This is a power-oriented mode in which you tend to stand up for your rights, defend a position you believe is correct, or simply try to win and have your own way. The competing individual pursues her own concerns at the expense of another by sometimes using force, pulling rank, exerting coercive power, or arguing.[2] When you're competing, you're unwilling to relinquish your goals for any reason. Conflict resolution becomes a take-it-or-leave-it, win-lose proposition—negotiation is not an option.

A woman who adopts a competing style with other women may, under certain circumstances, be perceived as violating the Power Dead-Even Rule, and it is for this reason that many women eschew it. When competing, you're essentially saying, "My ideas are better than yours," or "My needs are more important than yours." When a woman appears too confident, aggressive, selfish, or self-serving (which can be characteristics of the competing style), other females often see her behavior as a violation of the Power Dead-Even Rule, particularly if this woman tends to advance her own agenda instead of that of the group.

Competing certainly has its proper place, however. Not all competing behavior is odious to women, and sometimes a win-win resolution is impossible. A competing conflict style may enable a woman to see to it that her ideas are implemented for the sake of attaining a team goal and making a project the best it can be. When decisive action is called for in a bottom-line situation, the ability to use the competing style effectively is definitely a leadership plus. If you're going after a great job, an incentive-linked bonus, or the last seat available on an airplane, you may have no choice but to compete. And if you're dealing with someone who predominantly uses this style, you might need to adopt a competitive style just to be heard.

Competing can be useful:

- When you need to take quick, decisive action, as in emergencies or when time is of the essence

- When your department needs a big win

- On important issues in which you must take unpopular actions like cutting costs, dismissing employees, disciplining, or imposing rules

- When you know you are right about issues that are critical to your or your organization's interests

- To defend against people who exploit cooperative behavior

Competing might have been the most appropriate conflict style in Scenario 2 in the Conflict Styles Questionnaire, for instance—the situation in which you and a best friend are vying for the same position. In the business world, it is important that women apply for situations that advance their careers. If not, men will be the only ones landing the dream jobs. Unfortunately, sometimes that means good friends will contend for the same job. If you find yourself in this conflict, it may be best to apply for the position and then talk with your close friend about the dilemma it poses. In order to avoid a violation of the Power Dead-Even Rule, the winner must be gracious and, perhaps somewhere down the road, assist the loser in obtaining her own dream assignment.

There are drawbacks to using competing as your dominant conflict style. Ask yourself if you are surrounded by "yes" men and women. Perhaps they are compliant because they've learned it's unwise to disagree with you, and they've simply given up trying to influence you. Unfortunately, this can insulate you from receiving vital information and alternative viewpoints. Your employees may also fear admitting ignorance or uncertainties to you. In competitive climates, people fight for influence and respect, often pretending to be confident when they're not. Employees trapped in this situation can feel less able to ask for information or outside opinions, thereby cutting off avenues for growth and learning that could benefit the whole department.

COLLABORATING: "TWO HEADS ARE BETTER THAN ONE"

A collaborative approach to conflict involves your attempt to work with another person to find solutions that fully satisfy both of you. You might seek out new alternatives and solutions in brainstorming sessions together. When collaborating, you and another party might explore a disagreement to learn from each other's insights, resolve a condition that could have otherwise pitted you against each other for resources, or find a creative solution to an interpersonal problem.[3]

In addition to preserving and strengthening the self-esteem of everyone involved in the conflict, collaborating preserves relationships. Consequently it is one of the preferred conflict styles for women.

Collaborating can be useful:

- When you need to find a mutual solution if conflicting interests are too important to be conceded or ignored

- If you need to gain another person's buy-in by including her issues in a consensus you've crafted together

- If you want to build relationships by understanding others' perspectives or resolving animosities

- When you want to combine ideas from people with varied views

Collaboration might have been the best conflict style to have chosen in Scenario 5 of the Conflict Styles Questionnaire: your boss wants you to add sections to a report, but you feel this is a waste of time. Having a discussion with her about the issue may generate payoffs for both of you. Sharing perspectives with your boss could increase your understanding of how she thinks and her appreciation of your thought processes. This can help build your rapport and the relationship. Besides, when you combine your ideas, the resulting report can be all the better for it.

Collaboration does have its downside, however, especially if it's your only way of dealing with conflicts. It can require lots of time and energy, and you may find yourself discussing issues in depth that do not deserve this kind of attention. Trivial problems don't require optimal solutions; involving everyone in a decision can bog down the process. In addition, others may perceive an overuse of collaboration as your desire to minimize risk or an unwillingness to take responsibility. You may come across as being tentative and exploratory. And in order for collaborating to be effective, both parties have to choose the same style—you can't collaborate with someone who only wants to compete with you. Sometimes your collaborative behavior may fail to elicit the other party's response in kind. When you insist on collaboration, you may miss cues indicating defensiveness, strong feelings, impatience, competitiveness, or conflicting interests.

Avoiding: "Leave Well Enough Alone"

Avoiding is the opposite of collaborating. Avoiding conflict means you fail to pursue immediately your own concerns as well as those of the person with whom you are in conflict. You neither address nor resolve a conflict but rather overlook it, pass the buck, go into hiding, or stall. This all sounds very negative, but avoiding might take the positive form of diplomatically side-stepping a conflict, postponing an issue for a more propitious moment, or withdrawing from a potentially threatening situation.[4] It can be quite useful if a relationship is vital whereas the conflict is trivial.

Avoiding can be useful:

- When you believe a concern is relatively insignificant or when other, more pressing issues loom

- When your cause is hopeless and you believe you're wasting your time. For example, you may be frustrated by situations you have little power to change such as national policies, someone's personality, or directives from on high.

- When the benefits of a confrontation aren't worth the damage it might do

- When tempers are too hot and people need time to regain perspective and composure. Postponing a conflict can reduce tension so that your department returns to a productive level.

- When you don't have enough information and must put the problem on hold until you have the facts in place

- When you're less well equipped to resolve the conflict than others

- When the problem is only a symptom of a larger issue

Avoiding is the most appropriate conflict style in Scenario 6 of the Conflict Styles Questionnaire, the one in which your area report is always relegated to last during the monthly meetings. Cheryl, the agenda scheduler, will be gone before the next discussion. There is no point in creating conflict and defensiveness, because she will no longer be the one making those decisions. When you pass her in the hallway, wish her success in her new job. But be sure to ask the new person taking over her duties for how much time you'd like to be accorded. It's important that you represent your area at the meeting and that others hear your group's concerns and issues.

If avoiding is your dominant conflict style, you may find small issues can escalate when you don't deal with them. And decisions made by default (because you haven't confronted them) can limit your success and the productivity of your organization. Also, if you gravitate toward avoiding, others may have trouble getting your input. They won't know where you stand or how best to work with you because they can't glean enough information from you to be effective. They may feel they're pulling teeth to ascertain your opinions or concerns and may eventually stop asking you for your contribution.

If you tend toward avoiding and hold a leadership position, it may also appear that your employees are tiptoeing around an elephant in the middle of the room; sometimes a dysfunctional amount of energy can be devoted to steering clear of pressing difficulties. Your coordination of tasks and productivity can suffer. You may feel harried and overwhelmed by the sheer volume of unfinished business that keeps piling up. In that case, you'll need to devote more time to setting priorities. Decide which issues are unimportant and delegate them. Finally, when you avoid conflict you must ask yourself whether you have crossed into passive-aggressive behavior; that is, refusing to confront someone whom you perceive as having hurt you, but retaliating behind her back instead by clamming up, being terse and unhelpful in interactions, using stalling tactics, or other forms of indirect aggression.

Accommodating: "Kill Your Enemies with Kindness"

Accommodating is the opposite of competing, as a person who is accommodating can be submissive and compliant. In fact, she may neglect her own concerns to satisfy those of a person with whom she is in conflict. The accommodating mode incorporates an element of self-sacrifice, taking the form of selfless generosity or charity, obeying another person's order when you would prefer to do otherwise, or yielding to a viewpoint in opposition to your own.[5]

Accommodating on minor issues enhances goodwill. Admitting you're wrong and conceding a point give others permission to do so too.

Accommodating can be useful:

- When you're wrong. Owning up to this will gain you power chips in future conflicts.

- When the outcome matters more to the person with whom you are in disagreement than to you

- To build up power chips for other issues that may be more important to you in the future

- When you know you're going to lose, and additional conflict will only hurt you

- When preserving harmony and avoiding disruption are especially important

- To help your employees develop by letting them take the lead and learn from mistakes that aren't too damaging

Accommodating is a good choice in the first scenario of the Conflict Styles Questionnaire. Cynthia has always been willing to trade weekends with you, so now would be a good time to be supportive and give her some chips. Consequently, you agree to change weekends with her, even though you don't want to. Besides, if you refuse to cover for her without a good excuse, you may lose her as an ally in the future.

The downside to accommodating can be that your ideas and concerns don't get the attention they deserve. Continually deferring to others' concerns can deprive you of influence, respect, and recognition. It also robs your organization of your potential contributions. Many women default to accommodating because they were brought up to be nice and get along. However, if accommodating is your predominant style, it can lead to a permanent decrease in your power and self-esteem. If you are constantly helping others reach their goals at the expense of your own, you could be seen as a martyr, or you could lose your personal boundaries. The balance in power will be skewed, and you may perceive everyone else as more valuable than you are. That, in turn, could lead to resentment and injurious behavior.

Moreover, being overly accommodating can lead to lax discipline. Rules, procedures, and assignments are crucial for you and your organization. It is important that there be consistency in how you carry out policies and procedures.

Compromising: "Split the Difference"

Compromising falls between competing and accommodating. Your objective in compromising is to explore the difficulties on each side of an issue and then work together to find an expedient, mutually acceptable solution that partially satisfies both parties. It's a form of sharing. You've each made your positions known. It's a question not of either side dominating or retreating but of exchanging concessions—I'll give in on A if you give in on B—because you realize that continuing to disagree will not further your cause. It might mean splitting the difference or seeking a middle ground.[6]

Neither party gets all that she wants, but you're each willing to back down for the sake of reaching an accord. Compromising helps in building trust and keeping open lines of communication. It also helps you to stay focused on the big picture because you are attuned to both sides' needs. This adheres to the Power Dead-Even Rule. Neither party wins big and gets everything she wants, but both believe they get something, and it's perceived as even. Compared to collaboration, compromising can be a more expedient way to move ahead. You split the difference and move on.

Compromising can be useful:

- When the outcome doesn't matter that much to you, and compromise avoids additional conflict

- You and your opponent have the same clout and are strongly committed to diametrically opposed positions as in labor and management or real estate buyer/seller negotiations

- When you want to get a quick, provisional resolution to complicated issues

- If you haven't been able to resolve your issues using collaboration or competition

Compromising would be an effective style for managing the potential conflict in Scenario 3 of the Conflict Styles Questionnaire. Because the report can be easily divided, allowing you to play with the graphics and Abby to write the narrative, there's no reason to seek a more complex or divisive resolution.

As with the other conflict styles, however, there are drawbacks to emphasizing compromise over other approaches. For instance, you will need to be mindful of your bottom line and how much you're willing to give up. If not, you may come away from a compromise feeling as if you've gotten a raw deal. This can cause resentment and prompt a squabble.

Moreover, you may concentrate so heavily on the practicalities and tactics of compromise that you lose sight of the principles, values, and long-term objectives of your cause. A heavy reliance on bargaining and trading can create a cynical climate of gamesmanship that can undermine interpersonal trust and deflect attention from the merits of issues under consideration.

If a relationship is important, compromise might be less advisable than collaboration or accommodation because it has greater potential to damage relationships. For instance, returning to Scenario 1 of the Conflict Styles Questionnaire, if you offered Cynthia only Saturday rather than both weekend days, she might be offended, feeling that she had traded you whole weekends whenever you requested them in the past. She might consider evening the score, refusing to accommodate to your needs the next time you asked to trade a weekend. In other situations, however, such as when you're closing a real estate transaction and will most likely never see the buyers or sellers after the deal is completed and therefore don't have a great investment in the relationship, compromise might be the best strategy.

Your Colleague Quotient

None of these conflict preferences exists in a vacuum: among co-workers, the interaction of various styles can give rise to secondary conflicts. For example, if you prefer to avoid conflict but you're working on a project with a person who favors competing, your very good ideas may never get implemented. Often women prefer the avoiding style. But a joint project executed by two female colleagues who both have such a penchant may turn out to be mediocre because neither has spoken up to challenge the other's limited ideas. Conflict styles can create their own problems if we're unaware of them; we need to choose overtly which is the best style for a given situation.

Many people use only one or two styles when embroiled in difficult situations. But flexibility to switch in and out of various styles has an impact on how effective others perceive you to be. An effective colleague deals with conflict situations in a thoughtful and forthright manner and doesn't waste much time in destructive gossip. When conflicts arise with a co-worker, she takes into account the ramifications as far as her long-term association with that person is concerned. She respects others, and they respect her. She preserves her own and her co-workers' self-esteem. She recognizes that many times it is worthwhile to collaborate. However, occasionally, especially in time-bound situations or those in which the issue is unimportant, she understands that collaboration takes too long, and she may take a competing or accommodating style.

The following score sheet will help you ascertain how effective and adaptable you are as a colleague in choosing a situation-appropriate conflict management style based on your responses to the questionnaire that opens this chapter. With this new knowledge, you can more easily determine which styles you may want to develop for future use.

Your Colleague Quotient

Go back to the Conflict Styles Scorecard on p. 219. Find your circled response to each scenario—the one that received the most points—and transfer the corresponding letter to the "Option Selected" column below. If, for example, you gave your highest score (4 or above) to option "e," to Scenario 2, write "e" in the Option Selected column.

Now look at the right-hand columns where we have assigned a particular value to selected answers. From the example below, you can see that if you chose "e," you would score 2 points. If you chose "d" you would receive 1 point. Any of the other possibilities would give you no points. Write the new point value in the middle column called "Number of Points Earned."

(continues)

Here's how the scoring would work with our original example:

The person in the next cubicle speaks too loudly on the phone and drives you batty. You:

_____ a. Don't mention it. After all, she has the right to speak any way she wants.

__1__ b. Avoid being in the area when she is on the phone.

_____ c. Tell her in no uncertain terms to pipe down.

__2__ d. Promise to help her on her assignments or do her some other favor if she lowers her voice.

(4) e. Brainstorm with her about what you can both do about the acoustics problem.

Scenario	Option Selected	Number of Points Earned	(either 2, 1, or 0)
Example:	e	2	e = 2 points; d = 1 point

After you've transferred your answers and assigned them a new point value, total up your points to determine your score.

Scenario	Option Selected	Number of Points Earned	(either 2, 1, or 0)
1.	_____	_____	b = 2 points; e = 1 point
2.	_____	_____	e = 2 points; b = 1 point
3.	_____	_____	e = 2 points; a = 1 point
4.	_____	_____	c = 2 points; d = 1 point
5.	_____	_____	c = 2 points; a = 1 point
6.	_____	_____	a = 2 points; e = 1 point
7.	_____	_____	a = 2 points; e = 1 point

8.	_____ _____	a = 2 points; b = 1 point
9.	_____ _____	b = 2 points; d = 1 point
10.	_____ _____	a = 2 points; e = 1 point

Total Points Earned _____ (20 points maximum)

See Appendix B for an answer key and the rationale behind which choices are the most effective.

EVALUATING YOUR SCORE

Now here's how to interpret your Colleague Quotient score. If your total points earned were:

16–20, you're in the stratosphere! You have an uncanny and rare ability to appropriately utilize the various conflict management styles. Keep up the outstanding work in dealing effectively and professionally when conflict arises.

11–15, excellent! You are well versed in your ability to use conflict management styles depending on the difficult situations you face. You sense which approach would be the best for resolving the conflict in a productive manner while continuing to preserve your important relationships.

6–10, very good! You are more effective than some professionals at resolving conflict; however, you could use some improvement in this important area of communication. You probably have intermittent success in dealing with conflict situations with your co-workers. When clashes arise, it is critical to think carefully about the ramifications when it comes to your long-term relationship with that colleague. An important part of successful conflict management is taking into account your self-esteem and that of your colleague. Continue to practice the various styles of conflict management and you will become more versatile and effective in developing collegial relationships with other professional women in your life.

5 or less points, danger! You may be embroiled in catfights and may even be unaware of how many. You may be avoiding and accommodating conflict to the point that your own needs are never met, or you may try to approach each situation by collaborating, when this may not be the most effective style. Start today to study the different styles of conflict management and practice them.

CONFLICT WITH DIFFICULT WOMEN

Even if you have mastered the appropriate, situational use of conflict styles and are a good colleague, it is possible that you will have the misfortune of crossing paths with someone who is terrible at conflict resolution because she uses the styles inappropriately. Imagine, for instance, that you've asked Heidi to take more responsibility for a project than she'd originally agreed to. She really doesn't want this extra work, but because she is habituated to an accommodating conflict style, she goes along with your suggestion without a peep. On the surface it seems as if your problem is solved, but actually it's just starting. Since Heidi believes she has given in when she shouldn't have (a better approach for her might have been to compete, collaborate, or compromise), she begins to feel resentful.

Predictably, at this point, the conflict goes awry. The Power Dead-Even Rule has been called into play, as Heidi feels indignant at the imposition of your will (i.e., power) on her. Because she is uncomfortable confronting you, her passive-aggressive behavior can emerge in the form of a catfight; she says nothing to you but gossips about you to your co-workers to balance the power chips. Her tactics may confuse you, especially if she has perfected the tools of indirect aggression that she learned so well as a child.

The woman you're struggling with may be less inclined to engage in head-on competitive conflicts but rather may fall into one of several categories according to her style: the gossip, the sniper, the clam,[7] the saboteur, the kitchen-sink fighter, the cabal queen, and the superbitch. By recognizing the tactics and hidden conflict style of your co-worker, you can identify and better manage any negative interactions with her.

Bear in mind that in each case, the strategy she uses holds some kind of payoff for the woman who engages in it. Much as it's tempting to think she's just an awful human being, remember that catfights take energy, and no one expends energy without expecting some benefit from it. For instance, although Heidi did not use an avoiding conflict style when she agreed to take more responsibility for the project (in fact, she used an accommodating style in the way she approached her conflict with you) her purpose and ultimately her payoff were to do damage but sidestep the consequences of her actions. With her destructive gossip, she sought to tear you down without your knowledge or the wrath that was sure to follow. Destructive gossip, sniping, clamming up, and sabotaging are a difficult woman's primary tools to diminish your power and self-esteem.

Let's look at each type of difficult woman:

THE GOSSIP

One of our correspondents wrote to us about her experiences at the hands of a gossip:

> I shared an office with an extremely competitive woman. She had two faces: One face was very supportive and helpful, but the other face used whatever information she received to enhance her position and make others look bad. As time wore on, I caught her telling untrue stories about me and other women in the organization.

How do you know if you're up against a destructive gossip? She attacks from behind, rarely to your face. She's often quite glib. If confronted, she will hide and act as if she has done nothing. In her attempt to build allies, she will talk negatively about you to co-workers but then behave as if she's your friend. Her payoff: She doesn't have to confront you directly. Although, like our correspondent's co-worker, she may be truly competitive at heart, her dominant conflict style seems to be that of avoiding as she will not confront directly.

THE SNIPER

A sniper will hide out in a crowd and work assiduously at getting others to take you less seriously by using rational-appearing indirect aggression (see chapter 5). For instance, if you're giving a presentation in a meeting, a sniper might say, "Ha, ha, ha. What an unusual idea. I've never seen anything like that." You can tell this is a put-down just from the way she has phrased her words.

So you respond, "You don't like what I'm recommending?"

"I didn't say that. I just thought it was so *unusual*."

One of our correspondents wrote to us about her experience with a sniping boss who, using a competitive mode of conflict, made no bones about directing frontal attacks at her:

> I had a female supervisor who had a penchant for making state-ments about me that I perceived as humiliating in front of me *and* my staff. I was always so taken aback that I didn't defend myself, feeling the less said, the sooner forgotten by all. Even-tually I was promoted to another position away from her. Shortly thereafter, I was in a meeting with quite a few other managers— and her—and she made a very derogatory (and unnecessary) re-mark about my department.

The sniper tries to get the rest of the group to invalidate your ideas as well, using all kinds of nonverbal cues like rolling her eyes, snickering, winking, and elbowing a colleague for agreement. Part of her strategy is to sway the group to go along with her ridicule. Sniping gives her more power while reducing yours; she feels as if she is controlling what's happening to you. Whether or not she attacks you directly, her payoff is to diminish you.

THE CLAM

A manager senses that Lisa, one of her employees, is unhappy. She gets the impression that Lisa is interviewing elsewhere. In order to ascertain what's going on, she calls Lisa into her office and asks, "Is everything going okay?"

"Sure, fine."

"Are you happy here?"

"Yeah."

"Is there anything you need from me?"

"No."

That's how a conversation proceeds with a clam—no information is shared, and there's little give-and-take in the interaction. The individual's facial expression is often clearly inconsistent with her words: she doesn't smile even though she says she's happy. She says she's "fine" when she really doesn't seem fine at all. She is apparently using an avoiding conflict style, but her mixed message is crazy-making for her manager. Women sometimes become clams when they want to communicate that something is wrong but they don't want to say what the problem is. They want you to care about the relationship so much that you can read their minds. Unfortunately, if you can't (and who can?), this provides them with ammunition for increased resentment.

The clam's lack of interrelatedness renders you awkward and ill at ease, throwing you off your game. In the process, she may conceal valuable information from you, even if it only relates to her state of mind. The reward for the clam is a feeling of being in control by withholding normal interaction from you. This increases her power and decreases yours.

The Saboteur

The saboteur will try to demoralize you any way she can, stealthily attacking your self-assurance or aggressively throwing obstacles in your path to success. She can disable your computer by willfully sending you a virus, refuse to pass along important messages, conveniently lose reports that must be filed on time, or undermine your good standing with your boss by making subtly derogatory statements such as "Candace? Haven't seen her all day. You know, I frequently have trouble finding her."

The saboteur uses a competing conflict style. In her mind, her needs supersede yours. Her payoff is to prevent you from succeeding by destroying your reputation or your output, thereby leveling the playing field.

The Kitchen-Sink Fighter

The kitchen-sink fighter uses a direct, competing style to turn any complaint you might have in a work situation into a complaint *against* you. For example, in the middle of a conflict about her failure to produce a report on time, Samantha may try to divert you with: "But you came to the meeting late last month, you didn't tell me my fax had arrived last Wednesday, and you didn't inform me that the corporate VP is coming next week for a site visit. . . ." She stores up a kitchen sinkful of past transgressions large and small, and then dumps them all on you in an effort to divert attention from her mistakes.

Her payoff is to avoid addressing any wrongs she may have committed by taking an offensive rather than a defensive position. She is trying desperately to keep intact her self-esteem and power.

The Cabal Queen

The cabal queen can use a variety of the preceding techniques to create disruption for a woman who she believes violated the Power Dead-Even Rule. Her goal is to draw as many people as possible onto her side in a conflict with another woman so as to inflict the greatest damage on her opponent while heightening her own sense of power and self-esteem.

At a large social-work agency, Stella, a newly hired supervisor, became embroiled in a clash with one of her case managers. Stella was a perfectionist who felt insecure in her new position, and so she took to carefully monitoring the work of her staff. This approach offended one of the case managers, Jane, who had worked at this agency for ten years. She felt she was being micromanaged and she was angry that Stella didn't respect her experience and expertise.

Enraged at what she perceived as Stella's violation of the Power Dead-Even Rule (Stella's assertion of power was making Jane feel that her own power was diminished), she began to give incomplete bits of information—just enough to respond to Stella's questions, but not enough for her to supervise appropriately. Then Jane solicited support from the other case managers. She talked negatively about Stella and told stories about her personal life. Soon the other case managers joined forces with Jane in undermining Stella's authority, rolling their eyes and winking at one another in meetings, clamming up, and generally making Stella's life miserable.

At first, Jane's behavior served as a complaint about her treatment at Stella's hands; later it became fun for her as she gained power by rallying her co-workers. Jane had metamorphosed into the informal leader of the agency; whenever Stella would give direction during a staff meeting, the rest of the staff would look to Jane for her reaction. In this win-lose situation, Jane was the victor.

Whereas a gossip does her damage privately one co-worker at a time, the cabal queen brings together many people to diminish the standing of her adversary. Jane's is just one example of cabal queen behavior. Other cabal queens instigate work slowdowns and sick-outs or department-wide refusals to put in overtime. Unlike the gossip or the saboteur, the cabal queen may not desire anonymity. Because most of the co-workers involved could name who's behind all the trouble, a cabal queen would derive power from being acknowledged as the agitator. She uses her informal sway over the group to deplete the power of her target—that's her payoff.

The Superbitch

This is a rare kind of difficult woman, but one who looms large if she's in your life because of her capacity to be destructive. She is manipulative in a conniving way behind the scenes, and if that doesn't work, she becomes overtly controlling and hostile. She blames when it's her fault and takes credit when it's not her due. She tends to be self-centered, to the point of seeming narcissistic: interactions, concerns, and attention revolve around her and her needs at the expense of her co-workers. This type of prima donna uses honeyed phrases and behavior if she wants something from you and is actually extremely socially competent and astute. However, should you cross her by denying her exactly what she demands, she may suddenly turn on you in a destructive rage in a way that can leave you shocked and immobilized.

Mia told us a story about her latest encounter with a superbitch at her company. Mia had just given birth to her first child and was home on maternity leave. A week and a half into her leave, she got a call from Gwen, a woman executive who was not her boss but who had significant power in the organization. Gwen told Mia, "You have to come in tomorrow for a critical meeting with our client."

Mia, thinking that Gwen had forgotten her situation, began to explain, "But Jake is only ten days old. I'm still recuperating, and I'm pretty exhausted."

That didn't seem to stop Gwen. "You have to be here. It's not optional."

"Why don't you talk to Ginger about it?" Mia countered, thinking her boss would come to her defense.

"I've already spoken to her, and she agrees," Gwen said curtly. End of conversation.

Mia hung up the phone and burst into tears. She was at a loss, because her boss had apparently been included in this decision. She pulled herself together and managed to make the meeting. But when she got to the office, she was vexed to discover Ginger's shock at seeing her. Gwen had lied to her about approaching Ginger—that conversation had never taken place.

The superbitch can be found at lofty levels in organizations, especially those that focus only on the bottom line. She is able to deliver the numbers, but she can leave a wide swat of bodies in her path. Often the superbitch provokes passive-aggressive behavior in female co-workers because they are afraid to confront so powerful and destructive a force—even in women who normally pride themselves on dealing directly with issues and avoiding catfights. The superbitch's payoff is getting her way, and often she is successful.

How to Defuse Specific Types of Difficult Women

Most of the difficult women we described above feel somehow justified in their misbehavior, whether it's Lisa clamming up or Jane fomenting a cabal, they are reacting to real or perceived violations of the Power Dead-Even Rule. (The superbitch, in contrast, is blind to the Power Dead-Even Rule because she believes the world revolves around her.) However, just because these women feel their behavior is making things "right" between you doesn't mean you have to put up with it if you feel it's actually hurting you. There are ways to contain and control destructive behavior based on the conflict-styles model we presented in the first half of this chapter. The key is first to identify the payoff this woman is seeking through her actions, and then actively to deny her that payoff. The following are some specifics that can help you defuse difficult women and put a stop to their attacks.

Silencing the Gossip

Many women, when faced with dealing with a gossip, will say, "I'm just not going to honor her remarks with my time and energy. What she's saying is untrue anyway, so why should I address it?" Unfortunately, this avoiding style allows the gossip to continue doing damage. In dealing with a gossip, it's usually best to air the conflict. Open the lines of communication in a nonthreatening way by first asking her if there's a problem between you. Your strategy is to get in the gossip's face, but in an appropriate way. Since her payoff in gossiping is doing damage to you without having to own up to her behavior, your goal is to eliminate that payoff by bringing her actions out in the open.

Bring up the remarks you believe originated with the gossip, and then ask her if it's *possibly* true that she said these things about you behind your back. Be sure to pose this as a tentative question—as in "possibly true"—not a statement like "I have twelve witnesses." Giving her an out with the word *possibly* will help to defuse her defensiveness.

She will probably still be defensive, though, and will say something like "Oh no, I'd never say that about you." If so, counter by thanking her with "I'm so glad, because I would hope that if you had a problem with me or anything about me, you would come and talk with me directly."

Don't expect this to solve the problem instantly. Before long, you will probably again be hearing that she has been talking behind your back. Again, you must get in her face with the same strategy. Expect the cycle to repeat several times. Over the long haul, she will learn that if she talks about you, it will get back to you, and you will confront her. This is exactly what the gossip wants to avoid, and it will gradually help extinguish her behavior.

Disarming the Sniper

The best way to deal with a sniper who uses group dynamics to undermine you is to enlist the aid of the group to reduce the sniper's power. If a sniper ambushes you during a meeting, you might say, "Vicki, I'm sensing that Joan has a problem with what I'm recommending. What do you think about my suggestions? How about you, Bob?" Faced with individual feedback from group members, the sniper is no longer able to hide out among them, and you have denied her the hit-and-run payoff she seeks.

Prying Open the Clam

To deny the clam's payoff of controlling the conversation and thereby exerting power over you, your global strategy should be to find ways to get her to talk. Take her away from the office environment, perhaps by going out to lunch or for coffee. Removed from familiar surroundings and sitting down with you one-on-one with no ringing phones or other distractions, she'll find it more difficult to be quiet. During your conversation, be sure to pose open-ended questions that begin with "What?" "Where?" "When?" "How?" "Who?" These are difficult to answer with a monosyllabic "yes" or "no." Rather than asking "How is your job going?" which might elicit a short "Fine," which you know you can't trust, you might inquire:

- "What do you like about your job?"

- "What's one thing that you would change about your job to make it more rewarding or interesting?"

- "Where do you want to go in this company?"

When soliciting this input, use an expectant stare, looking at your colleague with your lips slightly parted instead of pursed. This is a nonverbal technique that encourages give-and-take conversation. If the clam doesn't respond right away, don't rescue her by throwing out another question or suggesting your own answers to the original ones you posed. Just continue to look at her inquiringly. If the conversation continues to be strained, talk about the sparse dialogue. You might say, for instance, "I have a sense that something is not being said here, and I don't know what it is. I believe it's a problem and I think we need to talk about it. Is it something I've done?"

If you still cannot loose a gush of information from the clam, continue your efforts by saying something like "I don't know why I feel this way, but I really believe there is something wrong between us. It's important to me that we talk about it if there's a problem." Be sure to make the problem about you so that she doesn't become defensive. "Was it what I said in the meeting last week?" When you ask questions about yourself, you are essentially shrinking your own power while potentially increasing the other woman's self-esteem. Also, your show of interest can help balance a power deficit between you.

There are some clams who, despite your best efforts, will simply continue to withhold. In these cases, you may need to say, "I've done all I can in this situation. I value our relationship, so when you're ready to talk with me, I'll be available."

Confronting the Saboteur

Like the gossip, the saboteur must be dealt with head-on because her pay-off is to hit and run. When you reveal to the saboteur that you're on to her game, she will have a harder time concealing her destructive behavior. Go to the saboteur and tell her what you've seen her do to hurt you, when and where. Explain how you perceive the negative consequences of her actions, for instance: "Because you didn't give me those messages, I missed a meeting that's vital for our department's budget. I had planned to propose new computers for all of us." Then ask for her input. She will most likely deny the sabotage and say you're imagining things.

In order to deny her the payoff she seeks of undermining your success and power, you will need to repeat this process of confrontation until she realizes she can't get away with sabotaging behavior without your challenging her. If the sabotage continues unabated, you may need to discuss it with one of your higher-ups. Rather than tattling, ask your boss for advice on how to curb such behavior.

For long-term damage control with a saboteur, you'd be wise to develop a relationship with such a woman by building her power and self-esteem through appropriate chip management (see chapter 6). This may be very uncomfortable at first, especially because you believe the saboteur has done you wrong, and so it may seem self-defeating to look for ways to make her feel better about herself. But if you don't follow up with positive Power Dead-Even activities, you may find yourself in the same sabotage situation all over again—which wastes your time and energy.

Cleaning Up the Kitchen-Sink Fighter

Your overriding strategy with the kitchen-sink fighter is to deal with the issue at hand and not allow her to ensnare you in tangential arguments that she thinks she can win. Her payoff is evading the consequences of her actions, but by holding her to the issue at hand, you don't allow her to wiggle off the hook. For instance, if you are having a problem with Samantha about a late report and she counters your discussion of the issue by complaining about your tardiness for a meeting and the way you forgot to tell her about the VP's visit, make an effort to acknowledge the additional topics she has mentioned but bring her back to the issue at hand. You might say, "Samantha, I understand that you need to talk about my lateness and Charlie's visit, but right now let's focus on the late report."

Bear in mind that if you don't recognize the other issues, she will keep pointing them out. If she continues to pile it on, you could reiterate, "We'll talk about those issues as well, but right now I want to deal with the report that came in late."

One tactic that works well with a kitchen-sink fighter is to write down all the distractions she raises. You might say, "I've jotted down these other problems so we won't forget them, but let's get back to the topic at hand." She may back off since you've so clearly demonstrated that you've listened to what she was saying. You may or may not need to come back to them later.

DETHRONING THE CABAL QUEEN

Because a cabal queen gleans power from the group, your first challenge is to identify the instigator. If you feel an entire group of people has formed a coalition against you, observe the group's behavior during meetings. Does one person do most of the talking and send the lion's share of the negative signals you feel are directed against you? Do the others all look to her for approval after making an underhanded comment or gesture?

Once you've identified the disgruntled individual, separate her from her power base. Meet with her one-on-one to unearth and resolve the issues that are undermining the relationship. As in the case of the gossip and saboteur, you'll need to confront the cabal queen about her behavior. Tell her what you've seen her do to hurt you, when and where. Explain how you perceive the negative consequences of her actions. Ask for her input. She may deny your perceptions and claim that you're imagining things, but don't be deterred. You may need to repeat these confrontations until the cabal queen ceases her provocative and agitating behavior and the group falls back into line.

If these steps prove ineffective (because the cabal queen now has so much power and may be unwilling to relinquish it), it might be advisable to call in a mediator to work first with the two of you and then, if need be, with the whole group to establish team standards (see chapter 11).

Containing the Superbitch

The superbitch's payoff is to control and get her way. Because she is such a destructive force, if you're thinking about working with her, and you have a choice in the matter (like volunteering to work on her committee), you might reconsider. Here is one situation where avoiding may be an excellent style. We have spoken to many women who have quit their jobs or transferred to other divisions to get away from such a virago. If you leave her sphere of influence, she can't control you.

But if you're stuck with a superbitch in your life, follow the first rule of swimming with sharks: Don't bleed. That is, don't let on to her that she's getting to you. It will only feed her attacks. Do not try to fight back in kind by being as vicious as she seems to be—she is a world-class combatant with lots of experience, and you're bound to lose if you're new to this game. Rather, your strategy should be to establish your limits and stand up to her within the context of what you believe to be right. Mia, for instance, might have told Gwen, "I know you need me to come in tomorrow, but it's simply impossible. I will speak to Ginger about this, and let her know that despite my desire to attend the meeting, I just don't have the wherewithal yet."

From this point on, you would be wise to watch your back. You know what you're dealing with. You might want to verify the truthfulness of any other statements or demands she makes. And be ready to parry a frontal attack in the future, because it's sure to come.

Principles for Managing Conflictual Situations

Conflicts in the workplace aren't just limited to people who use techniques like the ones we've described above. There is a whole range of conflict-inducing situations that are beyond the confines of this book—about the best way to manage employees, about differing work habits (some people are notoriously punctual whereas others always stretch deadlines), about how to make strategic decisions, about who gets credit for what, and on and on.

But there are some general rules for resolving conflicts that you can use regardless of the style of the person you're having a problem with and re-gardless of your own predominant conflict style. There are basically three options for dealing with conflict. You can:

- *Fix it:* Find some way to change a negative situation.

- *Learn to live with it:* Find some way to tolerate or ignore it.

- *Leave it:* Get out of the situation altogether.

Imagine the following interaction: A co-worker is complaining that the accounting department requires her employees to input extra data every day. "My employees have to work overtime, and it's going to hit my budget hard. The bean counters don't care . . ."

You suggest that she bring her objections to the accounting department: a fix-it approach. "Have you ever tried to talk to those guys?"

She replies, "They don't care what's going on in my area."

To which you might say, "I guess you're going to have to live with it."

"Live with it? I can't live with it. It's going to cost me my job!"

"Well then, maybe you'll have to leave."

"Leave? I finally got four weeks' vacation. I'm not leaving now!"

Here, in a nutshell, are all three options. There are those among us who, as in the example above, act like martyrs and refuse to accept the limits of these options—but martyrdom doesn't get you anywhere but stuck in your problem. Because leaving a job to cope with a difficulty is not always logis-tically or financially feasible and living with the trouble can be destructive to your peace of mind and even your health, the first option—fixing the problem—is often the most viable.

When you choose this option, you will find that there are three targets for change. You can change:

- *The person with whom you are in conflict:* The problem here is that you can't "make" a person be different from who she is.

- *The system:* It is quite possible to make small or broad modifications in the status quo. If you're really unhappy about how our country is governed, you might, for example, feel motivated to run for Congress. That's a big move, but you might also make small changes. In one office that consulted with us, the staff was in the habit of coming in late for work. Management reprimanded the employees several times, and after each lecture the situation improved . . . temporarily. Finally, the executives decided to change the system; they installed a time clock. End of discussion; end of problem.

- *Yourself:* Your actions and responses are the most easily changeable element in a difficult situation. When you can't change others and you can't change circumstances, you can always change your own attitudes and behaviors. Ironically, this often brings commensurate changes in the behavior of a person with whom you are in conflict or in the conflict situation itself.

Changing Yourself

You can have success in resolving conflictual situations if you find productive ways to alter your own attitudes and behaviors in response to a conflict. We recommend that you use a fix-it approach. Before you respond to a problem, step back and pull your personal reactions out of the situation. Become strategic in your thinking. Here are some tactics you can keep in mind as you change yourself in order to manage difficult situations more productively.

1. Come to Grips with Your Emotions

When you're stuck in your emotions about any difficult situation (feeling hurt, angry, or afraid), it's easy to mismanage the conflict. It's important to extricate yourself from how you're feeling about the people and circumstances around you so that you can become more purposeful about dealing with them. Sit down and ask yourself what your primary goal is, what's likely to help you achieve that goal, how you see the situation, and how you should proceed in light of these insights.

2. IDENTIFY THE CONFLICT STYLE

If your conflictual situation involves others, it is important for you to identify their conflict styles, and your own, in a clearheaded manner. In this way, you can see if the conflict is due to incompatible personal styles and, if so, strategize ways to make the styles more harmonious. If you're dealing with an avoider and you're competing over an issue, this is only going to cause the avoider to run farther and faster. Also, you might not be using the style that's appropriate for this particular conflict. You need to step back and say to yourself, "Should I be accommodating or would collaboration be a more appropriate style?" Consciously choose your style rather than coasting along on autopilot.

3. ASCERTAIN AND THEN DENY THE PAYOFF

You must determine what the person with whom you are in conflict is trying to accomplish with her negative behavior and then find a way to counteract it. For instance, a competing woman typically gets her way by badgering and being verbally aggressive. You may be tempted to acquiesce to her demands because it's so uncomfortable to be yelled at, but this will only encourage her belief that her loud mouth is effective. Instead, firmly hold your ground, repeating statements such as "I understand that you want to take on this new account, but it has been assigned to Alice." This communicates to her that she's not going to get her way, no matter how loudly she yells.

4. BE CONSISTENT

When coping with a difficult situation, whether through changing your own conflict style or altering the way you communicate with the person with whom you are in conflict, the most important thing is to remain steady in your new behavior and attitude. You must be unswerving in denying the difficult woman her payoff; the strongest kind of behavioral reinforcement is intermittent and variable. Think of a gambler pulling the arm of a slot machine. Her belief that one of a hundred yanks on the lever might pay off is enough to keep her there mesmerized, pulling on it over and over again. If you deny a difficult person her payoff, you have to deny it consistently because giving in every now and then is enough to keep her hooked on her problematic behavior.

However, she might step up her efforts once she feels deprived of her reward. The gossip may gossip more; the sniper may snipe more, believing her level of effort is inadequate. Hang in there and remember that if you are assiduously consistent, eventually the lack of payoff and the negative consequences you've instituted will stop the behavior.

5. CONFRONT, CONFRONT, CONFRONT

A difficult situation will not resolve itself without effort on your part. Whether it's taking action to reiterate team performance standards in your department or making a conscious choice to become more collaborative when dealing with your team members who would rather avoid issues, you will have to face the problem head-on.

6. ADHERE TO THE POWER DEAD-EVEN RULE

Look for ways to obey the Power Dead-Even Rule by maintaining your self-esteem and power as well as that of your colleagues. This will help you resolve any ongoing conflicts and keep the imbalances from leading to conflict in the future.

UNDERSTANDING CONFLICT STYLES and knowing how to settle disagreements are important tools for all women at work, whether they are trying to do their very best creative work without expending unnecessary energy on office conflicts or simply enjoying a harmonious and fulfilling professional environment free of negative interactions. Conflict resolution skills are also essential for women who are eager to hone their leadership abilities and ascend in their careers. In the following chapter, we will explore ways to develop key skills that will help you become a competent and inspiring leader, especially of female employees.

TEN

How to Be
an Effective
Female Leader

THE ENGLISH PRESS frequently referred to former Prime Minister Margaret Thatcher as "bossy." Would anyone think of Tony Blair as "bossy?" Probably not. It should come as no surprise that the band of acceptable behavior for women in leadership roles is smaller than that for men; it's another double bind in which we can become mired. You work in a hierarchal system where you must behave hierarchically in order to be successful. But at the same time, female employees who unconsciously live by the Power Dead-Even Rule will be offended by the very behavior in which you, their leader, need to engage in order to accomplish your goals.

Several years ago, a comparative description of businessmen and -women circulated through corporate break rooms and company bulletin boards. Although it is humorous, it illustrates well this double standard in business.

How to Tell a ...		
BUSINESSMAN	*FROM A*	BUSINESSWOMAN
He's aggressive.		She's pushy.

He's good at details.	She's picky.
He loses his temper (because he's so involved in his job).	She's bitchy.
He's depressed.	She's moody.
He follows through.	She doesn't know when to quit.
He isn't afraid to say what he thinks.	She's mouthy.
He exercises authority.	She's bossy.
He's well dressed.	She's a clotheshorse.
He's confident.	She's conceited.
He climbed the ladder to success.	She "slept" her way to the top.

Today, we're living and working in a half-changed world. Many women have found windows in the glass ceiling through which they are climbing.[1] We have more opportunities, options, and power than ever before. But it's still not a totally level playing field. Regardless of where you are in the corporate structure, whether you work in a creative, high-tech, academic, service, financial, manufacturing, or entrepreneurial environment, if you find yourself in a leadership position—and we define this in the broadest sense to mean that you have *the ability to accomplish goals through others*—you must behave differently than a man. You face many unique challenges: you may have to consider how you present and carry yourself, what you wear, which battles to choose, how to manage friendships with former co-workers whom you now supervise, and how to discipline an employee without coming off as too critical or too soft.

For one thing, you could easily be perceived as violating the Power Dead-Even Rule merely by accepting your new role. You may have worked hard for your advancement, but once you're playing hardball with the big boys, do the women below shout, "Hurray, we've got a woman at the top"? Often not! Instead, we might hear them yelling, "Bitch, bitch, she's nothing but a bitch." If you are going to be successful, you need support from the women below you. But you must demonstrate a high-performance, hard-nosed approach to getting things done. Otherwise, you will fail in the eyes of your male counterparts. This is a tall order. And it is one of five primary paradoxes that you face as a female leader in today's society:

THE POWER PARADOX

Power is synonymous with masculinity. It's often the boy who sounds most self-assured, the one whose voice is left unchallenged, who's the leader of the pack. Confidence carries over to the adult male perception of leadership in organizations. Men grow up to value a powerful leader who gives direction and then acts self-assuredly about the direction he has given. Conversely, power is the antithesis of femininity because the latter has traditionally been equated with passivity, weakness, and accommodation. Of course, some girls may be more persuasive than others, but they're still not considered the "boss." Girls rarely get to play leadership roles, so practicing those skills usually begins with a woman's first managerial position. Even during the rare occasions when a girl is selected as a leader, it's usually because of her popularity. In fact, once she stops being nice, she's labeled "bossy" and is soon ousted from her position.

The Catch-22 for us today is that in the business world, organizations care very little about your being "nice." They are far more focused on your ability to achieve the company's goals through others. As Chris Lee, the managing editor of *Training* magazine put it, women in management "must be perceived as tough enough to overcome female stereotypes, but at the same time they are penalized if they appear too 'masculine.'"[2]

THE PERFECTIONISM PARADOX

Study after study find that women outscore men in most management categories. According to one investigation of about 6,400 managers of which nearly 2,000 were female, researchers found that the women did better than the men on twenty-eight of thirty management skill areas including problem solving, planning, controlling, managing relationships, leading, and communicating.[3] Despite our many talents, however, women do fall down significantly in risk taking. When we were girls, many of our teachers encouraged us to focus on details and praised us for neatness, good penmanship, and following the rules. In our minds, perfectionism became an attainable ideal. Most likely, at the same time we were also discouraged from taking risks for fear of producing imperfect work. These strategies might have helped us in school, but as adults in the business world, when we focus on perfecting details and risk avoidance, we can mistakenly believe we are enhancing our position when in fact the opposite may be true.

For instance, perfectionism is a nasty habit that can cause us to fear that no one is capable of doing the job as well as we can. Unfortunately, this anxiety can prompt us to micromanage our employees—we intrude when, in fact, we should be delegating. Not surprisingly, employees find it quite irritating to be micromanaged, as the volume of complaints we've heard about overbearing female bosses clearly attests. Some can see this meddlesome involvement as an insulting power move—"She hovers over me like a mother hen!" "What makes her think she knows how to do this better than I do?"—and that can inadvertently trigger a nasty conflict. Besides, micromanagement is harmful to employees, inhibiting them from learning new skills, taking responsibility for their actions, or truly celebrating a success.

"My employee might make a mistake, and I will be blamed for it," you might fret. That's true. The only way humans learn is by doing a job themselves, however; and as a leader, you must give your imperfect employees the opportunity to develop and grow. Unless you let go of perfectionism and learn to delegate, you will be forever ensnared in tedious trivia.

The Caring Paradox

Despite the fact that many of us shy away from leadership roles, research has shown that we have great management qualities, especially those involving interactions with others that demonstrate caring. When comparing 127 male and female entrepreneurs, a recent study conducted by the National Foundation for Women Business Owners found that more than half the women emphasized right-brain intuitive thinking, which encompasses creativity, sensitivity, and values when making decisions. Predictably, the women thought of their businesses as family with a network of connections (they derived satisfaction from building relationships with customers and employees), whereas the men perceived their companies as hierarchies with clear rules and procedures.[4]

Women have an advantage in the area of nurturing employees, peers, and customers. However, our skill can cut both ways, especially because female employees often expect extra attention and encouragement from their women bosses. Jealousies bordering on sibling rivalry can arise among employees reporting directly to a female boss if those expectations are frustrated. If you're traveling frequently with one of your employees or spending lots of time with a new hire, the perception among the other women may be that she is getting more from you or is your favorite. If the other employees feel neglected, they can perceive it as a violation of the Power Dead-Even Rule, which may embolden them to sabotage you.

Moreover, when you care too much about your employees, you run the risk of becoming enmeshed in their personal lives. If you are empathetic and compassionate, it is tempting to "nurture" employees to the point where you begin to play psychiatrist. It is critical to remember that you could be placing yourself and your organization in jeopardy if you give the wrong advice; and most likely, you are unlicensed to give psychological guidance.

Your capacity to nurture and care for others can also backfire if it causes you to take back responsibility for a previously delegated task. William Oncken, a business seminar leader, calls accountability for work assignments a "monkey"; hence, there's a monkey on the employee's back until she completes the task.[5] The caring, ever-so-helpful female manager will follow up with her employee regarding the task. Her initial intent in checking in is to give input and support her employee. "How's that assignment going? Anything I can help you with?" But a monkey is agile, with long arms and legs, and frequently it will rebound onto the manager's back unless she is vigilant about this possibility.

Indeed, many female managers feel overburdened because they unwittingly carry so many monkeys on their backs. And, as in the case of perfectionism, if you've taken over employees' responsibilities, it's difficult for them to become truly empowered or learn to do assignments on their own. It's also exhausting for you and can prevent you from concentrating on the big picture.

The Friendship Paradox

Along with leadership comes the responsibility to maintain an appropriate emotional distance from your employees. Until that distance is properly established, you can have a hard time leading other females. Newly promoted women don't like this bit of bad news and often lament to us, "But I still like my old co-workers. I want to keep them as my friends." The friendship paradox presents a great dilemma to these women. We tend to be reluctant to set ourselves apart as leaders because we fear alienating our friends.

Our reply: "Unfortunately, you can't have it both ways. If you want to be the leader, you must accept that while you can and must be *friendly* with your employees, you can't have *friendships* with them." The U.S. military understands how difficult it is for men and women to be promoted from within and usually transfers a new leader to be in charge of a different team.

Anson Dorrance, the women's soccer coach at the University of North Carolina who trained eight of the players on the 1999 champion U.S. women's soccer team, explains, "It's hard for a woman to accept the responsibility of leadership, which is to criticize or influence her teammates in a direction they don't want to go in. A male wants to command his teammates, but a woman has to be forced into it. And she almost will not accept it if it interferes with her popularity. Women would rather be accepted by the team than lead them, because if they lead them properly, they're going to make some enemies, and it's not worth it to them."[6] By now we all recognize that the enemy making to which Dorrance alluded emanates from Power Dead-Even Rule violations.

Friendship with staff members holds other perils for leaders. As a woman, you may have an innate desire to make connections and open up to friends, but as a leader, one of your greatest challenges will be to keep your private life private. The closeness of friendship brings a great deal of richness and fulfillment, but it also brings a boatload of vulnerability to the leader. When someone knows the intimate details of your life, you are open to attack on a wide range of fronts. You can easily be made to look stupid, weak, or petty. And if, as a new leader, you inadvertently violate the Power Dead-Even Rule when fittingly giving assignments or holding employees accountable, your female staff can use your intimate information as a weapon to express their dissatisfaction with your actions.

The Femininity Paradox

"How come no one takes me seriously?" Donna asked us. Although she was stymied, it was plain to us what her problem was. A cute, petite young woman of twenty-eight, Donna was dressed to kill. She wore a tight sweater with a plunging neckline and a short, figure-hugging skirt. Her open-toe high-heeled sandals gave us all a great view of her bright red toenail polish. Donna's long hair and dangly earrings completed the picture of a woman ready for a fun night at a club. Although she was quite feminine and attractive, unfortunately this was not the serious, businesslike image her firm wanted their junior attorneys to project.

Balancing femininity with leadership can be a problem for some women. Men simply don't have to deal with the issue that dressing in a provocative manner may incite catfights. In the movie *Erin Brockovich*, Julia Roberts drew the ire and cold shoulder of her co-workers because she flaunted her cleavage and curves. A jealous woman on your staff may be the first to use this as ammunition against you: "No wonder she got that promotion," she might say behind your back. "Look at how she's dressed."

Unfortunately, shallow as it may seem, inappropriate attire has ruined many a career. Because men are often attracted to provocative clothing from a visceral standpoint, other women may see dressing seductively as a power move as well as your attempt to undermine the respect and intellectual focus they have been working so hard to earn. You're not playing fair and you are diminishing your professional power. It's a question of your primary message at work: Are you a sexual being or a businessperson?

Respect the Difficulties

Great leaders know that leadership doesn't just happen: it takes insight, knowledge, practice, and an understanding of corporate expectations to become an effective leader. Because most women today have had scant opportunities to acquire or practice leadership skills while growing up, when we take leadership positions, we often feel as if we've been thrust into a storm-tossed sea without a life preserver. Men may be familiar with giving and taking orders, whereas many women are unaccustomed to orders, period.

According to management experts Paul Hersey and Kenneth Blanchard, the principal components of leadership are task focus (how, what, when, and where to get things done) and the cultivation of relationships (the two-way communication between the boss and the employee). These exist on continua. In the case of task focus, some employees need little direction and would be insulted if constantly told what to do and how to do it (those are the ones who would rightly protest that you micromanage them), whereas others require more guidance. At the extreme, task focus means the hierarchical command-and-control approach often adopted by men but uncomfortable for many women.

Similarly, the relationship component speaks to the fact that some employees need constant reassurance and feedback, whereas others are competent and confident and require only an occasional pat on the back. While this component may feel more natural to women, at its extreme, the cultivation of relationships means that no decisions are reached without negotiation—a flatter, more feminine approach, but one that can impede progress.

Leadership may feel like an impossible balancing act. If you're too controlling, your employees may dig in their heels and move at a snail's pace to counteract your direction. Catfight-prone women may resort to sabotage or worse. On the other hand, if you're too warm and open, your department may be filled with love, but achievement may suffer when employees spend far too much time dealing with personal issues instead of working. Besides, you may end up taking too much of the responsibility for work production upon yourself.

Striking a balance between the assignment you are charged with accomplishing and the well-being of the team is the challenge of leadership, and it's an especially complex undertaking for women who face the leadership paradoxes we've outlined above. Without a clear understanding of how to manage others appropriately, you can drown when tossed into a position for which you have not been prepared. But there is an answer. It is possible to learn leadership skills that will help you navigate what might become treacherous waters.

The following strategies will help you become a better leader in the contemporary environment by depersonalizing some of the difficult decisions you must make, especially when exerting power or doling out critical feedback. They will help you distinguish being *friends* from being professional *colleagues*. They will help you become more conscious and strategic in your management choices. These skills include setting S-M-A-R-T goals, using a situational leadership style, disciplining a backsliding employee, giving appropriate feedback, and finding a mentor. These are applicable when you are called upon to lead both genders, but are especially helpful if you want to avoid destructive conflicts with female employees.

SKILL #1: LOOK AT THE BIG PICTURE

Because leadership is the ability to accomplish goals through others, it's clear that you cannot lead anyone else until you understand exactly what those goals are. You must understand the "big picture" of the goals set for your department: how your department fits into your company's mission and how your company fits into your industry as a whole. Gaining big-picture perspective involves stepping back from the day-to-day work flow and focusing on your department's overall strengths and objectives.

In leading any group, whether it's a staff of three or a corporation of several thousand, it's vital to determine the organization's mission. You must discover what matters most to your boss and to your company and then figure out how this will be measured. What are your company's explicit and implicit current and long-range goals? What are you and your team being paid to achieve? How will you know when you've successfully accomplished these objectives? What are your department's and your company's future aspirations?

The answers to these questions aren't generally spelled out in a nice, neat package for you. To get the information you need, you may have to do some research and investigative thinking. Some ways to start are:

- Talk to your boss.

- Read your corporation's mission statement and annual reports and make sure you understand what the financial reports mean.

- Research the history and culture of your organization.

- Ask co-workers about spoken and unspoken rules regarding the corporate culture and how people are expected to behave.

- Familiarize yourself with the full range of products and services your company provides.

- Research your company's various customer groups.

- Find out about your competitors—their strengths and weaknesses.

- Memorize your company's organizational chart.

Along with understanding your organization's big picture, you also must grasp its expectations of you personally. Is your mandate to decrease spending and turnaround time? Or have employee morale and turnover been a problem that you're expected to fix? Expenses and turnover are easy to gauge, but employee morale can be subjective. Learn how these more subjective issues are weighted. How will your accomplishments be measured? You must clarify these goals with your boss as you enter your new leadership position.

Understanding the big picture also means having a fair assessment of yourself. This is one of the hallmarks of a good leader. What are your strengths and weaknesses? Recognizing and appreciating your own talents increases your self-esteem, and an awareness of your weaknesses helps you to identify areas in which you need to improve as well as develop a capacity to cope with these flaws. When you have this accurate view of yourself, you know to surround yourself with team members who have an appreciation of the same strengths you do, and who are strong in areas in which you're weak. For example, if you like to concentrate on the vision for the future and you aren't very good at details (and frankly don't like to get bogged down in them), it would behoove you to hire a few employees who are great at details and to celebrate their talents.

SKILL #2: SET S-M-A-R-T GOALS

Once you know the parameters of your company's needs and your own abilities, you must also develop an understanding of your employees' roles and responsibilities. Sometimes these delineations are unclear. The second step in effective management, therefore, is to define your employees' roles with them. Managers who say "I'm not sure what I want from you, but I'll know it when I see it!" are among the most frustrating to work for. How can employees perform if they don't know what's expected of them at all times? These expectations and goals become particularly helpful when an employee is struggling with a performance problem. When you focus on the goal, you depersonalize the feedback. The discussion revolves around why the employee did not fulfill the goals to which she had committed herself.

A good way to clarify expectations is to set what we call S-M-A-R-T goals. S-M-A-R-T is an acronym for: Specific, Measurable, Achievable, Results-oriented, and Time-bound. These are all aspects of well-thought-out goals.

Specific: Goals that are specific focus on outcomes an employee will achieve. For example, "I will acquire five pieces of property for the company during one year." Specific goals also focus on process—the activities in which you will engage continuously in order to reach the previously established outcome, as in "In order to purchase those properties, I will maintain positive relationships with banks that will result in my ability to negotiate lending rates at or below market."

Measurable: Measurable goals specify a precise dimension—the standard by which you know the goal has been reached. Such goals might include increasing sales by 10 percent or cutting overtime by 40 percent over the next year.

Achievable: Achievable goals are expectations that are realistic and reasonable. Sometimes an achievable goal can be a stretch, but the possibility does exist that it can be reached. For instance, "Our department will maintain sufficient competent personnel on duty every day during the next year" may be difficult, but it is an achievable goal. In contrast, "All employees will have perfect attendance during the next year" is an unattainable goal because such a high standard depends on variables beyond management's control.

Results-oriented: When you create a results-oriented goal, you use action verbs to lead toward an effect. One results-oriented goal would be: "I will actively play a part in the success of my department by contributing ideas, increasing productivity, and responding quickly to my teammates." A statement such as "I'll be a good team member" is too vague to be an identifiable goal. Instead of the more passive "Summer interns will be at the company for three months," a results-oriented goal might state, "At the end of three months, summer interns will know how to prepare a profit-and-loss statement, use PowerPoint to create presentations, and develop a departmental budget."

Time-bound: Time-bound goals delineate deadlines. You might commit to achieving your mission by 3 P.M., by Wednesday, by April 30, or by the end of the fiscal year. Time-bound goals might include statements such as: "Our department adheres to the 'Sunset Rule,' which means that all client calls will be answered before the end of the business day on which the client initially contacted us." Or: "We will reach our sales revenue goal of $1.2 million for the parts department by July 31."

When S-M-A-R-T goals have been set, it's easy to assess whether you have reached them because they are so concrete and quantifiable. And, by setting S-M-A-R-T goals for your team, not only are you asserting "I know what I want; have confidence in me," but you're also saying, "I believe you are capable of achieving these goals. I have confidence in you!"

SKILL #3: FOLLOW THE SITUATIONAL LEADERSHIP MODEL

Just as your employees will respond better to goals that respect their abilities, so will they perform more highly for leaders who have adjusted their approach to suit the individuals they supervise and situations in which they find themselves. To treat a dependable, knowledgeable, experienced employee as you would a new trainee would do your team members and your organization a disservice. You manage an employee based on his or her competence and commitment level, *not* the style that is most comfortable for you. In fact, you may have to override your preferred management style because it simply is not the style the employee deserves.

Paul Hersey and Kenneth Blanchard's Situational Leadership model will help you tailor your management approach to your employees' needs.[7] What's more, it's one of the best ways to sidestep many of the leadership paradoxes we've listed earlier in this chapter. It can help you strike a balance between coming on too strong (thereby violating the Power Dead-Even Rule) and being too warm and fuzzy (thereby undercutting your department's productivity and rendering yourself too vulnerable). The Situational Leadership model shows you how and when to focus on relationships, when to concentrate on the job, how and when to delegate tasks, and what to do when an employee backslides and requires discipline.

According to Hersey and Blanchard, there is no single style of leadership but rather a sequence of four styles: directing, coaching, supporting, and delegating. These styles are progressive, meaning that an effective leader will progress from one to the next as the skills and needs of her employees evolve.

DIRECTING

▼

COACHING

▼

SUPPORTING

▼

DELEGATING

Directing is the most controlling style, whereas delegating is the least. Your employee's *competence and commitment* to do a task dictate which leadership style you choose with her—the more competent and committed your employee, the less directive you're likely to be and the more you will move toward delegating. Women leaders are often most comfortable with the middle two styles—coaching and supporting. These styles emphasize a leader's relationship with her employee and are the most collaborative. But good female managers must also be directive or delegating when the situation calls for these approaches. Let's look at which styles are best in which situations.

Directing: "Let me explain to you exactly what I need"

This style is appropriate when an employee has low competence (is new to a job), low commitment (doesn't feel like doing it), or both. Directing involves one-way communication: a manager explains to the employee how to go about achieving the task, and the employee does it. This style is useful when the employee needs instruction in order to be successful. Directing is especially valuable when:

- An employee is new or is just beginning to learn a new skill.

- You have a problem with an employee who is not committed to doing a good job, and you need to take charge of the situation.

- Time is limited.

- No alternatives are possible (as when a new policy or procedure is handed down from above).

- You must win this goal, project, or negotiation. If not, your job, your department, or the company will go under.

Recently, when a CEO client of ours learned about the directive style, she remarked, "I just hired an experienced senior marketing vice president with a salary of two hundred thousand dollars. Do I still have to use a directive style with her?" Our answer was "Yes, you do." But you can adjust this style slightly with someone who is very experienced. It would be unwise to lecture her on *how* to do her job—if she's a pro, she should know that already—but you should communicate to her your goals and expectations for her position. You should also warn her about political potholes—if, for instance, there's bad blood between two executives. In this case, your directiveness would be about expectations rather than methodology. Every employee, no matter how experienced or expensive, needs to know your S-M-A-R-T goals, philosophy, expectations, and job requirements.

The directing style is best thought of as temporary. In the long run, competent workers learn their jobs and don't need to be told what to do. But if an employee can't or won't learn under your guidance, she may be ill equipped to handle the job, and you'd best find a better fit or be rid of her. The agenda of the directing style is "Get better or get out."

COACHING: "TELL ME WHAT YOU THINK ABOUT THIS"

During coaching interactions, a manager is somewhat directive, because the employee is still learning, but two-way communication exists between them. A coaching manager will solicit her employee's ideas and opinions in problem solving but retains control over the ultimate decision making. Coaching falls within the parameters of a flat, collaborative approach. It is a good style to use with female employees who are still learning but are progressing in their mastery.

SUPPORTING: "WHAT DO YOU SUGGEST?"

The supporting style of management works well with an employee who has gained greater competence and commitment to a task and has demonstrated she knows how to do it. Using this style, a manager would begin to allow her employee to take the lead in determining a plan of action or in solving problems. Dialogue moves the action forward, and a manager will often take the employee's opinions or suggestions unless she sees serious flaws in them. Transitioning from the coaching to the supporting style can be difficult because some managers find it easier simply to supply answers to their employees' questions rather than soliciting their employees' input. Some employees themselves may find the coaching style safer, as it can be frightening to fly on your own for the first time. The supporting style is a useful one to adopt, particularly among women, because it allows for give-and-take in working relationships.

DELEGATING: "LET ME KNOW IF YOU NEED HELP"

The delegating style is appropriate if an employee is fully competent and committed to her tasks. When delegating, a manager will give her employees responsibility without input or direct supervision. As Ken Blanchard once said, when managing in a delegating style, "Don't just do something. Sit there!" Delegating, like directing, involves more one-way communication, but this time, rather than the communication coming primarily from the manager, it's the employee who reports back to her boss on her progress or her ideas.

To shake off the micromanagement habit, be sure to delegate when circumstances are right—that is, when your employees demonstrate high competence and commitment to their tasks. As their leader, it may be up to you to increase their competence with training programs and other skill-building activities. Their commitment can flow from their loyalty to you and the department's goals if you know how to motivate them properly using positive reinforcement, power chips, and genuine warmth.

CHOOSING THE RIGHT LEADERSHIP STYLE

You may find that you're most comfortable coaching or supporting all your employees when, in fact, some weaker members of your team might benefit from directing while others are quite ready for you to delegate tasks to them. Your ability to match the most appropriate leadership style to an employee and then allow her to grow into the next phase, say from supporting to delegating, will benefit her as well as your entire department. Your appropriate guidance increases productivity, performance, and morale all around.

The following quiz will help you test your understanding of the Situational Leadership model—that is, when you should use which leadership style. There are right and wrong answers!

WHAT'S YOUR SITUATIONAL LEADERSHIP ACUMEN?

We all have a preference for a leadership style or styles, but employees deserve the styles they need, not the one we are most comfortable with. The following quiz will help you choose among directing, coaching, supporting, and delegating based on the competence and commitment of the employee. Pick the appropriate management style in the following situations.

1. You've hired a new employee who is anxious to excel, but she hasn't done this kind of work before. Do you:

(continues)

a. Give her an assignment and check in a week later to see if she has done it?

b. Ask her about her ideas and then let her run with the ball?

c. Tell her exactly what you expect, then monitor her to see if she's performing?

d. Discuss different ways to approach the work and then suggest to her what would be best?

2. Your employee has been on the job and knows how to do her work quite well. Today she comes to you with a problem that you know she can solve on her own. Do you:

a. Tell her to figure it out herself?

b. Discuss options with her but tell her which option to take?

c. Tell her what to do and monitor her closely?

d. Ask her what she would do?

3. You've been away from work for the past ten days with a sick family member. A significant assignment came up, and one of your employees started working on it without you. Although you have never assigned her this kind of work before, she is making great progress. Do you:

a. Discuss her approach and give her ideas about how to proceed?

b. Leave her alone and check in with her periodically?

c. Take the assignment back and do it yourself?

d. Talk it over with her but tell her how you'd like it done?

4. Your employee can do her work but often needs guidance from you. Lately her assignments have been coming in with mistakes. Do you:

a. Ask her how she plans to resolve this problem?

b. Review with her what the problems are and write a plan of action, then meet the following week to discuss it?

c. Sit down and clearly explain what you want and when you want it?

d. Leave her alone because she has been dependable and will probably get better with time?

Applying Hersey and Blanchard's theory to these questions, the correct answers would be:

1. c. A directing style is recommended because the employee is a novice.

2. d. A supporting style would be best, given her competence and commitment.

3. b. A delegating style is appropriate for an employee who can handle work independently.

4. b. A coaching style is needed because the employee requires more guidance to improve her performance.

SKILL #4: DISCIPLINE THE BACKSLIDING EMPLOYEE

Prior to this point, we've explained how to develop "green" employees through each of the four progressive leadership styles to the point where you can delegate to them. Now let's switch gears for a moment to explore how to handle a performance problem with a female employee using the Situational Leadership model. If she fails to fulfill her commitments and S-M-A-R-T goals, you must step in with some sort of disciplinary action. Discipline is an integral part of effective leadership; without it, the message you'll convey to all your employees is that performance doesn't matter. However, if the disciplinary action is not managed strategically, it can set you up for a catfight; as a result of an improperly handled confrontation, the employee may feel personally attacked and may believe her self-esteem and power are diminished.

Admittedly, correcting an employee's unproductive behavior can be difficult. Discipline is a sensitive issue for many women leaders and employees because it plays directly into the power paradox—you are asserting your authority over someone else. You may feel reluctant to do so if you tend toward avoiding conflict or if this person has been a friend. Alternatively, being unfamiliar with appropriate techniques or feeling insecure in your position, you may overcompensate and come across as too cold, strident, or punitive.

Unfortunately, neither extreme is constructive. Your ability to lead may be seriously impaired if you are unable to set appropriate limits with employees and then follow through consistently. Your area's output and morale can suffer because the reluctance to discipline can make you look like a weak manager and can hamper productivity. But if you become overbearing, your employees will resent you and feel as if you've treated them unfairly—possible violations of the Power Dead-Even Rule.

These issues may be compounded by an underlying tendency among employees to accept discipline better from a male manager than from a female one. A recent study emanating from Arizona State University in Phoenix found that even though women were as successful as men at changing their employees' unproductive behaviors, when it was a female who delivered the discipline, the people on the receiving end were less likely to believe the punishment was fair or to accept responsibility for their actions and more likely to think the manager didn't know how to do it properly. According to researcher Leanne Atwater, "Females may be more willing to accept discipline from a male because males are not expected to be compassionate or considerate. They may also be more accepting of their subordinate position to a male than a female."[8]

Employee attitudes such as these make your leadership role all the more difficult. But disciplining a backsliding employee is not impossible. There are effective ways to handle it. First, bear in mind that your response to poor performance should be based on the significance of the infraction—quick and intense if the problem is critical or patient and moderate if it's less serious. The following steps will also help you pull an errant employee back into line:

1. VERIFY YOUR DECISION

Make every attempt to observe the problem yourself before you say anything to your employee. Be sure you are talking to the right person about the right problem. Then discuss the problem with your superior or your human resources manager. To protect yourself and your company from lawsuits, familiarize yourself with your organization's disciplinary procedures and be sure to follow them carefully.

Conferring with your superior also has a secondary purpose. Some female employees, especially if they refuse to take you as seriously as they would a male, may make an end run around you directly to your boss (who may be a man). If you haven't alerted him in advance, he may allow himself to be drawn into the problem—an eventuality you want to avoid, as it can prompt him to believe you are ineffective. When you keep your boss in the loop, he won't hear about the problem for the first time from the disgruntled person. He'll have the full story, not just her side of it.

2. GO INTO A REGRESSIVE MODE

Your next step is to determine the Situational Leadership style you've been using (directing, coaching, supporting, or delegating) and back up one style.

DIRECTING

▲

COACHING

▲

SUPPORTING

▲

DELEGATING

For example, if you've been delegating, step back to a supporting style.

Set up a private meeting with your employee. Raise your concerns with her by asking questions such as "I was surprised to see that your accuracy rate is way down. What's happening?" By discussing the problem in a nonaccusatory tone and private setting, you might discover that your employee is bored with this project or angry with you or someone else in the department. Then together come up with a list of S-M-A-R-T goals that are important for your employee to achieve: you might increase her attention to detail by proofreading all her work and improve her skill on the computer by having her take workshops.

From our experience, a manager's supportive attention helps get wayward employees back on track more than 90 percent of the time. But if supporting makes no difference, you may need to backtrack into coaching. This is where your previously established S-M-A-R-T goals will keep the discussion on a professional, rather than a personal, level. Your strategy here is to divert the conversation from *you and her* and focus it on *her and her agreed-upon goals.* The issue is her choice rather than your attitude. You might say, "We've agreed on these goals, but you're not achieving them." Then establish a schedule of regular meetings and written goals to be accomplished between the meetings. If after several weeks of this regimen, you're still not getting the performance you expect, tighten the noose further to more frequent meetings during which you take notes (the employee gets a copy of these). These written work plans and your formalized evaluations can serve as documentation if you must terminate the employee in the future.

Finally, if all else fails, you must back into the directing style. You might say, "Let me tell you exactly what I need you to do today. If you have a problem with this, come to me, and I'll give you additional directions." Give your employee the choice of changing her performance or accepting punishment, which might be a written warning in her personnel file. You might even ask her to define her own negative consequences should she continue to underperform. The idea is to avoid taking on the role of executioner but to make the disciplining process self-reprimanding. The problem is hers, and she needs to fix it.

We guarantee that your employee will chafe at this and will probably be rather cold toward you, especially if she knows how to accomplish the task in question. She may even quit. Nevertheless, in cases of incompetence or lack of commitment, it's important to stick with the directing style. As the leader, you're ultimately responsible for the quality of work that your staff delivers. This employee has had several chances to improve her performance and has chosen not to. She needs to change or get out.

3. KEEP IT PROFESSIONAL

If, during your discussions, your employee reveals a personal problem (she explains, for example, that her alcoholic husband is acting out again), do *not* advise her about what to do at home; this crosses the line between manager and counselor and draws you into the caring paradox. Never forget that you are a leader, not a shrink. You can be supportive by recommending that she contact the Employee Assistance Program (EAP) or Alanon, but your focus must remain on her workplace behavior; that's the area of your professional expertise. Don't adopt her personal problems as your own or allow a natural impulse toward empathy to interfere with the job she must do.

When managers start to feel sorry for their employees, they often provide those individuals with excuses for delivering low-quality work. You must keep standards high for all employees. That's the leadership role. If an employee needs a leave of absence, give her one. If she's ill and can't produce the same quality of work she has consistently generated, it may be time for the rest of the team (including you) to pitch in and help her for a limited time. However, don't lower the standards of excellence for the rest of your team because one person is having difficulty on the home front. This is not fair to your organization, the other employees, or yourself.

And by all means, *never* share disciplinary issues or employees' personal problems with other staff members. They'll get the message that you gossip, and their trust in you will be destroyed. Keep the issues confidential.

4. KEEP YOUR COOL

Be sure that all your conversations are carried out in an even tone. Asserting your authority with a recalcitrant employee does not mean yelling—an all-too-frequent and, as far as we're concerned, unprofessional occurrence in the workplace. In fact, in reviewing our correspondents' e-mails, we were truly shocked to discover how many complained about their female bosses screaming at them, or vice versa. "Really letting her have it" focuses both of you on the relationship, rather than the content, and instantly pushes your employee into defensiveness. Besides, telling off an employee makes you look as if you're out of control and a poor leader—an emotional dictator, perhaps—and will weaken your power, damage your relationships, and undermine your credibility. The goal is to maintain your composure and act like the one in charge of yourself as well as others.

If your employee yells at you, respond calmly; it's difficult to continue shouting at someone who speaks slowly and evenly. It helps to maintain eye contact. If you're in a public area and the altercation occurs in front of your other employees, invite the irate individual into your office to vent in private.

5. Fire Her If You Must

What happens to an employee who can't or won't perform? This doesn't mean she's a bad person. It just means she's in the wrong job. There has to be another place for her. Your conversation might go as follows: "Because of your many computer errors, you leave me no choice. I am now giving you a written reprimand. A record of this event will be placed in your personnel file. Starting immediately, you need to produce accurate computer reports. The next time your statements are incomplete or inaccurate, you will receive a suspension. Continued errors can lead to termination. You are a valuable employee here, and I believe you can be accurate. I want you to succeed in this." If the problem persists, be consistent in following through with the steps you've laid out.

It would be unwise to undermine your group's productivity by allowing a poor performer to go swimmingly along. Besides, she may become a great asset at another organization in a different role. Rather than continuing to send your nonperforming employee to still another training class, be direct with her, counsel her, and explore her areas of strength with her. And if you must, send her on her way. This demonstrates respect for her as well as your other employees and the organization as a whole.

Skill #5: Assert Your Authority

Acting like a leader doesn't mean you have to be cold or uncaring—only that you must define expectations and limits and consistently follow through to assert your authority. A troublesome situation we frequently encounter occurs with competent but noncompliant female employees, as when they refuse to comply with assignments their female bosses have given them. As the bosses describe it, the employees want control and won't take direction. In fact, we've heard some employees yell at their bosses, "You can't tell me what to do!" (as in the childhood taunt "You're not the boss of me!"). The truth of the matter is, however, if you are the leader, you *are* the boss of her. And, perhaps more important, the output of the department, which rests upon your shoulders, can be diminished by her insubordination. Knowing how to be directive is part of resolving the power paradox.

You can begin to settle the issue by calmly asserting your authority. Start out by affirming your S-M-A-R-T goals with the noncompliant employee. Your discussion should center on her level of attainment and commitment. You might say, "We agreed that you would finish this project by the end of January. We are three days into February, and it hasn't been done. Help me understand what's happening with this project and with our agreement." If the employee responds with "You're picking on me," you might repeat, "I need to understand why you have chosen to disregard our agreement" until you get a viable answer from her.

Understanding the power paradox and the dimensions of the Power Dead-Even Rule is essential to your success as a leader. By keeping the power and self-esteem of your employees in mind, you will be able to reach the organizational goals with your team intact. If, however, this employee continues to disrespect your authority despite your best efforts, it may behoove you to follow through with disciplinary action.

Skill #6: Give F-A-S-T Feedback

No matter what situational leadership style you choose in managing your team members, all your employees need clear input from you, their leader, as they move toward their goals. According to Ken Blanchard, working without getting feedback about one's performance is akin to playing night golf: you swing at the ball but don't have a clue where it goes. Employees are hungry for input. Frequently clients proudly proclaim to us, "I just leave my stars alone. I don't want to get in their way!" But in our experience, those stars, if asked, would be eager for feedback from their managers about their performance. Even stars can get distracted and veer from their objective; they need positive reinforcement to stay motivated and learn how they can get even better at what they do.

Everyone needs feedback to remain focused and enthused, but people who have a feeling preference (see chapter 6) especially want and need to hear that they're doing a good job. Women also seem to require more feedback than men, even when it's only to say they are on track. In a study of two hundred first-year graduate students in an MBA program at Case Western University it was found that women seek out feedback more frequently than men do. Indeed, the women in this study took the opportunity to incorporate the frequent feedback they had solicited into their self-reflection, enabling them to get a more accurate picture of their role in certain events. This was in contrast to the men in the program, who relied primarily on formal channels of feedback like yearly reviews.[9]

Drawing on a concept developed by business writer Bruce Tulgan, we suggest adopting the following guidelines for providing feedback to your employees. Tulgan created an acronym, F-A-S-T feedback, meaning input that is Frequent, Accurate, Specific, and Timely.[10]

- *Frequent:* Giving an employee feedback once a year and expecting her behavior to change is like dieting only on your birthday and expecting to lose weight. Provide regular feedback about assignments or other professional behaviors.

- *Accurate:* Whether positive or negative, you are on shaky ground if you take hearsay as truth. Be sure you've observed firsthand any behavior you are commenting upon.

- *Specific:* Detail what made the behavior so good or so bad. "Your presentation was succinct and logical," you might say. "The comparisons with our competitors painted a clear picture for us about future positioning." Employees are likely to repeat behavior you have reinforced in this positive way and have a better chance of stopping negative behavior that you've clearly and specifically identified.

- *Timely:* Generally, the longer a pattern persists, the more it becomes ingrained. Behavioral researchers say that it takes twenty-one days for behaviors to become habitual. This can be good news and bad news. If an employee has been performing well in a certain area, after three weeks she will probably continue to perform well. If she has been performing poorly, unfortunately, those actions will also become ingrained. It is important to give feedback to employees as soon as you notice noteworthy positive or negative behaviors. The closer in time that an act is either praised or corrected, the better the chance of reinforcing or stopping that behavior.

NINE WAYS TO GIVE EFFECTIVE FEEDBACK

Tulgan's F-A-S-T feedback model tells us what good feedback looks like. But how do you know how and when to give it? If you give feedback too critically, your employee may become defensive. If you praise too frequently, she may become habituated and stop listening. If you dwell on the negative, you may perpetuate the problem. The following are nine strategies to give effective feedback that will help you avoid these pitfalls:

1. *State your feelings about the situation.* Yes, managers have feelings too, and sometimes employees cause us to become frustrated, concerned, and angry. Leaders worry that sharing their feelings with employees will make them vulnerable, but it's important that you identify them and get them out of the way before switching to problem solving. It is almost magical how you can become less emotional and more rational once you've identified your emotions and then expressed them out loud. By starting a conversation saying "I'm disappointed, upset, and frustrated," you also grab the employee's attention and set up for a more incisive discussion.

2. *Focus on the goal, not the mistake.* When an employee strays from a stated goal, managers often focus on what she did wrong rather than on what she was supposed to do right. For example, if Dana should start work at 8:00 but arrives at 8:20, you might say, "Dana, you're twenty minutes late! Go to your desk and don't let it happen again!" Greeting Dana like this can cause her to become defensive. She might stop listening to you, start justifying her position with a million excuses, or even cite times when you haven't been punctual. It would therefore be better to say, "Dana, I need you to be at your desk by eight A.M. to take incoming calls. You are the only customer service

rep on duty between eight and nine, and our clients have to be able to reach you to place orders and talk about our products." With such a goal-oriented approach, Dana will be better able to concentrate on the solution.

It can also be effective to state the harm that the employee's mistake has caused you and the department. You might say, "Dana, I'm upset and frustrated. Because of your tardiness, our customers are complaining. Two of your co-workers worked overtime yesterday to make up for your missed time. You need to fix this problem pronto."

3. *Ask your employee to repeat what you've said.* The truth about human communication is that most of us are more interested in what we're saying than in what's being said to us. We're better at talking than listening. Feedback, especially negative, will be better absorbed by an employee if you ask her to tell you what she thinks she needs to do based on your comments about her performance. Having her put the feedback in her own words will reinforce it.

4. *Move on.* Once you have given feedback, let it go. Don't continue to emit cues that you're dissatisfied with your employee's performance. Return to business as usual. If you believe she will mess up again, then sure enough, she will—it's a self-fulfilling prophecy. As an employee moves in a direction you'd like her to take, she will warm to your positive feedback. But if you continue to praise endlessly, she will become used to positive feedback, and it can lose much of its punch. When employees expect accolades, they don't have the same impact as when you give them sporadically and candidly.

5. *Avoid the sandwich approach.* By the "sandwich approach" to feedback, we mean delivering good news, then bad news, and then good news again. This is a way to soften the constructive criticism by tossing out a bit of praise first and ending on a positive note. Although you might believe this preserves that all-important relationship with your employee, we think it is confusing. Your employee may remember the praise at the beginning and the end but miss the meat in the middle. Consequently, her feelings may be spared but she neither hears nor deals with the bad news. Give the F-A-S-T feedback and then end with a statement such as: "I believe in you and am happy to be working with you."

6. Be consistent. Over the years, we've heard many complaints about bosses who play favorites with certain employees. This is why it's important to dispense positive and negative feedback with an even hand. Personal feelings about your employees are natural, but as a leader, you must supersede them by being consistent and objective in your appraisals.

7. Chips are helpful when giving negative feedback. Managing your power chips so you have surplus with your employees will help you when it comes time to give unfavorable feedback because they may not hear it as negatively or become as defensive as they would if you'd been in chip deficit. Chips you might give as a leader include teaching an employee new skills (or sending her for training), giving Friday afternoons off for extra effort, being fair, recognizing good performance, and simply listening and caring.

8. Use positive reinforcement. Positive feedback can be a powerful management tool. When given in the form of F-A-S-T feedback, praise can dramatically improve performance by moving employees from needing constant direction to working independently toward the goals you've established. When you praise behavior of which you approve, your employee is apt to repeat the task to your liking and to learn and grow on the job. This is the simple principle of *operant conditioning*, which means praising the baby steps along the way to reaching a final goal.

To deliver your positive reinforcement, you can surprise your employees with a widely distributed memo extolling their recent achievements. Bring in doughnuts on a Friday. One of our clients started putting positive stickers on good reports turned in by her employees. Once she had depleted her sticker supply, her employees requested that she buy more. They liked their little rewards. Another manager intermittently wrote personal notes on the payroll stubs of employees who had shown superb performance. From our experience, money is not always the best incentive: many people prefer verbal or written validation and appreciation.

9. Beware of upside-down consequences. In giving feedback, you want to be careful that you don't inadvertently reward poor performance as you attempt to praise good performance. If you praise your employees for their preparedness for a recent meeting, you may also unwittingly be reinforcing them for arriving a half hour late to the meeting because they were finishing their work. One behavior you want; the other you don't. So you need to determine the behavior you want (attending meetings on time) and reward that behavior (by actually starting the proceedings promptly). Similarly, you might be tempted to overload your top performer with work because she is so capable. Instead of inadvertently punishing your star, you need to keep the lines of communication open, find out what projects would be particularly gratifying to her, and assign them to her. Give her chips that she specifically values to reward her excellent performance.

MENTORS

Developing your goal-setting and feedback-giving skills is an excellent way to increase your employees' satisfaction and performance level. This will, in turn, help you in your career ascent. But as you work at improving your abilities to lead others, you can benefit greatly by learning to follow. Most successful professionals, both men and women, have strong feelings of gratitude for the multiple mentors who help them along their career paths. We highly recommend mentors, in large part because leadership roles are unfamiliar to many women, who, when they finally have been promoted to the executive ranks, can greatly benefit from the wisdom and teachings of those who came before them.

In today's rapidly changing world, regardless of our title or skill level, we can need several kinds of mentors: professional, leadership, technical, financial, family, physical, spiritual. The mentor relationship works particularly well for women because it is a perfectly balanced exchange of power and self-esteem. A powerful, experienced woman augments the skills and as a result increases the self-esteem of her charge. Her charge, in exchange, augments the power and self-esteem of her mentor by treating her with respect and acknowledging her greater power.

Even though an airplane in flight has a destination, wind turbulence blows it off course 99 percent of the time. Just like airplanes, we can also easily be blown off course, even when we know where we're headed. It's simply smart business to identify a mentor who will help you get to your destination by limiting how much time you stray from your goals.

How to Find a Mentor

Mentors don't grow on trees. Although it's flattering to be approached by a colleague seeking your advice, being a mentor is a commitment of time, energy, and professional leverage. It is wise to remember this as you search for someone to coach you. You are not doing your mentor a favor; she's doing one for you.

In looking for a wise voice to guide you as you strive to become a better leader, keep the following guidelines in mind:

1. *Determine your goal and/or destination.* A professional mentorship can help you improve as a leader, project manager, communicator, team player, and/or meeting facilitator. Knowing the area(s) in which you need advice will help you pinpoint a mentor with particular experience or expertise in these areas.

2. *Develop a relationship.* It's hard just to walk up to a stranger and ask, "Will you be my mentor?" Potential mentors are all around you: a peer, a boss, someone in another area of the company, even someone in another organization or a woman whom you've met at a professional association. Mentor-protégée alliances are most naturally developed as an evolving relationship with someone you know or are getting to know. It's also a good idea to develop mentor-type relationships with more than one person. A broad range of supportive relationships will give you several different perspectives from which to draw insight.

3. *Reach out.* It's important for you to cultivate your mentor and not the reverse. Call her. Meet for lunch. Stop by her office and ask for advice: "I have a dilemma and don't know what to do. May I have a few minutes of your time?" Talk about why you feel you need help in a specific area, and why she would be the ideal helper.

4. *Agree upon how your relationship will work.* The role of the mentor is to support, not to rescue. Trust is critical. When we mentor clients, we meet initially for several hours to define their goals and to get a sense of each

other. Then we usually follow up with weekly phone calls or face-to-face meetings to review progress. Discuss with your mentor the mechanics of your relationship: how often you will meet, what you will focus on, how you are to receive feedback, issues of confidentiality, and so on. You might also ask your mentor for a list of books, tapes, or periodicals she recommends to enhance your insights into your area of interest. Define ways in which you could be of service to your mentor, too.

5. *Celebrate success as partners on a team.* You are not entitled to a mentor's help. She is being generous in giving you her time, energy, and thoughtful insights. It's important to be humble and express gratitude to her. Be respectful and appreciative and treat any success that comes your way as a joint achievement.

BEING A MENTOR

Some of the best thanks you can give your mentor is to share her wisdom with those coming up behind you. Indeed, as a leader, you may be called upon to mentor promising employees. This can also be a growth relationship for you. Your protégée will become part of your own supportive network; she may keep you in touch with a different pool of developing ideas and technologies. Besides, you may learn things you never realized you knew as a result of having to explain them to someone else.

What should you do when someone has selected you to be her mentor, and how can you establish and maintain a mutually beneficial relationship? Here are a few pointers:[11]

1. *Make sure you agree on the focus.* With your protégée, determine the outcomes and goals of your partnership. What exactly is your protégée trying to learn or change? Will you give input where she has questions or warn her about impending problems? Sit down early on and discuss if what she is concerned about is a skill deficiency that someone else wants her to "fix" or if she herself is eager to improve certain skills.

2. *Determine how you will give advice.* Your goal is to communicate with your protégée in a way that minimizes her feeling controlled or coerced. It's im-

portant to determine early on whether she would like to receive advice only when she asks for it or if she would be receptive to your asking, "Could I give you a suggestion?" and waiting for her to say "yes" before doing so.

3. *State your advice and feedback in the first person singular.* Many of us are tempted to start with "You ought to . . ." "You should . . ." because we all like to give advice. Unfortunately, these sorts of statements can raise defenses and cause resistance. Instead, try "What *I* found helpful . . ." and "What worked for *me* . . ." By referring to yourself, you don't sound critical or judgmental of your protégée. You are simply giving her the benefit of what you have learned or experienced, not telling her what you believe she should do.

4. *Avoid "why" questions.* Direct communicators use "Why?" to help them get the picture. But more women are indirect communicators. "Why?" instantly puts an indirect person on the defensive. She may feel judged and vulnerable when queried in this manner. If, as the mentor, you are curious, try: "Help me understand . . ." This can be much less disconcerting.

Some other useful questions you might ask:

- "What have you learned about your project that you didn't expect to learn?"

- "How is this project different from the last one you managed?" "How is it similar?"

- "If you could handle that situation again, what would you do differently?"

5. *Adopt a hands-off approach.* People learn best by participating rather than watching. If you were teaching your protégée how to use a machine, you might be tempted to reach over her shoulder and say, "Let me show you . . ." Don't give in to this impulse! Not only would you infringe on her space, but she also wouldn't learn as much as she would if she pushed the buttons and moved the levers herself.

BEING YOUR OWN MENTOR

Our roles as mentor and protégée can last a lifetime. But we also need to rely on our own wisdom to stay on course. Periodically you need to ask yourself how satisfied you are with your life professionally, personally, physically. What advice would you offer yourself? What cautions might you urge? Where do you think you need development? Are you evolving, stuck in place, or going backward on your life's journey? These may be difficult questions to answer, but they are essential to your becoming a strong and effective leader. Employees sense when you're not genuine, and it's frightening for them to follow someone they believe they can't trust.

One of the best tools is a mirror—really look at yourself and your behaviors. Would you want to have yourself as a leader? Or as a team member? Give yourself a performance appraisal. And make sure that your physical appearance inspires confidence as well. Dress like the person in your company who is holding the position you'd like to attain. Think of your appearance as a support for the expression of your ideas, not as its own end goal. Accentuate your ideas.

EVERY NEW YEAR'S DAY, we compile a list of our accomplishments of the previous year and the goals for the next twelve months. Yes, we really do state them as S-M-A-R-T goals. We develop individual goals and family goals. We believe women must be leaders and full participants in all aspects of their lives, and that means taking charge of your aspirations and dreams.

And although being a female leader can sometimes feel difficult and stressful, with a sense of humor and humanity it is possible to overcome the problems you encounter. By dint of your position, you may also be blessed with opportunities to make changes in the status quo. Once you grasp how to assert your authority without triggering female conflicts, you can go on to create a winning, high-performing team, one that achieves all that it sets out to accomplish and more. In the next chapter, we will give you some pointers on how teams develop and flourish.

ELEVEN

Building a Dream Team

IN BUSINESS CIRCLES, the idea of team building has become increasingly popular as mergers make companies more unwieldy. So it seems as though every group of people gathered for whatever reason is a team. "Hey, there's the rides-the-same-train-home team." "Look, it's the standing-in-the-hallway-at-this-moment team." Management experts, however, define *team* as "a small number of people with complementary skills who are committed to a common purpose, performance goals, and approach for which they hold themselves mutually accountable."[1] A team is a structured functional unit that has its own set of objectives, rules, and conventions.

In today's global economy, teams are more important than ever, and as businesses expand through telecommuting and the Internet, team membership can be ever more diverse and far-flung. Over the past twenty years, a lot of energy has been expended studying high-performing teams to understand how and why they work. Researchers have found that a group of individuals does not become a high-performing team overnight or by chance. It takes time, effort, and attention from all the members and especially the coach to build a dream team.

A dream team is one in which:

- Team members understand and agree on goals, objectives, and priorities.

- There is clarity about job roles and responsibilities.

- Member resources are fully recognized and utilized.

- Procedures are effective; team members support these procedures and regulate themselves.

- The team has well-established and agreed-upon approaches to problem solving and decision making.

- There are open and well-used lines of communication.

- There is a high degree of trust among members.

- Conflict is dealt with openly and worked through.

- Leadership roles are shared among members.

- Teammates are open and authentic in discussions; they listen, understand, and feel understood.

- Team members show genuine concern for one another.

- The team experiments with innovation and tries out creative approaches.

- The team acknowledges and celebrates success.

Building a powerful team and managing those who may not be friends but who can combine talents to get the job done are the focus of this chapter. We will explain the steps to forming and growing a high-performing dream team as well as the particular challenges that managing female teammates can pose. And we will show you how to combine the principles of team building with the unique strengths of women to form supportive, growth-inspiring Girl Gangs.

PITFALLS FOR FEMALES ON TEAMS

When we consult with teams composed mostly of women, we've noticed unique issues among them that have the potential to impede performance and pull the teams apart. Many workplaces are filled with what we call a "carbon-monoxide culture." Carbon monoxide is an odorless, colorless, and *deadly* gas. It is a stealthy killer, seeping into the workplace and doing great damage before anyone recognizes its presence. Some sure signs of carbon-monoxide poisoning at the office include rampant catfights, gossip, unwarranted criticism, finger-pointing, power struggles, defensiveness, turf battles, and sabotage among team members. One workshop participant told us her office was so filled with carbon monoxide that some of her teammates would "stab you in the back and then turn you in for having a concealed weapon!"

Power Dead-Even Rule violations within teams are a significant source of carbon monoxide. Two women on the 2000 U.S. Olympic swim team, Dara Torres and Jenny Thompson, had lost their capacity to be effective teammates. Their rivalry became personal enough that their coach was forced to ask them to practice at different times and at different pools. Here's how a sports writer described their shared moment of glory as they received their medals for tying for second place at the Sydney Games.

> Dara Torres stepped on the bronze platform first and scooted all the way to the right. Jenny Thompson stepped on next and took a giant step to the left. Torres shifted her shoulders in one direction. Thompson moved her hips in the other direction. Torres looked up. Thompson glared down. Medals around their necks, the two American swimmers were supposed to be standing together in glory. They looked, instead, as if they were standing together in a stalled elevator.[2]

Some say Thompson started the bad blood by becoming jealous of the attention lavished on Torres when she joined the Stanford-based club. Others say that Torres, returning to swimming after a ten-year absence, demanded too much notice. Whichever is the truth, somewhere behind this infusion of toxicity lurks a violation of the Power Dead-Even Rule that set these teammates at odds with each other and tainted the environment for all.

Let's look at some other factors that can hurt female teammates and prevent teams from functioning in top form:

1. Catfights

The propensity to engage in catfights can render team building a challenge for any leader. Difficult women such as the gossip, the sniper, the saboteur, the cabal queen, and the superbitch can pump great volumes of carbon monoxide into the office, creating factions, destroying trust, and undermining cooperative endeavors.

2. Lack of Familiarity with the Rules of the Game

Like conflict resolution and leadership, accepted standards for appropriate team membership and team building may be less familiar to women than to men. One of the lessons boys learn early on is how to play with people they may not like. The big, mean, rough-and-tough kid may be obnoxious, but his social skills are irrelevant. He is someone you want on your team because he's going to help you win the game.

Girls play with friends who are nice. If a child isn't pleasant, other girls are unlikely to choose her as a playmate. As a result, women often prefer to have people on their teams whom they like, and they may be reluctant to choose objectionable teammates who are talented in a critical area. Pleasant teams are wonderful, but often it's more beneficial also to have an outspoken team member who is unafraid to contribute his or her truth and mix it up a bit.

3. Reluctance to Engage in Overt Conflict

Team solidarity grows out of successful conflict resolution. But the culture of women dictates that we avoid overt conflict, which can interfere with a team's ability to coalesce into a cohesive group. Without direct conflict during "official" team meetings, you'll soon find the hallways clotted with groups of women engrossed in "real" meetings in which they gripe and gossip about one another. Such indirect aggression tears at the heart of any team.

4. Internal Competition

As in the U.S. women's swim team, female-to-female competition can destroy team spirit. Unfortunately, if team leaders are unaware of this dynamic, they can create situations in which the Power Dead-Even Rule is inadvertently violated.

Carl took over the management of a six-person office equipment sales team (five women and one man). Firmly believing that competition is what gets a salesperson's juices flowing, he set up a challenge among the employees reporting directly to him, pitting one against the other in weekly and monthly sales figures. This strategy had been highly profitable for him in the past, and he saw no reason to abandon it now. But he hadn't taken into account the gender ratio of his team, and suddenly, without his understanding why, a formerly well-functioning group became disagreeable and bitter. The women began bad-mouthing one another to him. They complained that they weren't getting their customers' messages, and the support staff was dragged into the fray; they promptly processed paperwork for their favorite salesperson but dragged their feet when it came to the others.

Competition can bring out the worst in female indirect aggression. Because most of us are unschooled in how to compete without taking the battle personally, women placed in this situation are prone to becoming entangled in nastiness. The saleswomen in Carl's department were vying for the same resource—a place in the sun as the top performer—a prototypical source of hostility among females.

5. Difficulty Taking a Leadership Role

Anson Dorrance, the male coach of the University of North Carolina's women's soccer team who had previously coached eight of the players on the winning U.S. team, spoke with us about the reluctance female team leaders can have in taking charge. Conflicts can arise, he explained, "if women start to become presumptuous about what they know. But then they develop an attitude of 'If none of us rise above a certain level, we can all be friends.' I see this when I train them. Unfortunately, that attitude makes all the women wonderfully mediocre."

We see this female team-building dilemma in a small but irritating way when we schedule workshops with women's networks. It can take forever to book a speaking engagement. No one will take responsibility for making decisions unilaterally, down to so petty a detail as choosing the day of the week the organization will hold the program. The women don't want to step on one another's toes. They don't want others to get mad or hold their audacity against them forever. They focus on the interpersonal problems that could occur if an individual makes a decision for the team.

It's inefficient when everyone on a team has to collaborate on every single decision. To maximize the team's performance, someone has to take the lead.

6. Difficulty Being a Follower

The reverse situation can also occur—women don't like other women to tell them what to do, and that attitude can easily devolve into a destructive conflict. Although this mind-set is widespread, it can come to the forefront when women of different generations interface. Often younger women who are new to a team expect to have as much power and impact on the group as its official leaders and long-standing members. When these young women are denied a sense of equality, they typically voice complaints to a male executive about "those power-hungry women who are bossing everyone around."

Not only does this create problems for the leadership of the team, but such behavior can also undermine its value and contribution within the organization at large. These complaints can encourage a perception among male leaders that "these women just can't get along, and goodness knows, we'd be crazy to put them in leadership positions."

We aren't saying that younger or lower-ranked women shouldn't have influence—they just need to earn it first. It's a matter of honoring the power of those who are in the leadership positions without resentment that could be destructive to the team. If you want your team's efforts to be successful, you must have good followers as well as good leaders, particularly in a hierarchical system. That means allowing other women to be in power, even though it violates the Power Dead-Even Rule.

7. Other Generational Tensions

Friction that undermines the team can exist between female baby boomers, who are now more senior in their organizations, and younger Gen-X women. For instance, big disparities in one's work ethic can split along generational lines. The baby boomers may say, "I had to pay my dues. I answered the phones, worked weekends, and stayed late on Christmas Eve. What do you mean 'I'm not gonna'?"

For their part, the Gen-Xers may say, "Just because you sacrificed your life to your job doesn't mean I'm going to be crazy enough to follow in your footsteps!" Impasses like these can interfere with teamwork and may promote a constant underlying sense of conflict.

8. Tensions Between Mothers and Nonmothers

Today, many organizations offer perks in the form of flex time, job sharing, and reduced hours or travel schedules for the benefit of working parents. Although this makes life easier for the nation's working mothers, it can also be a divisive factor among females on a team. Women who avail themselves of these legal and acceptable company policies may still run afoul of their female colleagues who can feel put-upon if they have to pick up the slack in the workload or if the working mother leaves at her normal appointed time but in the midst of a company crisis. Often the women who don't have children complain that they're being punished for their nonparental status.

Overcoming Pitfalls: How a Group Becomes a Team

These pitfalls can destroy team cohesiveness and productivity. But for women to be successful in today's business world, we must set aside ingrained habits and learn how to be high-performing team players. If you are the team's leader, you are responsible for flushing the carbon monoxide that these attitudes can generate from your workplace. That means creating a positive work environment for your male and female team members. (Susan frequently offers oxygen masks to clients as desktop gifts in order to remind them to provide their teams with sufficient oxygen.) You pump in fresh air by engaging in productive conflict; by relying on Situational Leadership, S-M-A-R-T goals, and F-A-S-T feedback; by honoring the Power Dead-Even Rule among female team members and snuffing out catfight behavior; by respecting your employees and maintaining nurturing relationships with them; and by good communication and attentive listening.

You also create a winning team by understanding and adhering to the dynamics of team building. There are certain steps that all high-performing teams follow in order to achieve an effective synergy. Let's look at these more closely.

Groups never start out as a team. Usually they simply begin as a set of individuals milling around, trying to sniff one another out. Each person wants to discern who's on her side and will support her, who may sabotage her, and who'll be indifferent to her. As this wary group of individuals begins to gel into a team, it progresses along two major axes:[3]

- *Task focus:* This dimension concerns the coordination of activities to do the job.

- *Process focus:* This concerns the interpersonal relationships among team members.

If the task and process dimensions do not develop roughly simultaneously, coaches and teams can fail to achieve their goals. For instance, the CEO of a cardboard box manufacturer asked us to help him develop a strategic plan for his organization. He was, above all, focused on the task of increasing productivity and profits. While consulting with this company, we discovered its unprofitability was essentially due to the employees' dislike for one another. They sabotaged one another's equipment, hoarded supplies, and undermined one another in numerous other subtle ways. The CEO's absolute focus on productivity (the task) to the exclusion of interpersonal relationships (process) was destructive and ultimately hampered performance and undermined revenue.

It can be equally damaging to focus solely on the process but neglect the task at hand. In another case on which we consulted, the management team at a psychiatric hospital was constantly concerned about how everyone was feeling (process). The CEO, a psychiatrist, made sure that all conflicts were out in the open and that interpersonal relationships were constantly addressed. Although this made for a relatively pleasant work environment, the team failed to market the facility and often neglected to bill patients for services rendered (task). When we were called in to help with the hospital's strategic plan, the facility was already in bankruptcy. Although these examples are rather extreme, it's clear that group members must focus on the task to be done as well as the interpersonal relationships among them as the group grows into a team.

THE FOUR PHASES OF TEAM DEVELOPMENT

How does a group develop into a high-performing team? By progressing through four stages of development. Those stages are: Forming, Storming, Norming, and Performing. Let's take a closer look at them:

1. FORMING

The Forming stage is a period during which group members physically begin to meet, to set goals, and to create a team identity. During the Forming phase, team members are dependent on their leader for protection, assurance, and direction. Protection means that if another group lobs a bomb in on your team saying, for instance, "That's our territory; you're not supposed to be doing this," the leader will handle it. Because the team at this stage is still quite new, it needs strong guidance, and the members need encouragement from their leader at the very outset. Connie Gersick, professor of human resources and organizational behavior at UCLA, has found that the tone set in the first few minutes of the initial meeting of a project team is the one the team has to live with for the rest of its history.[4]

There is very little rocking of the boat or challenge to the status quo during Forming. If, at this point, someone on the budget committee were to propose a new idea about how to proceed, she would probably be shot down. Although the team is concerned with social appropriateness, often little listening occurs at this stage. People will put their hands up to be called on, and they'll make position statements rather than interact on a topic. They talk *at* each other instead of *to* each other. Weaknesses are covered up, objectives are unclear, and personal involvement is low—"I just do what my area is supposed to do; I don't worry about marketing. It's not my territory."

A good deal of time might be expended creating a mission statement. The team might wordsmith it to death, put a lovely frame around it, hang it up on the wall, and then ignore it, because the group isn't cohesive enough yet to hold one another accountable for the goals it describes. Very little is accomplished in this stage other than people getting to know one another a bit more.

Some groups can get stuck indefinitely in the Forming stage. Pat was invited to do team building with the thirteen leaders of a nonprofit association. The team had been with the same leader for four years. Pat used an assessment tool to diagnose their stage of development and found that after all that time, this group was still in Forming. She was almost embarrassed to share these results with the executive director, a polite southern woman named Charlotte.

But in talking with Charlotte about her findings later that evening, Pat discovered why this team hadn't progressed beyond the first stage. Charlotte believed "good people don't get into conflicts." Pat also learned that she had been brought in as a consultant because Charlotte wanted her to silence a "mouthy" woman on the team.

"But you desperately need her," Pat explained to Charlotte. "She's the only one who will risk bringing up the problems everyone else is complaining about in the hallway." Pat's last words to Charlotte were "You really need to get into these conflict issues with your group, or you'll never have a team." That is, without conflict they would never move into Storming, the next stage.

2. STORMING

Storming is a stage in which people become fed up with always being "nice" and disingenuous about problems and actually start talking about them. On any team, it's a given that you're going to have conflict. If you put a group of people together and ask them to move roughly westward at the same time, they *will* differ about how to do that. Paradoxical as it may seem, conflict is essential to team development. The best decisions occur when all teammates can state their ideas and then allow those insights to be debated and built upon. In fact, an important part of our consulting practice is working with teams to *increase* their ability to have healthy conflict and disagreements. When leaders boast to us that their teams never argue and always get along well, we respond, "Then you don't have a team!" If a group never differs, the decisions they reach will only be fair to middling.

During Storming, group members usually demonstrate increased listening and concern for one another. Also during this phase, content and relationship problems are voiced, personal feelings are introduced, factions may begin to form, and pecking orders may take shape. The group might begin to consider wider options and goals, and their overall mission and purpose. There is also more defensiveness, competitiveness, polarization, and focus on *who's* right rather than *what's* right for the organization. The inherent lack of unity at this phase leads to increased tension. Little is accomplished.

Storming is essentially the adolescence of the team's life. Members test out their roles, challenging one another and especially their leader. They might say, for instance, "Are you going to make all the decisions, or do we get some say around here?" Members are trying to take on responsibility, and managers *must* nurture this kind of conflict. Unfortunately, some leaders can see this as a potential loss of control; they may clamp down on more assertive individuals, which can inhibit them from becoming more responsible, participative members.

All teams have disagreements as to how to achieve their goals, even if the members agree on the goals to be met. The key to creating a cohesive team is learning how to manage and resolve such conflicts in a productive way.

Because of the potential for hurtful conflict, Storming can be a particularly treacherous time for female relationships. One of your friends may have joined the other side against yours. Pecking orders can disturb the power equilibrium among peers. Competitiveness and polarization may lead to sabotage and backbiting, and they can create situations that are permanently damaging and debilitating to a team. You must engage in conflict at this stage, but you must do so in a productive way: be careful what you say, how you say it, and to whom.

Susan was asked to do team building with members of a Young Presidents' Organization (YPO) forum. This particular forum had four people in it and had been cohesive and intimate. They were adding two new members and wanted to return to this closeness as quickly as possible.

Susan quickly noticed that they were extremely socially appropriate—a sure sign that they were still stuck in the Forming stage. But during their first coffee break, Jill, one of the members, took Susan aside and said, "There's a bunch of crap going on around here. People have been stabbing one another in the back." When they reconvened, Jill confronted the rest of the group in pointed language and was able to kick the team into Storming. It's quite common for groups to get stuck either just before the Storming phase, because they shy away from conflict, or during Storming, because they're deeply engaged in unproductive, destructive conflict.

Once team members understand the dynamics of team development, they're more likely to see Storming as group growth rather than dysfunction or personal attack. After their first blowup, informed team members have actually asked us with glee, "Is this Storming? Did we finally get there?" They embrace it rather than push it away. If you or anyone on your team is concerned about the level of discord emanating from your group, it is reassuring to understand that the discord is a positive part of the developmental process.

3. NORMING

The Norming phase follows the tumult of Storming. During Norming, group members begin to accept their roles and the other members of the team along with their idiosyncrasies. The purpose of this phase is to create group norms and standards. Norms are the group's written and unwritten rules of conduct and expectations. They can be informal, such as "No one comes to a meeting more than five minutes late," or they can be formal, written rules of conduct for the whole team such as "Be honest and dependable," "Deliver what you promise," or "Stand behind and support team decisions."

There's more probing on the interpersonal level and into team dynamics. Team members might say, "You haven't spoken up lately. Is there anything you want to contribute? Is something troubling you?" People feel the ability to express their emotions more openly. Risky issues are debated. The mission statement becomes real now because team members hold one another responsible for it. "We say our employees are our number-one asset, but what you're talking about doing here doesn't sound like we value our employees at all!" More listening occurs. The team develops an esprit de corps.

Frequently we are called in to work with groups to increase their listening skills, and we find that they know how to listen, but they just don't want to! Coaches of successful teams serve as role models for listening and insist that team members listen to one another. It's one of the hallmarks of a high-performing team.

Conflict still occurs during Norming, but it centers on how the team is going to solve a problem rather than who's right and who's wrong. For instance, Pat was team building with a group of middle managers who had just finished a round of employee performance appraisals. At one point, team member Judy said, "Hold on a minute. Although we haven't used any of our employees' names, we know one another's employees well enough to figure out who's who. I think that violates employee confidentiality, and I don't think we should be having this discussion."

During the break Miranda approached Pat and said, "Several of us were offended by Judy's comment. Can we bring this up when we go back into the meeting?" When the meeting reconvened, Pat said, "Miranda, is there something you want to say?"

Miranda took a deep breath and jumped in. "Judy, I was offended by what you said before the break. I'd like us to talk about it." Soon Shelly joined in with "Let me give you my perspective." Then Sam added, "I was troubled, too. Let me tell you what bothered me."

The team then proceeded to have an elegant exchange about the balance between wanting to help one another in their management work and their fear of breaching employee confidentiality. They pondered, searched for, and eventually identified a win-win solution. As a result of this conflict and the ensuing discussion, the group created norms to which all could adhere.

4. PERFORMING

This phase is difficult to reach. A team in the Performing stage can diagnose and solve problems and make expedient, suitable decisions. Risky issues are openly debated, the team is highly flexible in terms of how tasks are accomplished, and the leader tends to behave just like any other teammate. Members make maximum use of their energies and abilities. An eye is always kept on the mission and goals to ensure that the team is moving in the right direction. Strong interpersonal norms prevail, and the group tends to have insight into the interpersonal process. Members are highly productive and reach their goals.

Pat witnessed a high-performing team in action when she sat in on a board meeting for a large, nonprofit organization dedicated to a medical issue. Several of the members had served on the board for nearly twenty years. The organization had been invited to present their issues before a congressional committee in Washington, and the team was facing the delicate situation of choosing whom from among them they would send as their representative. If this team had been in the Forming stage, the physician with the most seniority on the board would have been a shoo-in for this plum assignment. But the team had an eloquent discussion about who would be the most persuasive and articulate person to promote their goal of increased visibility and funding. They selected their newest member, a bright young physician who had been a board member for only three months.

In a high-performing stage, everyone is equal. The leader tends to be facilitative rather than directive. The team begins to manage its own issues and opts for collaborative decisions. Power Dead-Even Rule violations are less frequent because the power is more equitably balanced among team members. Teammates enjoy sharing the limelight with one another and celebrating. Members are often close to one another, which feels particularly comfortable for women, and work interdependently. Each member takes responsibility and feels accountable for her own part but also looks to see how she can help her teammates reach their common goals.

Women usually point outward when successful, attributing their achievements to others. When on a high-performing team, you may point outward, but the other members will be pointing at you.

Team Building Through the Stages

No matter which stage of development your team is in, there are key principles that will help you move your group to the next level. Here is your strategy for each level:

1. Forming: *Show Strength*

Taking on the mantle of leadership in a group can be awkward, especially because during the Forming phase this would require you to act with authority. You must provide structure, assurance, and direction; clarify the agenda and goals; and keep the group focused. The Power Dead-Even Rule may come into play here, and you may fear that you're acting too forcefully when you assert your influence. Additionally, the women on your team may resent your position. It's critical to give clear directions about the S-M-A-R-T team goals and be aware of the overall group developmental process as the new group comes together. Without directive behavior from a leader, a team can't get its wheels moving.

If you are a member of a woman-led team, you must allow your leader to give directions and help you focus on the work to be done. It's a fact of life. Some women are in leadership positions. If you want to advance an activity or agenda, often you can do so more effectively if there are leaders and followers within the team. It can be hard to appreciate that having powerful women leading the team in a hierarchy will get you farther than a random sample of women running the effort haphazardly, but that's the way the system works.

2. Storming: *Welcome Conflict*

If you're going to start team building, you must be able to finish it, even though that means getting involved in conflict. Teammates will begin opening up and taking risks. They'll feel hopeful and excited. An already-toxic situation can be exacerbated if a newly opened door suddenly and irrevocably slams in the members' faces because you cannot tolerate or don't know how to properly conduct conflict.

Men are used to jockeying for position, making their views known, and forming ephemeral coalitions, but women are not. Women are often indirect with one another and can easily resort to indirect aggression at this stage. Disagreements may go underground and cliques may form. Disgruntled female team members are likely to say to one another, "Is Marilyn going to make all the decisions?" "We'll show her. She's going to pay for trying to be so bossy." "We're not children."

But by using productive conflict resolution and leadership techniques, your team can push through this difficult phase. Allow for differences; focus on the problem, not the person; and discuss underlying values and beliefs. If you are leading a team in which mothers are in conflict with nonmothers, for instance, it might be time to collaborate. You could call the parties together and say, "We understand, Alyssa, that you want time to be with your child, and we understand, Jenna, that you can't be expected to do one hundred twenty percent of your job. Let's see if we can figure out a way to meet everyone's needs." When you do this, you also subvert catfight behavior and build trust. You're attacking the problem directly rather than allowing it to fester in a more covert way.

3. NORMING: *FOSTER TRUST*

Both genders find this stage more satisfying than Forming and Storming. But because of their tendency to be less direct, women may have a tougher time than men in confronting other team members when they see them violating a norm. For example, a group norm might be: "All team members will speak positively about the team to outsiders." If Carrie witnesses Ellie gossiping about a teammate, she may be uncomfortable talking to Ellie about her transgression. A trust-inducing environment, however, makes this kind of confrontation easier.

The basis for teamwork and the binding element in all high-performing teams is trust. To develop a team that cultivates trust among its members you must practice and insist upon:

- *Honesty:* the avoidance of lies or exaggerations

- *Openness:* a willingness to share information and ideas, to disclose your own feelings, and to listen to others

- *Consistency:* the ability to do what you say and say what you do. Your behavior and the concomitant results are predictable.

- *Respect:* the capacity to treat all employees with dignity and fairness. This includes your ability to allow workers to make mistakes and learn from them.

- *Supportiveness:* the capacity to reinforce others when they offer ideas and opinions

- *Competence:* the willingness to prepare adequately and to exhibit excellence in results

Trust often grows through open communication. Listening is a key ingredient in developing trust. Listening is *not* waiting for your turn to talk! It means giving your full attention to another team member and wanting to know what she means by her words.

Finally, make sure that competition among team members is not among the group norms you've established. If your group is composed mostly of women, it would be most productive if any competition was external to the team. Saleswomen, for instance, might compete with other sales teams or regions. Or they could compete against their own numbers from last year. If you're the manager, realize that competition among the women on your team probably won't create the dynamic you're hoping for.

4. PERFORMING: *HANG ON TO WHAT YOU'VE GOT*

It's difficult to get to the Performing stage, but once you're there, you must keep working on team building to sustain peak output. Teams can regress if attention is diverted from their development and functioning. Pat once worked on team building with a manufacturing company that was on the brink of bankruptcy. But after meeting quarterly for several years in team-building sessions, the company's financial situation became so positive it was able to go public. Soon, it began acquiring businesses around the world.

There was a downside to the explosive growth, however. Because the acquisition process took so much time and energy, the company suspended the team-building sessions for a year, and everything began falling apart: teammates had destructive conflicts; they withheld information; they stopped supporting one another. Because of the erosion of trust, manufacturing problems developed that hurt the bottom line.

A high-functioning team will suffer from inattention. This was a tough lesson for this company to learn, but the president quickly made the necessary adjustments. He has now elevated quarterly team building to one of the organization's highest organizational priorities. Teams are not static entities; they evolve over time. If conscientious team building is abandoned, a high-performing team can revert to earlier, more turbulent, less productive phases. But given constant care and attention, a high-performing team will continue to grow, flourish, and exceed expectations.

Great leaders also encourage team members to celebrate their achievements and savor their victories. Celebrations can actually build team confidence, which leads to a greater ability to take risks, and thus more winning. When goals are reached, reward your team. Chances are you'll be celebrating more successes in the near future.

A Winning Team

It can be great when a female team works well together. We were quite taken by the teamwork demonstrated during the Women's World Cup Soccer Games played in 1999. The American team was a tight unit that supported one another and used its cohesiveness to win.

Anson Dorrance told us that although he saw the potential for destructive conflicts on his team, citing "women's enormous expectations of each other" and their acute sensitivity to "pick up any potentially negative nuance," he also appreciated the capacity of women to bond. "It's unbelievable," he said. "Women connect in a very profound and real way that men never get to. And once the teammates are cemented, it's such a deep connection; the rewards are incredibly rich."

Nike wanted to promote Mia Hamm, a key member of the team, and asked if they could create an ad about her exclusively. According to Dorrance, "Mia wanted Nike to promote *the team.*" She wouldn't do the spot unless the other women were included. The commercial that eventually ran features player Brandi Chastain leaving a dental office saying, "Oh my gosh, I just got two fillings." Hamm stands up and says, "Then I'll get two fillings." Other teammates follow suit. They've won their title together, and they'll reap the rewards together. That's one of the marvelous benefits of close, positive teamwork among women. When we learn to avoid the pitfalls of Power Dead-Even double binds and function as high-performing teams, the possibilities for success can be boundless.

The Power of Girl Gangs

As the world watched the Women's World Cup soccer team play China one afternoon in July 1999, they saw an example of what women can accomplish when they banish catfight behavior. The team members supported one another, praised one another, and celebrated one another's victories. This was truly a group that understood the strength of the Power Dead-Even Rule. In finding ways to maintain power equity among themselves, they simultaneously enhanced the effectiveness of everyone on the team. Rather than squabbling with one another for the limelight, thereby undercutting their chances for success, they elevated one another and their team to the stratosphere.

Their success echoes Margaret Mead's wise statement, "Never doubt that a small group of committed individuals can change the world. In fact, that's all that ever has." In our work together, we have found this to be true, especially for females. When a group of women forgo their negative behaviors and leave behind destructive ways of relating, when they band together as a force for change, they can become a powerful source of social transformation. Women's suffrage, the expansion of women's roles in the workplace and in politics, the Equal Rights Amendment, the movement to understand rape as an act of violence rather than a crime of passion, the criminalization of spousal abuse, the fight for economic parity (equal pay for equal work), the end of legal and employment discrimination, the exposure of sexual harassment in the workplace, the support of female reproductive rights, the establishment of women's study programs—these changes for the good all began as small movements among women.

When female colleagues become what has recently been dubbed a "Girl Gang"—a group of women who fiercely support one another, protect one another, and help one another toward success—however that may be measured[5]—they inspire greatness in one another. These groups of committed, cooperative, collegial women serve many purposes: they act as agents of change, power bases, antidotes to loneliness, and sources of protection. Female alliances help to keep females free.

GIRL GANGS SUPPORT CHANGE

In the summer of 1994, three tenured women faculty in the School of Science at MIT began to discuss the quality of their professional lives. Each had felt her career trajectory was less promising than those of her male colleagues. But they were unsure whether this was an experience unique to each of them individually. They even questioned whether their perceptions were accurate or whether they were just overly sensitive. In coming together and exchanging notes, however, they recognized a pattern. They had all experienced lower salaries than their male counterparts, smaller laboratories and office spaces, fewer awards, restricted access to resources, and exclusion from significant roles in their departments.

They polled their 14 women colleagues in the School of Science (in contrast to 194 men in the same school), who immediately recognized the problem and validated their perceptions. Within a single day, a group of 16 tenured female faculty at MIT formed a Girl Gang intent on exposing and correcting the inequity of female exclusion and invisibility in their departments. They requested of their dean that a committee be established to improve the status of women in the School of Science, writing: "We believe that unequal treatment of women who come to MIT makes it more difficult for them to succeed, causes them to be accorded less recognition when they do, and contributes so substantially to a poor quality of life that these women can actually become negative role models for younger women."[6]

Their voices were heard. The committee they'd requested was established and did its work. In 1999, it made many recommendations to improve the status of and ensure equity for senior and junior female faculty members as well as suggestions on how to increase the number of women professors at the school. Soon equity committees were created at all five schools at MIT. Then, in January 2001, MIT convened a meeting with the presidents, chancellors, provosts, and twenty-five female professors from nine top research universities, including Harvard, Yale, Princeton, Stanford, Cal Tech, and the University of California, Berkeley, to discuss the equitable treatment of women faculty in science and engineering. This renowned group agreed to analyze the salaries and proportion of other university resources provided to women faculty and to "recognize that this challenge will require significant review of, and potentially significant change in, the procedures within each university, and within the scientific and engineering establishment as a whole."[7]

The efforts of sixteen women working together led to systemic reevaluation and potential change, not just in their own departments or university but across the country as well. The sixteen MIT female professors are a marvelous example of women pulling together to create systemwide institutional change.

GIRL GANGS AS A POWER BASE

Although they have disparate philosophies and espouse various politics from liberal to conservative, the women of the U.S. Senate have banded together in their very contentious workplace as a group, another Girl Gang of sorts. They make a point of meeting regularly for "power coffees" and dinner. In fact, in a book entitled *Nine and Counting: The Women of the Senate*, they described the purpose of these meetings as "neither plot hatching nor deal making. It is, rather, a familiar ritual among women colleagues everywhere—that uniquely female manner of lending support by sharing experiences, describing challenges, and talking about issues they care about."[8]

Although they do not espouse a singular women's agenda, the female senators do sometimes unite behind a piece of legislation that has implications for women. And they revel in the power that their positions afford them. As Mary Landrieu, the Democratic senator from Louisiana, acknowledged, "I like having power. But it's not power for power's sake. Power shouldn't be something you want because it lifts your ego. It's power to do more good than you can do without it."[9] Each of these remarkable women has this power to do good, and each has joined with her female colleagues to create a collective power-base that supports them all in their important work.

GIRL GANGS AS AN ANTIDOTE TO LONELINESS

For some women, the bond created with a group of women at work can dispel the isolation that arises when their careers put them in predominantly male settings. Author Harriet Rubin documented the formation of one Girl Gang at a staid, hidebound corporation. One executive there, who requested anonymity, was about to leave this organization because she could no longer tolerate the loneliness that grew from working with dozens of high-achieving men—but no women—for seven years. When her female boss got wind of her new job offer, she gave the disgruntled employee an opportunity to create her own department and hire whomever she wanted.

The leader hired five women, and according to Rubin, "The change was immediate. The loneliness, isolation vanished. Just as important, the quality of the work changed and improved. . . . These women make their own rules, and that alone gives them a sense of control over their own destiny." According to the leader of this Girl Gang, "We are all there for one another. We look after one another, help one another. I'm so happy."[10]

As a female executive in the male-dominated gas and oil industry, Karyl Lawson's world was filled with men: she had a husband, a son, and almost exclusively male colleagues. She felt a huge void in terms of female professional friends. In 1994, she created the Women's Energy Network of Houston with only six members—all female attorneys in the industry. The following month, each woman brought a female professional friend/colleague; and the month after that, the membership doubled again. The organization grew exponentially, and today the Women's Energy Network has over 350 members.

When we asked Karyl what motivated her to create this Girl Gang, she told us, "I felt I was losing out on a good part of my life, and I wanted to fill that emptiness." This group now has an additional, perhaps more altruistic, focus. It now sponsors an annual fund-raising event to benefit local charities helping women and children.

We are sure that there are hundreds, if not thousands, more of these grassroots female-oriented professional and networking organizations across the country, each providing camaraderie, support, and helpful alliances for women who abandon their catfighting ways and coalesce to encourage one another's career successes.

GIRL GANGS AS PROTECTION

Some Girl Gangs form because their members need refuge in a hostile work environment. In the nursing field, for instance, a woman can find herself in a precarious, no-win situation when a stressed-out male physician begins yelling at her. Although the nurse may not deserve this abuse, she can't simply turn on her heel and walk away from him, because that would be tantamount to insubordination. But nurses have been known to unite in order to help a co-worker under attack like this. They typically call a "Code Pink"—a signal that lets the other nurses know that one of them is being besieged. Whoever is free among the rest of the nursing staff rushes to the side of the threatened woman. Acting as supporters, they stand next to her and

witness the barrage. This audience usually dampens or halts the vitupera-
tion; the physician is too embarrassed to continue. Later, the nurses report
the attack to a manager.[11]

Prior to nurses standing up to such berating behavior by physicians,
very few male doctors were disciplined for raunchy jokes or violent or
scathing outbursts. The tide is changing. Hostile work environments are no
longer tolerated, and physicians have lost privileges for such unprofessional behavior. Laws against this sort of harassment accompanied by stiff
penalties are largely the result of Girl Gangs exposing these issues and
pushing for change.

CREATING YOUR OWN FEMALE NETWORK

We have seen how a nonhierarchical, "flat" relational structure grows from
our biogenetic heritage and seems natural among women. Research has
shown that women are better at interacting in small networks than in
the sprawling multitiered associations that men prefer. These closer groups
allow for the intimacy many of us need. In some instances, an interlocking
network of connections can help women to create mutually beneficial
alliances.

Consider the recent formation of an international women's business
network for female executives, founded by Elisabeth Fuchs. An entrepre-
neur and owner of a midsized bottled mineral water distributing company
in Germany, Fuchs constructed this group to allow for intimacy without a
central controlling mechanism. The group is made up of what she calls relational "knots," groups of two or more women who forward professional
contacts to one another, serve as sources of information, and provide mentoring. Fuchs set out the rules and bylaws for her organization as follows:

- There are no rules; there are no bylaws.

- As in a real network, all knots (relations) are independent and
  self-responsible.

- Each knot is responsible for the relationship to her direct
  neighbor knot.

- We have direct links to other knots and are indirectly linked with all others in the network.[12]

The sharing of power, as depicted in Fuchs's organizational chart, makes for the possibility of wonderful relationships, especially because no one woman holds all the power.

Bear in mind that this is a female-alliance-building group. It is not trying to force change by going against established social systems or conventions in an organized way. When women begin to work toward large social changes, we must join forces in a somewhat more organized fashion. Perhaps this is why the feminist movement failed to have the success it could have had in equalizing pay for equal work and in supporting opportunities for women: within this large social movement there was no leader or common voice. Instead, there were many smaller splinter groups that pulled against one another.

When our goal is to form a critical mass in order effectively to stand firm against large institutions, we need to be able to behave hierarchically to deal with these like-minded organizations. Some of us must allow other women seemingly to violate the Power Dead-Even Rule as they take on the leadership positions to move the group forward toward its goals.

An organization needs a clear mission, roles, and quick decision-making. This may be best accomplished with leaders and followers. We believe this can be achieved by keeping in mind the Power Dead-Even Rule: create a culture that provides for chips to enhance self-esteem no matter what the members' level. Some of us must also let go of our ego-driven needs for power and learn to be loyal followers too, for the sake of the greater good.

THE EPITOME OF CARING

The truth of the matter is, most women care deeply about other women—we are all in this together. Without women in our lives, we feel lonely and incomplete. Author and journalist Natalie Angier teaches us that women "fall in love" with their female friends. These friendships help us define ourselves because they foster the sharing of our deepest thoughts, feelings, beliefs, and experiences.

Under duress, women will come to one another's aid; we will stand by steadfastly with support, nurturance, and love. We will pitch in when called upon to help one another. We will offer a shoulder to cry on and a warm embrace when feelings are hurt. We will celebrate one another's victories, large and small. We have come to expect that of one another, and usually our expectations are fulfilled.

IN THIS BOOK we have examined the darker side of why women behave toward one another the way they do, and what you can do to counteract some of the most painful aspects of working with other women. We know from experience and from contact with thousands of women in the workplace that most female-to-female relationships are truly wonderful. But nearly every woman we've spoken to bears the scars of at least one difficult experience.

It is our hope that by recognizing the previously invisible Power Dead-Even Rule as the enormous stumbling block in women's relationships that it is, you can now use its principles to find powerful allies and friends among women in the workplace. By utilizing some of the techniques we've suggested in these pages, we hope that you will find a way to turn workplace conflict into powerful alliances, to the benefit of all involved.

Women are our greatest potential workplace resources. Even as we strive to move forward, at all levels, we still share inequities in pay and opportunities as well as the potential for harassment and invisibility. If we can cast off our negative tendencies and join together in potent Girl Gangs, we will be emboldened to celebrate our common strengths and address our mutual needs. Squabbling among ourselves, we will continue to struggle; united toward a common purpose, we can change the world.

A FINAL WORD

MANY WOMEN ASK US, "Now that I understand the Power Dead-Even Rule, I can see how it's creating problems with the women who work with/for me. But what can I do about it?" Since female-to-female dynamics are invisible to most women, you will have a hard time fixing problems unless you put language to them. In our offices, which are primarily female, we joke about the flat culture of women as much as possible. We laugh when someone says, "Oh, the Power Dead-Even Rule strikes again!" If we have to violate it—we're stuck at the airport, it's ten minutes before the plane leaves, and we must dole out twelve assignments over the phone—we often preface our requests with "Now I'm going to have to violate the Power Dead-Even Rule, but . . ."

Some companies even incorporate information about male-versus-female power structures into their everyday corporate culture. For instance, at the California headquarters of a major insurance company, when a man becomes boastful and dominates a team meeting, other executives around the conference table will make little hand signals indicating a triangle or pyramid. They're letting him know he's behaving hierarchically. By the same token, if a woman becomes self-deprecating and says, "This is no big deal, but . . ." her teammates will smile in recognition and place their hands horizontally fingertip to fingertip, showing how she has flattened the power interaction. Everyone laughs and has fun with the concepts and the

differences. And most important, this insight helps defuse potentially dis-
ruptive conflicts.

What else can you do to avoid woman-to-woman workplace conflicts?
You might:

·   Find or become a mentor.

·   Join or start a women's group in person or on the Web. On the Internet,
    a few isolated women can connect with a larger group of like-minded
    women without depending on the top-down flow of information. The
    sharing of experiences and resources helps build confidence and al-
    liances, and change can snowball as more and more women become
    involved.

·   If there's a woman in your life with whom you're having a problem,
    make a resolution to adopt some of the strategic insights and tactics of-
    fered in this book to deal with her constructively *now!*

APPENDIX A

BOOKS ON SELF-ESTEEM

Author	Title	Date/Publisher
Terry Bragg	*31 Days to High Self-Esteem: How to Change Your Life So You Have Joy, Bliss & Abundance*	Paperback 1997, Peacemakers Training
Nathaniel Branden	*The Art of Living Consciously: The Power of Awareness to Transform Everyday Life*	Paperback 1999, Simon & Schuster
Nathaniel Branden	*Honoring the Self: The Psychology of Confidence and Respect*	Paperback 1985, Bantam Doubleday Dell
Nathaniel Branden	*How to Raise Your Self-Esteem*	Paperback 1988, Bantam Doubleday Dell
Nathaniel Branden	*The Six Pillars of Self-Esteem*	Paperback 1995, Bantam Doubleday Dell
Nathaniel Branden	*Taking Responsibility: Self-Reliance and the Accountable Life*	Paperback 1997, Simon & Schuster

Author	Title	Date/Publisher
Nathaniel Branden and W. G. Bennis	*Self-Esteem at Work*	Hardcover 1998, Jossey-Bass
Dorothy C. Briggs	*Celebrate Your Self: Enhancing Your Self-Esteem*	Paperback 1986, Doubleday
Suzanne E. Harrill	*Affirm Your Self Day by Day: Seed Thoughts for Loving Yourself*	Hardcover 1998, Innerworks
Matthew McKay and Patrick Fanning	*Self-Esteem: A Proven Program of Cognitive Techniques for Assessing, Improving, and Maintaining Your Self-Esteem*	Paperback 2000, New Harbinger
Claude M. Steiner	*Scripts People Live: Transactional Analysis of Life Scripts*	Paperback 1990, Grove/Atlantic

APPENDIX B

CONFLICT STYLES QUESTIONNAIRE ANSWER KEY

HERE IS AN EXPANDED VERSION of the Conflict Styles Questionnaire you took in chapter 9. In this appendix we give you detail on all ten scenarios. We've also explained not just the first choice but also the second, because in real life you may need a Plan B.

1. Your job requires that you and others in your department work every other weekend. You were on last weekend. Although you don't have any activities scheduled for the coming weekend, you are looking forward to having the time off. Cynthia, your co-worker, has just approached you and asked if you would work for her next weekend so she can spend time with her new boyfriend. In the past, Cynthia has always been willing to trade shifts with you when you've asked her to cover for you. You:

    a. Tell her you'll think about it and then duck whenever she comes around. (avoid)

    b. Agree to change with her even though you really don't want to. (accommodate)

    c. Tell her, "Sorry, can't do it. I was looking forward to having next weekend off." (compete)

    d. Tell her, "I was looking forward to the weekend off, but I'll trade one of the two days with you." (compromise)

    e. Suggest the department get together to develop a system whereby employees who don't mind exchanging weekends can be the first ones approached for swapping. During that meeting, you can bring up Cynthia's dilemma and conjure up weekend coverage for her. (collaborate)

Rationale for Scenario #1

(b) Accommodating is a good choice for "colleagues" in this example. Cynthia has always been willing to trade weekends with you, and it is a good time to be supportive and give her some chips. Not only is this a great opportunity for you to reciprocate, but also if you don't cover for her without a good reason, you may lose an ally who has helped you in the past. *2 points*

    (e) Collaborating would be a secondary choice. This could provide a long-term solution to the weekend-coverage issue and help with Cynthia's immediate need. However, you might not be able to hold such a meeting before the next weekend, so this solution may not be optimal for Cynthia's short-term problem. *1 point*

2. You are applying for a job that seems to be perfect. Trouble is, you just found out one of your closest friends has also applied for it. You:

    a. Don't mention it to your friend and hope the topic doesn't come up. (avoid)

    b. Talk with her about the situation and try to figure out a way for both of you to get a great job like this. (collaborate)

    c. Tell your friend that if she wants you to pull out as a candidate you will. (accommodate)

    d. Agree to pull out of the competition if she will. (compromise)

    e. Expect she'll try to compete for the job just as you will. (compete)

Rationale for Scenario #2

(e) Competing is appropriate in this case. In the business world, it is important that women apply for jobs that will advance their careers; otherwise men will be the only ones landing the dream jobs. Sometimes that means good friends will go after the same position. We recommend that you apply for the job and then, at some later point, talk with your friend about the dilemma; this is just a fact of life in the business world. The winner must be gracious, however, and perhaps assist the loser in obtaining another dream assignment. *2 points*

(b) Collaborating with your friend is also a recommended choice in this scenario. Head-on competition with a friend often ends with a win-lose outcome, but the friendship could be the real loser. By talking openly with your friend about career goals, you can help each other reach your career goals. *1 point*

3. You and your co-worker, Abby, have just finished a successful project and now must write a report for your joint boss. This report is of secondary importance because your boss has been involved every step of the way. You disagree about how to do this report because you grasp information best if it is laid out in graphics while Abby prefers to process information in narrative form. You:

   a. Go ahead with the narrative approach. The report isn't that important. (accommodate)

   b. Hang in there and insist on the graphics. (compete)

   c. Don't talk with her about it. (avoid)

   d. Meet with Abby to see if you can come up with a third way that works for both of you. (collaborate)

   e. Suggest that she use narrative form for the part she is doing, while you use graphics in your part. (compromise)

Rationale for Scenario #3

(e) Compromising is best here because the report can be easily divided, allowing both of you to do what you do best. Besides, because your boss is up to speed on the project, you need not spend a lot of time hashing out alternative solutions. *2 points*

(a) Accommodating is a good second choice. Because the report isn't that important, accommodating and doing it her way may earn you some chips. It's probably not worth the effort to collaborate. *1 point*

4. Your boss has just created a new incentive program in your office. For the next month, when customers call in for support services, they will be rating you and your colleagues. The employee with the highest rating will get a free weekend at a luxurious resort. You feel awkward competing with co-workers whom you consider dear friends. You:

   a. Keep mum on the issue. (avoid)

   b. Agree to participate but make it clear up-front you won't take the award if you win. (compromise)

   c. Go for it! You'd really enjoy the weekend. (compete)

   d. Talk with your boss about the negative impact you see this having on the team and try to change his mind. (collaborate)

   e. Go through the motions but don't put your heart into it. (accommodate)

Rationale for Scenario #4

(c) Competing is our choice in this case. Incentive programs work well in all-male departments, and women thrive best when our relationships are intact. However, in these kinds of competitions, if the women decide to avoid or accommodate, the men will always win the luxurious weekends as well as the visibility necessary for promotions. If you do win, be aware that you have violated the Power Dead-Even Rule and will need to be gracious in victory. *2 points*

(d) Collaborating with your boss is our distant second choice for this scenario. Depending on your boss's receptivity and how much he or she understands the Power Dead-Even Rule, you may be heard. However you may be misunderstood and be labeled as "unsportsmanlike," "weak," or "afraid to lose." *1 point*

5. Your boss wants to meet with you to discuss sections she believes you need to add to the report you have written requesting new office equipment. You think this is overkill. You:

  a. Do what she tells you to do. (accommodate)

  b. Hide from her in hopes she may forget all about it. (avoid)

  c. Meet with her to find out why she thinks the added information is necessary and explain your perspective. (collaborate)

  d. Let her know that this is wasting your time and ask her to rethink the request. (compete)

  e. Do as much as she makes you but not any more than you have to. (compromise)

Rationale for Scenario #5

(c) Collaborating would have many payoffs for you and your boss. Sharing perspectives with her could increase your understanding of how she thinks. Plus a meeting of the minds might merge your insights, resulting in a better report. All this will build your rapport and relationship with your boss. *2 points*

  (a) Accommodating is a good second choice if you are in a time crunch to meet the report deadline, or if it really isn't all that important to you. *1 point*

6. Cheryl is responsible for coordinating the agenda for a monthly meeting related to a major computer conversion. You have noticed you are always the last to report on what's going on in your area. By then, some members have left the room and the rest are bored to death and anxious to leave. As a result, your area always gets short shrift. You have heard Cheryl is taking a job with another company in a month. You:

  a. Don't bring up the agenda with her. (avoid)

  b. Sit down with her to see if you can come up with another option that meets both your needs. (collaborate)

c. Tell her you are fed up with being last on the agenda and expect this to end. (compete)

d. See if you can get her to agree to put you in the first half of the meeting half of the time. (compromise)

e. Ride it out for the next month. (accommodate)

Rationale for Scenario #6

(a) Avoiding is the most appropriate choice here. Cheryl will be gone before the next meeting, so there is no point in creating conflict and defensiveness. When you pass her in the hallway, wish her success in her new job. *2 points*

(e) Accommodating is a backup style for this scenario. However, once Cheryl has departed and the new agenda coordinator is appointed, meet with her to discuss other options for your report. *1 point*

7. You are working on a project with Felicia. She is quite junior to you and has much less experience but is creative and knowledgeable about the topic. She keeps telling you how the project should be done. Even though it looks very good so far, you are increasingly uncomfortable with Felicia's assertive behavior. You:

a. Allow her to take the lead in the project. (accommodate)

b. Conceal that her approach is bugging you, keep your head down, and hope to get through the project. (avoid)

c. Divide the project in half, and let her do her part the way she wants to. (compromise)

d. Make it clear you are the senior person and will be calling the shots. (compete)

e. Tell her that you value her creativity and knowledge and that you would like to brainstorm ways for both of you to have a positive impact on the project. (collaborate)

Rationale for Scenario # 7

(a) Accommodating is appropriate in this case. Felicia is adding some great ideas to the project and both of you will be contributing to its success. By allowing her to utilize her creativity and knowledge in conjunction with your experience, you both win. If the project gets off track, you can always use your expertise and redirect Felicia before any missteps take place. *2 points*

(e) Collaborating is a good second choice here. When your next joint assignment with Felicia comes along, you will have already established an open way of working together. You and Felicia will brainstorm ideas and reach consensus on how to implement them. *1 point*

8. You know it's not a big deal, but it bugs you that Heather, a critical member of your support system, who also orders the soft drinks and coffee for the office kitchen, always buys Coke instead of Pepsi. She defiantly states that Coke is superior, but you're a Pepsi fan. When you've talked with her about buying both Coke and Pepsi, she makes lame excuses like "I'd have to go to two sources." You:

    a. Don't talk with her about it. It's not worth getting her hackles up. (avoid)

    b. Bring your own Pepsi. (accommodate)

    c. Tell her you'll bring up the issue with the office manager if she doesn't address your request. (compete)

    d. Call a meeting in the department to discuss how supplies are ordered. (collaborate)

    e. See if she'll buy Pepsi half the time and Coke half the time. (compromise)

Rationale for Scenario #8

(a) Avoid the Coke-versus-Pepsi challenge. This issue is trivial compared with other office problems and seems to have become a bit too emotionally laden for Heather. You need to take the high road, especially because Heather is critical to your business success. *2 points*

(b) Accommodating is the second most effective choice. Bring your own Pepsi and don't make a big deal about it. You want to continue to build and nurture your relationship with Heather. *1 point*

9. You and another manager are sending some employees to a conference. Eileen thinks you should split the cost because your department has a larger training budget. You think she should pay more than you because she's sending more people. You:

    a. Let her know that you will not pay for her employees. (compete)

    b. Sit down with her and brainstorm a variety of approaches for finding additional funding. (collaborate)

    c. Agree to split the costs as she wishes. (accommodate)

    d. Suggest that your joint boss decide and agree to abide by her decision. (compromise)

    e. You don't mention it, hoping the finance manager will charge her budget for Eileen's employees' attendance. (avoid)

Rationale for Scenario #9
(b) Collaborating is a good choice here. This is a good chance for a win-win. The other options create win-lose outcomes. And losers have long memories. *2 points*

(d) Compromising by having your boss decide may be a second choice, depending on your boss. If your joint boss likes to be involved in budgetary decisions, it would be appropriate to include her in the problem solving since her employees have reached an impasse. If your boss prefers her managers to work things out on their own, we recommend doing just that. *1 point*

10. Your department and another are working on a big project. You are all absolutely swamped and up against a tight deadline. There are a lot of thankless tasks associated with the project, and unfortunately the other department is trying to get your department to be responsible for them. You:

a. Propose that your department take on the menial tasks every other week. (compromise)

b. Don't mention it; it will cause too much conflict. (avoid)

c. Be the bigger person and take on the work. (accommodate)

d. Clearly state that you will not do the other department's "junk work." (compete)

e. Call the employees of both departments together to brainstorm the best solution. (collaborate)

Rationale for Scenario #10

(a) Compromising would be an appropriate style for resolving this conflict. The thankless tasks must be done, but there has to be a fair way to distribute them between departments. The idea of alternating these duties weekly accomplishes that goal, especially if there is no time for another meeting. *2 points*

(e) Collaborating could be a secondary choice here. If there is time to get the employees together to do some brainstorming about this issues, collaborating may spawn new solutions for performing the important but menial tasks. At the same time, such a meeting will take time, which is in scarce supply. *1 point*

NOTES

Introduction

1 Kaj Björkqvist, K. Osterman, and K. M. J. Lagerspetz, "Sex Differences in Covert Aggression among Adults," *Aggressive Behavior* 20 (1994): 27.

2 Richard Driscoll, "Will Women Be Better Managers? Gender Conflict at Work," *Transitions: The Journal of Men's Perspectives* 19 (1999).

3 Judith Briles, *Women to Women 2000: Becoming Sabotage Savvy in the New Millennium* (New Horizon Press, 1999).

4 Kathleen Collins, "New Economy Friendship," *Working Woman*, September 2000, 16.

5 Carol Gallagher with Susan K. Golant, *Going to the Top* (New York: Viking, 2000), 5.

One: The Golden Triangle

1 Jean Baker Miller, "The Development of Women's Sense of Self," in *Women's Growth in Connection*, Judith V. Jordan, Alexandra G. Kaplan, Jean Baker Miller, et al. (New York: Guilford Press, 1991), 15.

2 Gallagher, 51.

3 Susan A. Murphy, "A Study of Career Values by Generation and Gender" (Ph.D. diss., the Fielding Graduate Institute, 2000).

4 J. French and B. Raven, "The Basis of Social Power," in *Studies in Social Power*, ed. D. Cartright (Ann Arbor: University of Michigan Press, 1959).

5 Matthew McKay and Patrick Fanning, *Self-Esteem* (Oakland, Calif.: New Harbinger Publications, 2000), 1.

6 Carol Gilligan, *In a Different Voice* (Cambridge, Mass.: Harvard University Press, 1982), 17.

7 Alfons A. M. Crijnen, Thomas M. Achenbach, and Frank Verhulst, "Comparisons of Problems Reported by Parents of Children in 12 Cultures: Total Problems, Externalizing, and Internalizing," *Journal of the American Academy of Child and Adolescent Psychiatry* 36, no. 9 (September 1997): 1276.

8 Deborah Tannen, *You Just Don't Understand: Women and Men in Conversation* (New York: Ballantine, 1990), 100.

9 Sue Wick and Laura Williams, "The Impostor Phenomenon," *Women in Cell Biology* 20, no. 10. Also P. R. Clance and S. A. Imes, "The Impostor Phenomenon in High-Achieving Women: Dynamics and Therapeutic Intervention," *Psychotherapy: Theory, Research, and Practice* 15 (1978): 241–47.

Two: The Power Dead-Even Rule

1 Kathleen Jacobs, "In Praise of Power," *Working Woman*, November 2000, 22.
2 Ibid., 24.
3 Shad Helmstetter, *What to Say When You Talk to Your Self* (New York: Pocket, 1987), 52.
4 Ibid., 192.

Three: From the XX Files

1 Cited in Natalie Angier, *Woman: An Intimate Geography* (New York: Houghton Mifflin, 1999), 293.
2 Sarah Blaffer Hrdy, "Natural Born Mothers," *Natural History*, December 1995, 38.
3 Shelley E. Taylor, Laura Cousino-Klein, Brian P. Lewis, et al., "Bio-Behavioral Responses to Stress in Females: Tend-and-Befriend, Not Fight-or-Flight," *Psychological Review* vol. 107, no. 3 (July 2000):28.
4 Angier, 284.
5 Frans de Waal, *Peacemaking Among the Primates* (Cambridge, Mass.: Harvard University Press, 1989), 51.
6 Ibid., 53.
7 Deborah Blum, *Sex on the Brain: The Biological Differences Between Men and Women* (New York: Penguin, 1997), 71.
8 De Waal, 1989, 48.
9 Ibid., 52.
10 Ritch Savin-Williams, "Dominance Systems among Primate Adolescents," in *Dominance, Aggression, and War*, ed. D. McGuinness (New York: Paragon, 1987), 153.
11 Cited in Blum, 72.
12 Angier, 296.
13 De Waal, 1989, 51–53; also Frans de Waal, *Good Natured: The Origins of Right and Wrong in Humans and Other Animals* (Cambridge, Mass.: Harvard University Press, 1996), 124.
14 Barbara Smuts quoted in Angier, 297.
15 Angier, 297.
16 De Waal, 1996, 91–92.
17 Angier, 304.
18 De Waal, 1989, 53.
19 Angier, 299.
20 Anne Moir and David Jessel, *Brain Sex: The Real Difference Between Men and Women* (New York: Dell, 1999), 48.
21 Ibid., 55–57.
22 De Waal, 1996, 121.
23 Moir and Jessel, 17, 55–57.
24 Witleson cited in Moir and Jessel, 46.
25 Blum, 218.
26 Sarah Blaffer Hrdy and C. Sue Carter, "Hormonal Cocktails for Two," *Natural History*, December 1995, 34.
27 Irina Bosse, "Oxytocin: A Hormone for Love." *futureframe science* Web site, September 24, 1999.
28 Erica Goode, "Women Are Found to Respond to Stress by Social Contact, Not by Fight or Flight," *New York Times*, 14 May 2000.

29 M. M. McCarthy, "Estrogen Modulation of Oxytocin and Its Relation to Behavior," in *Oxytocin: Cellular and Molecular Approaches in Medicine and Research*, ed. R. Ivell and J. Russell (New York: Plenum Press, 1995), 235–42.

30 D. Jezova, E. Jurankova, A. Mosnarova, M. Kriska, and I. Skultetyova, "Neuroendocrine Response During Stress with Relation to Gender Differences, *Acta Neurobiologae Experimentalis* 56 (1996): 779–85.

31 R. L. Repetti, "Effects of Daily Workload on Subsequent Behavior During Marital Interactions: The Role of Social Withdrawal and Spouse Support," *Journal of Personality and Social Psychology* 57 (1989): 651–59.

32 Taylor et al., 20.

Four: Lessons from Childhood

1 Robert J. Stoller, "A Contribution to the Study of Gender Identity," *International Journal of Psychoanalysis* 45 (1964): 220–26.

2 Angier, 287.

3 Sandra L. Bem, "Gender Schema Theory and Its Implications for Child Development: Raising Gender-Aschematic Children in a Gender-Schematic Society," *Signs* 8 (1983): 598–616.

4 Michael Lewis, "Parents and Children: Sex Role Development," *School Review* 80 (1972): 229–40.

5 Lori A. Roggman and J. Craig Peery, "Parent-Infant Social Play in Brief Encounters: Early Gender Differences," *Child Study Journal* 19 (1989): 65–79.

6 Alyson L. Burns, G. Mitchell, and Stephanie Obradovich, "Of Sex Roles and Strollers: Male Attention to Toddlers at the Zoo," *Sex Roles* 20 (1989): 309–15.

7 Lillian Glass, *He Says, She Says: Closing the Communication Gap Between the Sexes* (New York: Perigee/Berkley, 1993), 68.

8 Jean Berko Gleason and Esther Blank Greif, "Men's Speech to Young Children," in *Language Gender Society*, ed. Barrie Thorne, Cheris Kramar, and Nancy Henley (Rowley, Mass.: Newberry House, 1983), 140–50.

9 Tannen, 154.

10 Dana Crowley Jack, *Behind the Mask* (Cambridge, Mass.: Harvard University Press, 1999), 23.

11 Dorothy Clark-O'Neil, personal communication, 2 November 2000.

12 Jack, 57.

13 Anne Campbell, *Men, Women, and Aggression* (New York: Basic Books, 1993), 21.

14 Taylor et al.

15 "Jill Barad," *Los Angeles Times Magazine*, 27 June 1999, 34.

16 John Gottman and Nan Silver, *Why Marriages Succeed or Fail* (New York: Fireside, 1994), 142.

17 American Association of University Women and the Wellesley College Center for Research on Women, *How Schools Shortchange Girls* (Washington, D.C.: American Association of University Women, 1992), 10.

18 Janet Lever, "Sex Differences in the Games Children Play," *Social Problems* 23 (1976): 478–87.

19 Ibid.

20 Cited in Maureen Dowd, "Boys Going Batty," *New York Times*, 25 October 2000, national edition, A31.

21 Eleanor Maccoby, "Gender and Relationships: A Developmental Account," *American Psychologist* 45 (1990): 513–20.

22 Robert S. Weiss, *Staying the Course: The Emotional and Social Lives of Men Who Do Well at Work* (New York: Free Press, 1990), 256.

23 Gottman and Silver, 482.

24 Lever, 1976, 484.

25 Ibid., 485.

26 Gottman and Silver, 142.

27 Lever, 1976, 482–83.

28 Janet Lever, "Sex Differences in the Complexity of Children's Play." *American Sociological Review* 43 (1978): 481.

29 Gottman and Silver, 143–44.

30 Marjorie Harness Goodwin and Charles Goodwin, "Children's Arguing," in *Language, Gender, and Sex in Comparative Perspective*, ed. Susan U. Philips, Susan Steele, and Christine Tanz (Cambridge: Cambridge University Press, 1987), 200–48.

31 Kathleen Deveny, "Chart of Kindergarten Awards," *Wall Street Journal*, 5 December 1994, B1.

32 Myra Sadker and David Sadker, "Sexism in the Schoolrooms of the '80s," *Psychology Today* 19 (1985): 57.

33 Edward B. Fiske, "Lessons: Even at a Former Women's College, Male Students Are Taken More Seriously, A Researcher Finds," *New York Times*, 11 April 1990, national edition, Living Arts Section.

34 Deanna Kuhn, Sharon Nash, and Laura Brucken, "Sex Role Concepts of Two- and Three-Year-Olds," *Child Development* 49 (1978): 445–51, cited in Diane Carlson Jones, "Power Structures and Perceptions of Power Holders in Same-Sex Groups of Young Children," *Women and Politics* 3, no. 2/3 (Summer/Fall 1983) (www.haworthpressinc.com).

35 Deborah Best, John Williams, Jonathan Cloud, et al. "Development of Sex Trait Stereotypes among Young Children in the United States, England, and Ireland," *Child Development* 48 (1977): 1383, cited in Diane Carlson Jones, "Power Structures and Perceptions of Power Holders in Same-Sex Groups of Young Children," *Women and Politics*.

36 Dorothea Braginsky, "Machiavellianism and Manipulative Interpersonal Behavior in Children," *Journal of Experimental Social Psychology* 6 (1970): 97.

37 Diane Carlson Jones, "Power Structures and Perceptions of Power Holders in Same-Sex Groups of Young Children," *Women and Politics*.

38 Anne Campbell, "Staying Alive: Evolution, Culture, and Women's Intra-Sexual Aggression," *Behavioral and Brain Sciences* 22, no. 2 (April 1999): 203–52.

39 Deborah Tannen, *Talking From 9 to 5* (New York: Morrow, 1994), 36–37.

40 Ibid., 36.

FIVE: THE "BITCH FACTOR": INDIRECT AGGRESSION

1 Kirsti M. J. Lagerspetz, Kaj Björkqvist, and Tarja Peltonen, "Is Indirect Aggression Typical of Females? Gender Differences in Aggressiveness in 11- to 12-Year-Old Children," *Aggressive Behavior* 14 (1988): 403–14.

2 Eleanor E. Maccoby and Carol Nagy Jacklin, *The Psychology of Sex Differences* (Stanford, Calif.: Stanford University Press, 1974).

3 L. Tiger and J. Shepher, *Women in the Kibbutz* (New York: Penguin, 1977), reported in Anne Moir and David Jessel, 61.

4   Taylor et al., 8.

5   Angier, 288.

6   Ibid., 261–63.

7   Kaj Björkqvist, Kirsti M. J. Lagerspetz, and Ari Kaukiainen, "Do Girls Manipulate and Boys Fight? Developmental Trends in Regard to Direct and Indirect Aggression," *Aggressive Behavior* 81 (1992): 117–27.

8   Angier, 289.

9   Kaj Björkqvist, K. Ekman, and Kirsti M. J. Lagerspetz, "Bullies and Victims: Their Ego Picture, Ideal Ego Picture, and Normative Ego Picture," *Scandinavian Journal of Psychology* 23 (1982): 281–90.

10 Campbell, 2000.

11 Jack, 190.

12 Angiers, 290.

13 Kaj Björkqvist, 118.

14 Jack, 190.

15 M. Wilson and M. Daly, "Competitiveness, Risk-Taking, and Violence: The Young Male Syndrome," *Ethology and Sociobiology* 6 (1985): 59–73, cited in Anne Campbell, "Staying Alive: Evolution, Culture, and Women's Intra-Sexual Aggression," *Behavioral and Brain Sciences*, 22, no. 2 (April 1999): 203–52.

16 Ibid.

17 Taylor et al., 10.

18 Campbell, 2000.

19 de Waal, 1989, 56.

20 Björkqvist et al., 30.

21 Benjamin Svetkey, "Legends of the Casting Call," *Entertainment Weekly*, 8 November 2000, 135.

22 Björkqvist et al., 30.

23 Jack, 189.

24 Liz Smith, "Why Gossip Is Good for Us," *Brill's Content*, May 1999.

25 Susan Mann Trofimenkoff, "Gossip in History" (Ottawa: Canadian Historical Association, 1985).

26 Liz Smith.

27 Jennifer Coates, "Gossip Revisited: Language in All-Female Groups," in *Language and Gender: A Reader*, ed. Jennifer Coates (Malden, Mass.: Blackwell Publishers Ltd., 1998), 226.

28 Tannen, 1990, 98.

29 Ibid., 118.

30 George C. Homans, *The Human Group* (New York: Harcourt Brace Jovanovich, 1950).

31 Jenn Shreve, "Sugar and Ice: Why Women Freeze Out Other Women." http://underwire.msn.com/underwire.

Six: The Goal Is the Relationship

1   Harriet Rubin, "Who or What Is Killing the Great Women of the Corporate World?" *Fast Times*, December 2000, 338.

2   Doria Lavagnino, "The Joy Work Club," *Working Woman*, September 2000, 16.

3   Debra A. Dinnocenzo, personal communication, 15 December 2000.

4   Kathleen Collins, 16.

5 Cited in Sandy Sheehy, *Connecting: The Enduring Power of Female Friendship* (New York: William Morrow, 2000), 82–83.
6 Jennifer Coates, "Gossip Revisited: Language in All-Female Groups," in *Language and Gender: A Reader*, ed. Jennifer Coates (Malden, Mass.: Blackwell Publishers Ltd., 1998), 229.
7 Ibid., 245.
8 Ibid., 230.
9 Ibid., 244.
10 Amy Halberstadt, Cynthia W. Hayes, and Kathleen M. Pike, "Gender and Gender Role Differences in Smiling and Communication Consistency," *Sex Roles* 19 (1988): 589–603.
11 Isabel Briggs Myers, *Gifts Differing: Understanding Personality Type*, 9th ed. (Palo Alto, Calif.: Consulting Psychology Press, 1986, and Kansas City, Mo.: Association for Psychological Type, 1992).
12 Sheehy, 32.

SEVEN: LOOSENING POWER DEAD-EVEN DOUBLE BINDS

1 Joyce Brothers, "Feeling Betrayed Because Best Friend Landed a Job," *Los Angeles Times*, 15 January 1998.
2 Laurie A. Rudman, "To Be or Not to Be (Self-Promoting): Motivational Influences on Gender Stereotyping," American Psychological Society, 30 June 1995.
3 Gallagher, 108–9.
4 Sheehy, 33.
5 Ibid., 85.
6 Gallagher, 85.
7 Ibid., 86.

EIGHT: HOW TO HAVE HEALTHY CONFLICT WITH ANOTHER WOMAN

1 Albert Mehrabian, *Nonverbal Communication* (Chicago: Aldine, 1972).

NINE: HANDLING CONFLICT WITH STYLE

1 The discussion of conflict and conflict styles grew out of Kenneth W. Thomas and Ralph H. Kilmann, *Thomas-Kilmann Conflict Mode Instrument* (Palo Alto, Calif.: Xicom, Inc., 1974).
2 Ibid.
3 Ibid.
4 Ibid.
5 Ibid.
6 Ibid.
7 The description of snipers and clams grew out of Robert N. Bramson, *Coping with Difficult People* (New York: Dell, 1988).

TEN: HOW TO BE AN EFFECTIVE FEMALE LEADER

1 Gallagher.
2 Chris Lee, "The Feminization of Management," *Training*, November 1994, 29.
3 Michael R. Perrault and Janet K. Irwin, "Gender Differences at Work: Are Men and

Women Really That Different?" *Advanced Teamware, Inc.*, Agoura Hills, Calif., July 1996. In another study of 676 male and 383 female managers at 211 organizations using 360-degree feedback to examine fifteen management characteristics, women did better on all measures including planning, decision making, coaching, evaluating, approachability, fostering teamwork, and empowering employees. Harris Collingwood, "Women as Managers: Not Just Different—Better," *Working Woman,* November 1995, 14.

4 Lee, 30.

5 William Oncken, "Management Time—Who's Got the Money?" *Harvard Business Review,* November–December 1974.

6 Anson Dorrance, personal communication, 13 July 1999.

7 Paul Hersey and Kenneth H. Blanchard, *Management of Organizational Behavior: Utilizing Human Resources,* 8th ed. (Englewood Cliffs, N.J.: Prentice Hall College, 2000).

8 Leanne Atwater, David A. Waldman, and James A. Carey, "Gender and Discipline in the Workplace: Wait Until Your Father Gets Home." Paper presented at the Academy of Management Annual Meeting, 2000, Toronto, Canada.

9 Susan Case and Lorraine Thompson, "Gender Differences in Student Development: Examining Life Stories, Career Histories, and Learning Plans," in *Innovations in Professional Education,* ed. Richard E. Boyatzis, Scott Cowen, and David A. Kolb (San Francisco: Jossey Bass, 1995), 135.

10 Bruce Tulgan, *The Manager's Pocket Guide to Generation X* (Amherst, Mass.: HRD Press, 1997), 42–43.

11 Chip Bell, *Managers as Mentors: Building Partnerships for Learning* (San Francisco: Berrett-Koehler Publishers, 1996).

Eleven: Building a Dream Team

1 Jon R. Katzenbach and Douglas K. Smith, *The Wisdom of Teams* (New York: HarperBusiness, 1993), 45.

2 Bill Plaschke, "Thrills . . . & Chills," *Los Angeles Times,* 22 September 2000, Section U, 1.

3 B. W. Tuckman, "Developmental Sequence in Small Groups," *Psychological Bulletin* 63 (1965): 384–99.

4 Connie Gersick, "Time and Transition in Work Teams: Toward a New Model of Group Development," *Academy of Management Journal* 31 (1988): 9–41.

5 Harriet Rubin, "Girl-Gang Members Are the New Mistresses of Misrule," *Fast Company,* May 2000, 342; Ann C. Logue, "Girl Gangs: They Got It Goin' On," *Training and Development,* January 2001, 24.

6 "A Study on the Status of Women Faculty in Science at MIT," *The MIT Faculty Newsletter,* special edition, 11 March 1999.

7 "Leaders of 9 Universities and 25 Women Faculty Meet at MIT, Agree to Equity Reviews," *MIT News,* 30 January, 2001.

8 Barbara Mikulski, Kay Bailey Hutchison, Dianne Feinstein, Barbara Boxer, et al. *Nine and Counting: The Women of the Senate* (New York: William Morrow, 2000), 3.

9 Ibid., 182.

10 Rubin, 344.

11 Christine Simms, "Don't Become a Casualty in the War of Words," *Springnet.com; Nursing Communities.*

12 Elisabeth Fuchs, personal communication, 1 April 2000.

REFERENCES

Alvarez, Lizette. "Feminine Mystique Grows in Senate." *New York Times*, 7 December 2000.

American Association of University Women and the Wellesley College Center for Research on Women. *How Schools Shortchange Girls*. Washington, D.C.: American Association of University Women, 1992.

Angier, Natalie. *Woman: An Intimate Geography*. New York: Houghton Mifflin, 1999.

Atwater, Leanne, David A. Waldman, and James A. Carey. "Gender and Discipline in the Workplace: Wait Until Your Father Gets Home." Paper presented at the Academy of Management Annual Meeting, 2000, Toronto, Canada.

Bell, Chip. *Managers as Mentors: Building Partnerships for Learning*. San Francisco: Berrett-Koehler Publishers, 1996.

Bem, Sandra L. "Gender Schema Theory and Its Implications for Child Development: Raising Gender-Aschematic Children in a Gender-Schematic Society." *Signs* 8 (1983): 598–616.

Best, Deborah, John Williams, Jonathan Cloud, et al. "Development of Sex Trait Stereotypes among Young Children in the United States, England, and Ireland." *Child Development* 48: (1983): 1977.

Björkqvist, Kaj. "Sex Differences in Physical, Verbal, and Indirect Aggression: A Review of Recent Research." *Sex Roles* 30 (1994): 177–88.

Björkqvist, Kaj, K. Ekman, and Kirsti M. J. Lagerspetz. "Bullies and Victims: Their Ego Picture, Ideal Ego Picture, and Normative Ego Picture." *Scandinavian Journal of Psychology* 23 (1982): 281–90.

Björkqvist, Kaj, Kirsti M. J. Lagerspetz, and Ari Kaukiainen. "Do Girls Manipulate and Boys Fight? Developmental Trends in Regard to Direct and Indirect Aggression." *Aggressive Behavior* 81 (1992): 117–27.

Björkqvist, Kaj, and Pekka Niemela, eds. *Of Mice and Women: Aspects of Female Aggression*. New York: Academic Press, 1992.

Björkqvist, Kaj, K. Osterman, and K. M. J. Lagerspetz. "Sex Differences in Covert Aggression among Adults." *Aggressive Behavior* 20 (1994): 27–33.

Blum, Deborah. *Sex on the Brain: The Biological Differences Between Men and Women*. New York: Penguin, 1997.

Bosse, Irina. "Oxytocin: A Hormone for Love." *futureframe science* Web site. 24 September 1999.

Braginsky, Dorothea. "Machiavellianism and Manipulative Interpersonal Behavior in Children." *Journal of Experimental Social Psychology* 6 (1970): 77–99.

Bramson, Robert N. *Coping with Difficult People.* New York: Dell, 1988.

Briles, Judith. *Women to Women 2000: Becoming Sabotage Savvy in the New Millennium.* New Horizon Press, 1999.

Brothers, Joyce. "Feeling Betrayed Because Best Friend Landed a Job." *Los Angeles Times*, 15 January 1998.

Bumiller, Elisabeth. "Clinton Campaign Confronts Erosion of Women's Support." *New York Times*, 22 February 2000, Metropolitan Desk.

Burns, Alyson L., G. Mitchell, and Stephanie Obradovich. "Of Sex Roles and Strollers: Male Attention to Toddlers at the Zoo." *Sex Roles* 20 (1989): 309–15.

Campbell, Anne. *Men, Women, and Aggression.* New York: Basic Books, 1993.

——. "Staying Alive: Evolution, Culture, and Women's Intra-Sexual Aggression," *Behavioral and Brain Sciences*, 22, no. 2 (April 1999): 203–52.

Case, Susan, and Lorraine Thompson. "Gender Differences in Student Development: Examining Life Stories, Career Histories, and Learning Plans." In *Innovations in Professional Education.* Edited by Richard E. Boyatzis, Scott Cowen, and David A. Kolb. San Francisco: Jossey Bass, 1995), 135.

Clance, P. R., and S. A. Imes. "The Impostor Phenomenon in High-Achieving Women: Dynamics and Therapeutic Intervention." *Psychotherapy: Theory, Research, and Practice* 15 (1978): 241–47.

Clark-O'Neil, Dorothy. Personal communication, 2 November 2000.

Coates, Jennifer. "Gossip Revisited: Language in All-Female Groups." In *Language and Gender: A Reader.* Edited by Jennifer Coates, Malden, Mass.: Blackwell Publishers Ltd., 1998), 226–53.

Collingwood, Harris. "Women as Managers: Not Just Different—Better." *Working Woman*, November 1995, 14.

Collins, Kathleen. "New Economy Friendship." *Working Woman*, September 2000, 16.

Crijnen, Alfons A. M., Thomas M. Achenbach, and Frank Verhulst. "Comparisons of Problems Reported by Parents of Children in 12 Cultures: Total Problems, Externalizing, and Internalizing." *Journal of the American Academy of Child and Adolescent Psychiatry* 36, no. 9 (September 1997).

Cuming, Pamela. *The Power Handbook: A Strategic Guide to Organizational and Personal Effectiveness.* Boston: CBI Publishing Co., 1981.

Deveny, Kathleen. "Chart of Kindergarten Awards." *Wall Street Journal*, 5 December 1994, B1.

de Waal, Frans. *Good Natured: The Origins of Right and Wrong in Humans and Other Animals.* Cambridge, Mass.: Harvard University Press, 1996.

——. *Peacemaking Among the Primates.* Cambridge, Mass.: Harvard University Press, 1989.

Dinnocenzo, Debra A. *101 Tips for Telecommuters.* San Francisco: Berrett-Koehler Publishers, 1999.

Dowd, Maureen. "Boys Going Batty." *New York Times,* 25 October 2000, National Edition, A31.

Driscoll, Richard. "Will Women Be Better Managers? Gender Conflict at Work." *Transitions: The Journal of Men's Perspectives,* 19 (1999).

Duff, Christina. "So, Would You Like to Come Up and See My Kid's Etchings?" *Wall Street Journal,* 17 November 2000, 1.

Fiske, Edward B. "Lessons: Even at a Former Women's College, Male Students Are Taken More Seriously, A Researcher Finds." *New York Times,* 11 April 1990, National Edition, Living Arts Section.

French, J., and B. Raven. "The Basis of Social Power." In *Studies in Social Power.* Edited by D. Cartright. Ann Arbor: University of Michigan Press, 1959.

Fuchs, Elisabeth. Personal communication, 1 April 1998.

Gallagher, Carol, with Susan K. Golant. *Going to the Top.* New York: Viking, 2000.

Gersick, Connie. "Marking Time: Predictable Transitions in Task Groups." *Academy of Management Journal* 32 (1989): 274–309.

——. "Time and Transition in Work Teams: Toward a New Model of Group Development." *Academy of Management Journal* 31 (1988): 9–41.

Gilligan, Carol. *In a Different Voice.* Cambridge, Mass.: Harvard University Press, 1982.

Glass, Lillian. *He Says, She Says: Closing the Communication Gap Between the Sexes.* New York: Perigee/Berkley, 1993.

Gleason, Jean Berko, and Esther Blank Greif. "Men's Speech to Young Children." In *Language Gender Society.* Edited by Barrie Thorne, Cheris Kramar, and Nancy Henley. Rowley, Mass.: Newberry House, 1983), 140–50.

Golant, Mitch, and Susan Golant. *Disciplining Your Preschooler and Feeling Good About It.* 3d ed. Los Angeles: Lowell House, 1997.

——. *Finding Time for Fathering.* New York: Ballantine, 1992.

Goode, Erica. "Women Are Found to Respond to Stress by Social Contact, Not by Fight or Flight." *New York Times,* 14 May 2000.

Goodwin, Marjorie Harness, and Charles Goodwin. "Children's Arguing." In *Language, Gender, and Sex in Comparative Perspective.* Edited By Susan U. Philips, Susan Steele, and Christine Tanz. (Cambridge: Cambridge University Press, 1987), 200–248.

Gottman, John, and Nan Silver. *Why Marriages Succeed or Fail.* New York: Fireside, 1994.

Halberstadt, Amy, Cynthia W. Hayes, and Kathleen M. Pike. "Gender and Gender Role Differences in Smiling and Communication Consistency." *Sex Roles* 19 (1988): 589–603.

Handelman, David. "Ms. President: Elizabeth Dole's Potential Run for America's Highest Office Has Set Minds Feverishly Speculating about a Once Remote Possibility: A Female President." *Bazaar*, March 1999, 371.

Heim, Pat, and Susan K. Golant. *Hardball for Women: Winning at the Game of Business.* New York: Plume/Penguin, 1993.

Helmstetter, Shad. *What to Say When You Talk to Your Self.* New York: Pocket, 1987.

Hersey, Paul, and Kenneth H. Blanchard. *Management of Organizational Behavior: Utilizing Human Resources.* 8th ed. Englewood Cliffs, N.J.: Prentice Hall College, 2000.

Holmstrom, R. "Female Aggression among the Great Apes: A Psychoanalytic Perspective." In *Of Mice and Women: Aspects of Female Aggression,* edited by K. Björkqvist and P. Niemela, New York: Academic Press. 1992.

Homans, George. C. *The Human Group.* New York: Harcourt Brace Jovanovich, 1950.

Hrdy, Sarah Blaffer. "Natural Born Mothers." *Natural History,* December 1995, 30–42.

———. *The Woman That Never Evolved.* Cambridge, Mass.: Harvard University Press, 1981.

Hrdy, Sarah Blaffer, and C. Sue Carter. "Hormonal Cocktails for Two." *Natural History,* December 1995, 34.

Jack, Dana Crowley. *Behind the Mask.* Cambridge, Mass.: Harvard University Press, 1999.

Jacklin, Carol Nagy. "Female and Male: Issues of Gender." *American Psychologist* 44 (1989): 127–35.

Jacklin, Carol Nagy, and Eleanor E. Maccoby. "Social Behavior at 33 Months in Same-Sex and Mixed-Sex Dyads." *Child Development* 49 (1978): 576–99.

Jacobs, Kathleen. "In Praise of Power." *Working Woman,* November 2000, 22.

Jezova, D., E. Jurankova, A. Mosnarova, M. Kriska, and I. Skultetyova. "Neuroendocrine Response During Stress with Relation to Gender Differences. *Acta Neurobiologae Experimentalis* 56 (1996): 779–85.

"Jill Barad." *Los Angeles Times Magazine,* 27 June 1999.

Johnson, Fern L., and Elizabeth J. Aries. "The Talk of Women Friends." In *Language and Gender: A Reader,* edited by Jennifer Coates. Malden, Mass.: Blackwell Publishers Ltd., 1998, 215–25.

Jones, Diane Carlson. "Power Structures and Perceptions of Power Holders in Same-Sex Groups of Young Children." *Women and Politics,* 3, no. 2/3 (Summer/Fall 1983) (www.haworthpressinc.com).

Katzenbach, Jon R., and Douglas K. Smith. *The Wisdom of Teams.* New York: HarperBusiness, 1993.

Kelly, Kate. "Meet the Smart New York Women Who Can't Stand Hillary Clinton." *New York Observer*, 17 January 2000, 7.

Kuhn, Deanna, Sharon Nash, and Laura Brucken. "Sex Role Concepts of Two- and Three-Year-Olds." *Child Development* 49 (1978): 445–51.

Lagerspetz, Kirsti M. J., Kaj Björkqvist, and Tarja Peltonen. "Is Indirect Aggression Typical of Females? Gender Differences in Aggressiveness in 11- to 12-Year-Old Children." *Aggressive Behavior* 14 (1988): 403–14.

Lavagnino, Doria. "The Joy Work Club." *Working Woman*, September 2000, 16.

"Leaders of 9 Universities and 25 Women Faculty Meet at MIT, Agree to Equity Reviews." *MIT News*, 30 January 2001.

Lee, Chris. "The Feminization of Management." *Training*, November 1994, 25.

Lever, Janet. "Sex Differences in the Complexity of Children's Play." *American Sociological Review* 43 (1978): 471–83.

———. "Sex Differences in the Games Children Play." *Social Problems* 23 (1976): 478–87.

Lewis, Michael. "Parents and Children: Sex Role Development." *School Review* 80 (1972): 229–40.

Logue, Ann C. "Girl Gangs: They Got It Goin' On." *Training and Development*, January 2001, 24.

Maccoby, Eleanor E., "Gender and Relationships: A Developmental Account." *American Psychologist* 45 (1990): 513–20.

Maccoby, Eleanor E., and Carol Nagy Jacklin. "Gender Segregation in Childhood." In *Advances in Child Development and Behavior*, vol. 20, edited by H. W. Reese, 239–88. New York: Academic Press, 1987.

Maccoby, Eleanor E. and Carol Nagy Jacklin. *The Psychology of Sex Differences*. Stanford, Calif.: Stanford University Press, 1974.

Mackoff, Barbara. *What Mona Lisa Knew: A Woman's Guide to Getting Ahead in Business by Lightening Up*. Los Angeles: Lowell House, 1990.

Madden, Tara Roth. *Women vs. Women: The Uncivil Business War*. New York: American Management Association, 1997.

McCarthy, M. M. "Estrogen Modulation of Oxytocin and Its Relation to Behavior." In *Oxytocin: Cellular and Molecular Approaches in Medicine and Research*, edited by R. Ivell and J. Russell, 235–42. New York: Plenum Press, 1995.

McKay, Matthew, and Patrick Fanning, *Self-Esteem*. Oakland, Calif.: New Harbinger Publications, 2000.

Mehrabian, Albert. *Nonverbal Communication*. Chicago: Aldine, 1972.

Mikulski, Barbara, Kay Bailey Hutchison, Dianne Feinstein, Barbara Boxer, et al. *Nine and Counting: The Women of the Senate*. New York: William Morrow, 2000.

Miller, Jean Baker. "The Development of Women's Sense of Self." In *Women's Growth in Connection*, edited by Judith V. Jordan, Alexandra G. Kaplan, Jean Baker Miller, et al., 11–26. New York: Guilford Press, 1991.

———. *Toward a New Psychology of Women*. Boston: Beacon Press, 1976.

Miringoff, Lee M. "Losing the Women." *New York Times*, 31 January 2000, editorial page.

Moir, Anne, and David Jessel. *Brain Sex: The Real Difference Between Men and Women*. New York: Dell, 1991.

Morrison, Ann M., and Randall P. White. *Breaking the Glass Ceiling*. New York: Perseus Books, 1987.

Murphy, Mary. "The Way She Is: Barbra Streisand." *TV Guide*, 22 January 2000, 18.

Murphy, Susan. "A Study of Career Values by Generation and Gender." Ph.D. diss., the Fielding Institute, 2000.

Myers, Isabel Briggs. *Gifts Differing: Understanding Personality Type*. 9th ed. Palo Alto, Calif.: Consulting Psychology Press, 1986, and Kansas City, Mo.: Association for Psychological Type, 1992.

Oncken, William. "Managerial Time—Who's Got the Monkey?" *Harvard Business Review*, November–December 1974.

Perrault, Michael R., and Janet K. Irwin. "Gender Differences at Work: Are Men and Women Really That Different?" *Advanced Teamware, Inc.* Agoura Hills, Calif., July 1996.

Plaschke, Bill. "Thrills . . . & Chills." *Los Angeles Times*, 22 September 2000, Section U, 1.

Repetti, R. L. "Effects of Daily Workload on Subsequent Behavior During Marital Interactions: The Role of Social Withdrawal and Spouse Support." *Journal of Personality and Social Psychology* 57 (1989): 651–59.

Roggman, Lori A., and J. Craig Peery. "Parent-Infant Social Play in Brief Encounters: Early Gender Differences." *Child Study Journal* 19 (1989): 65–79.

Rosener, Judy B. "Ways Women Lead." *Harvard Business Review*, November/December 1990, 3–10.

———. *America's Competitive Secret: Utilizing Women as a Management Strategy*. Oxford, England: Oxford University Press, 1995.

Rubin, Harriet. "Girl-Gang Members Are the New Mistresses of Misrule." *Fast Company*, May 2000, 342.

———. "Who or What Is Killing the Great Women of the Corporate World?" *Fast Company*, December 2000, 334–38.

Rubin, Lillian. *Just Friends*. New York: Harper & Row, 1985.

Rudman, Laurie A. "To Be or Not To Be (Self-Promoting): Motivational Influences on Gender Stereotyping." American Psychological Society, June 30, 1995. Paper presented at an APS meeting on this date.

Sadker, Myra, and David Sadker. "Sexism in the Schoolrooms of the '80s." *Psychology Today* 19 (1985): 53–57.

Savin-Williams, Ritch. "Dominance Systems among Primate Adolescents." In *Dominance, Aggression, and War*, edited by D. McGuinness, 131–73. New York: Paragon House, 1987.

Sheehy, Sandy. *Connecting: The Enduring Power of Female Friendship.* New York: Morrow, 2000.

Shreve, Jenn. "Sugar and Ice: Why Women Freeze Out Other Women." http://underwire.msn.com/underwire.

Simms, Christine. "Don't Become a Casualty in the War of Words." *Springnet.com; Nursing Communities.*

Smith, Liz. "3 Legendary Actresses Plus One." *Los Angeles Times,* 25 October 2000.

——. "Why Gossip Is Good for Us." *Brill's Content,* May 1999.

Stoller, Robert J. "A Contribution to the Study of Gender Identity." *International Journal of Psychoanalysis* 45 (1964): 220–26.

"A Study on the Status of Women Faculty in Science at MIT." *MIT Faculty Newsletter,* 11 March 1999, special edition.

Svetkey, Benjamin. "Legends of the Casting Call." *Entertainment Weekly,* 8 November 2000, 133–35.

Tannen, Deborah. *Talking From 9 to 5.* New York: Morrow, 1994.

——. *You Just Don't Understand: Women and Men in Conversation.* New York: Ballantine, 1990.

Taylor, Shelley E., Laura Cousino-Klein, Brian P. Lewis, et al. "Bio-Behavioral Responses to Stress in Females: Tend-and-Befriend, Not Fight-or-Flight." *Psychological Review,* in press.

Taylor, Verta, Nancy Whittier, and Cynthia Fabrizio Pelak. "The Women's Movement: Persistence Through Transformation." In *Feminist Frontiers 5,* edited by Laurel Richardson, Verta Taylor, and Nancy Whittier, 559. Boston: McGraw-Hill Higher Education, 2001.

Thomas, Kenneth W., and Ralph H. Kilmann. *Thomas-Kilmann Conflict Mode Instrument.* Palo Alto, Calif.: Xicom, Inc., 1974.

Tiger, L., and J. Shepher. *Women in the Kibbutz.* New York: Penguin, 1977.

Trofimenkoff, Susan Mann. "Gossip in History." Ottawa: Canadian Historical Association, 1985.

Tuckman, B.W. "Developmental Sequence in Small Groups." *Psychological Bulletin* 63 (1965): 384–99.

Tulgan, Bruce. *The Manager's Pocket Guide to Generation X.* Amherst, Mass.: HRD Press, 1997.

Weiss, Robert S. *Staying the Course: The Emotional and Social Lives of Men Who Do Well at Work.* New York: Free Press, 1990.

Wick, Sue, and Laura Williams. "The Impostor Phenomenon." *Women in Cell Biology* 20, no. 10

Wilson, M., and M. Daly. "Competitiveness, Risk-Taking, and Violence: The Young Male Syndrome." *Ethology and Sociobiology* 6 (1985): 59–73. Cited in Ann Campbell, "Staying Alive: Evolution, Culture, and Women's Intra-Sexual Aggression," *Behavioral and Brain Sciences,* in press.

INDEX

ABOUT THE AUTHORS

Pat Heim, Ph.D., is the coauthor of *Hardball for Women* and *Smashing the Glass Ceiling* and president of the Heim Group, which provides consulting services for organizations including General Mills, General Motors, IBM, Lucent Technologies, McDonald's Corporation, Microsoft, Polaroid, and Proctor & Gamble. She is the recipient of the 1999 Eli Lilly Women's Network Award and the 1998 KFC Wisdom Award. She lives in Pacific Palisades, California.

Susan A. Murphy, Ph.D., M.B.A., is a business and organization consultant, graduate school professor, and president of Energy Engineering, Inc. She has thirty years of consulting experience, having worked with organizations such as Bank of America, Shell Oil, Texaco, Duke Energy, Textron Aerospace, State Farm Insurance, NBC, and the U.S. Army and Navy. She lives in Rancho Mirage, California.

Susan K. Golant has authored/co-authored twenty-two books, including *Going to the Top, What to Do When Someone You Love Is Depressed,* and *Helping Someone with Mental Illness* (with Rosalynn Carter), which won the 1999 Outstanding Nonfiction Book Award from the American Society of Journalists and Authors. She lives in Los Angeles, California.

Left to right: Susan Murphy, Susan Golant, and Pat Heim

PAMELA DAVIS-KIVELSON

The Heim Group is a consulting firm, specializing in strengthening an organization's competitive edge through effective communication and leadership. We specialize in gender differences, helping men and women to communicate more effectively, and assisting organizations in keeping their best and brightest. Dr. Pat Heim, who has been leading the firm since 1985, is a nationally recognized expert in the areas of gender issues in the workplace. The Heim Group delivers and coordinates a wide variety of activities to support organizational transitions, improve team effectiveness, and enhance professional and managerial skills.

Visit our website at www.heimgroup.com, e-mail us at heimgroup@aol.com, or give us a call at (888) 917-7797.

Dr. Susan A. Murphy welcomes your phone calls and email messages. Please contact her at Business Consultants Group, Inc. (800) 644-2922 or Energy Engineering, Inc. (281) 442-1400. Dr. Murphy's e-mail is *DrSMurphy@Consult4Business.com* and website is *www.Consult4Business.com*